Literary Representation of Spanish Immigration in the United States of America (1900–1950)

CONTRIBUTIONS TO ENGLISH AND AMERICAN LITERARY STUDIES (CEALS)

Edited by Ingo Berensmeyer, Christoph Ehland,
Julika Griem, Andrew S. Gross and Antje Kley

Vol. 7

Francisco Javier Plañxart Pérez-Santalla

Literary Representation of Spanish Immigration in the United States of America (1900–1950)

Transculturation, Hybridization, and the Third Space

PETER LANG

Berlin - Bruxelles - Chennai - Lausanne - New York - Oxford

Bibliographic Information published by the Deutsche Nationalbibliothek
The Deutsche Nationalbibliothek lists this publication in the Deutsche Nationalbibliografie; detailed bibliographic data is available online at http://dnb.d-nb.de.

Library of Congress Cataloging-in-Publication Data

Names: Plañxart Pérez-Santalla, Francisco Javier, author.
Title: Literary representation of Spanish immigration in the United States of America (1900-1950) : transculturation, hybridization, and the Third Space / Francisco Javier Plañxart Pérez-Santalla.
Description: Berlin ; New York : Peter Lang, 2025. | Series: Contributions to English and American literary studies, 2366-5068 ; vol. no. 7 | Includes bibliographical references and index.
Identifiers: LCCN 2024049322 (print) | LCCN 2024049323 (ebook) | ISBN 9783631929612 (hardback) | ISBN 9783631929629 (ebook) | ISBN 9783631929636 (epub)
Subjects: LCSH: Immigrants in literature. | American fiction—20th century—History and criticism. | American fiction—21st century—History and criticism. | Spaniards in literature. | Cultural fusion in literature. | Spaniards—Cultural assimilation—United States. | Spaniards—United States—History—20th century. | LCGFT: Literary criticism.
Classification: LCC PS374.I48 P57 2025 (print) | LCC PS374.I48 (ebook) | DDC 813/.54093526912—dc23/eng/20241214
LC record available at https://lccn.loc.gov/2024049322
LC ebook record available at https://lccn.loc.gov/2024049323

Cover Image

Cover Design by Peter Lang Group AG

ISSN 2366-5068
ISBN 978-3-631-92961-2 (Print)
ISBN 978-3-631-92962-9 (E-PDF)
ISBN 978-3-631-92963-6 (EPUB)
DOI 10.3726/ b22549

Published by Peter Lang GmbH, Berlin, Germany

info@peterlang.com - www.peterlang.com

This publication has been peer reviewed.

Abstract

The aim of this work is to analyze twentieth-century literary representations of Spanish immigration in the United States of America set between 1900 and 1950, as reflected in the following books: *Chromos* (1948), by Felipe Alfau; *Windmills in Brooklyn* (1953), *Fiesta: A Novel of Modern Spain* (1960), by Prudencio de Pereda; *Pinnick Kinnick Hill: An American Story* (2003), by Gain W. González; *The Lower East Side Kid That Made It Good: The Autobiography of Claude Morell* (2008), by Claude Morell; and *Las hijas del Capitán* (2018), by María Dueñas. The variety of scenarios of these texts offers a wide picture of the experiences of these Spanish immigrants and the different strategies that they used to succeed in a new country, a new reality, while negotiating their identity between the new American culture and their native Spanish one. These six life stories will be examined to identify how they represent the history, use of language, and the cultural transformation in which the characters find themselves through their lives and how they evolve in the different spaces and times presented in these readings. This representation will be analyzed through the phenomenon of transculturation and hybridization and the theory of identity in the Third Space. The first chapter presents a theoretical framework of the concepts related to the cultural transformation that the characters in these works will experience. The second chapter focuses on the historical background and the representation of the Spanish community in the United States, more specifically in Harrison County and New York City, where all the stories connect. The third chapter focuses on the representation of witnessing and memory and offers a closer view of how they affect the main characters of these stories. The fourth chapter explores the use of language in the texts and how it is used both by the author and the protagonists of these stories in the different settings. The last chapter closes the cultural hybridization circle with an analysis of the different stages in which the identity of the Spanish immigrant transforms and how they are fully or partially assimilated into American society.

Contents

Introduction

Between 1820 and 1977, around 320,000 Spanish immigrants officially arrived in the United States of America, approximately 250,000 of them before 1950 (Rueda Hernanz 1993, 74). In other words, more Spaniards crossed the Atlantic Ocean to settle in what is now the United States of America than in any other period in history. The story of the Spanish migration to the American continent began with the arrival of the first Spanish explorers led by Christopher Columbus on October 12, 1492, to the Caribbean island of La Española. This event would initiate a series of voyages that would culminate in the establishment of the first successful settlements by Europeans of Spanish origin during the sixteenth century and the arrival of more Spaniards from the Iberian Peninsula (Blazquez Dominguez et al. 2011). For centuries, Spanish immigrants and their descendants have left written records of their experiences in all the countries that today form the American continent. In the case of the United States, this account of history is relevant because it focuses on the literary representation of those writers of Spanish origin who write about the last major period of Spanish immigration between 1900 and 1950 and how they choose to describe and interpret, in a subjective way, the cultural transformation experienced by members of Spanish communities in the United States.

In 2011, Alicante-born director Artur Balder directed the documentary *Little Spain* about a Spanish neighborhood in New York City located in the area around 14th Street, between Seventh and Eighth Avenue on the island of Manhattan.[1] The work, which was retrieved from relative obscurity, recounts the history of Spanish immigrants in the metropolis, and the documentary archive of the Spanish Benevolent Society, the oldest Spanish society in the United States, founded by Spanish immigrants in the nineteenth century, was a discovery for me and led to a fascination with the almost unknown history of those immigrants who crossed the Atlantic

1 *Little Spain*. Directed by Artur Balder. New York: Bluechromatic Productions, Chinstrap Films, Meatpacking Productions, 2011.

Ocean in search of a better life. This documentary was the genesis of my interest in the topic and spurred my curiosity to deepen my knowledge and begin to research the Spanish diaspora in the United States of America.

This monograph was born out of my passion for Spanish history and literature, two subjects that are not only intertwined when we talk about Spanish immigration in the United States but especially in the city of New York, where the growth of the arrival of Spaniards and its relevance during the second half of the nineteenth century and the first half of the twentieth century was overshadowed by other immigrant groups from the same period (Dolan 2010). This work will focus on a segment of the Spanish population that has remained invisible and forgotten for decades, not only by history but also by researchers and even by their own country. Special attention will be given to the Spaniards that migrated to the United States, and especially those who decided to stay in New York City and in Harrison County or, like in the case of Ros, nickname for Erostrato Varona in Prudencio de Pereda's *Fiesta: A Novel of Modern Spain* (1953), those who returned to Spain after years in the American country to reconnect with their Spanish roots. This little-known part of the United States' history and the underrepresentation of Spanish immigrants there have become an opportunity to explore a specific time and a space only studied by a few scholars.

The aim of this book is to provide evidence that there is a historical place for these invisible immigrants' stories, a place where they can be remembered and that can be used to show a process of cultural transformation. The depiction of Spanish immigration during the first half of the twentieth century (1900–1950) in the United States through literature is sparse; however, it is also a unique space where these Spaniards can find their place for representation. As a result, the specific goal of this work will be to study how this immigrant community is (re)presented in a few selected works, written by authors of Spanish origin, and to delve into their lives through the main characters and their narratives. This book tries to demonstrate that there is a cultural transition that these Spaniards experienced during the decades when they had to negotiate their identity and that it can be analyzed through literature based on and inspired by this period of history. The texts chosen prove that this transition can be traced using literature and thus construct a reliable literary representation of how the native Spanish culture of these immigrants merged with the dominant Anglo-American one.

The six stories selected will be examined to study the representation of memory, witnessing, and the use of language to identify the different states of cultural hybridity in which the characters find themselves throughout their lives and how they evolve in the different spaces and times presented in these texts. For decades, Spanish communities in the United States managed to preserve many features of their culture. The representation of the cultural transformation of the characters that portray these communities and their interaction with the environment shows a clear image of the Spaniards who settled in the country looking for a better life. This representation will be explored through the processes of transculturation and hybridization, as well as through the theory of identity of the Third Space.

These texts have been chosen for a few strategic reasons: first, because they are six of the scarce existing descriptions dedicated exclusively to the legacy of the Spanish community in the United States of America between 1900 and 1950. Second, because each text is set in a different but continuous temporal context that will give a specific and diverse perspective of the unique realities that could be found in the Spanish community during the first half of the twentieth century in the United States. And third, because they allow us to evaluate the legacy of twentieth-century migration. The contexts in which the texts are set include Spain, West Virginia, and New York City, in the boroughs of Manhattan, Queens, and Brooklyn. Therefore, the specifics of each text and the background of their authors will allow for a better understanding of this literature and how the writers represent the experience of Spanish immigration in the United States. Accordingly, I will focus part of my analysis on the process of cultural hybridity of these immigrants and the connection to their authors, as each one of these books is partly biographical and partly a memoir about how these invisible immigrants had to juggle their cultural transition in a new country to survive and thrive.

The breadth of the literature selected enables us to create a chronological timeline of the works to show the variety of spaces that constitute this analysis. The first text that introduces the Spanish immigrants to the American nation is *Pinnick Kinnick Hill: An American Story/Las colinas sueñan en español* (2003), by Gavin W. González, set in Harrison County, West Virginia. It begins in 1913, when the narrator's father becomes a local beer distributor. *Windmills in Brooklyn* (1960), by Prudencio de Pereda, is set in New York in the 1920s and narrates the childhood and youth of Prudencio with his family and their family friend, Agapito, around the world of the *teverianos*, or Spanish cigar sellers. *The Lower East Side Kid That Made It Good: The Autobiography of Claude Morell* (2008), by Claude Morell himself and edited by his daughter Teresa Morell, is set mainly in New York and begins in 1928, when eleven-month-old Claude arrives in the city with his parents. María Dueñas's *Las hijas del Capitán* (2018) is set in New York in 1936 and focuses on the lives of three young girls from Spain: Victoria, Mona, and Luz Arenas. *Chromos* (1948), by Felipe Alfau, follows the adventures of the narrator and his two friends during the 1940s in New York City. Finally, de Pereda's *Fiesta: A Novel of Modern Spain* (1953) is set in Spain in 1948, where Erostrato Varona, also known as Ros, returns to Mozares, his family's village in Burgos, fifteen years after his last visit to Spain.

In their analysis of the literary production on immigration, Konrad Bercovici's *Around the World in New York* (1924) and Julio Camba's *La ciudad automática* (1932) will be briefly explored, due to their framing of the literary period studied from 1900 to 1950, but will not be analyzed in depth as they are both considered travel literature with a comical, almost mocking tone, and they lack the presence of a story and a number of characters of Spanish origin where hybridization takes place. Other types of literary production from this time period and based on the experience of Spanish authors in the United States will not be taken into account, such as *Poeta en Nueva York* (1940), by Federico García Lorca, or *Exceso de equipaje: mis viajes a Estados Unidos, monólogos, películas, cuentos* (1950), by the Spanish writer and playwright Enrique Jardiel Poncela, due to their lack of connection to the phenomenon of cultural hybridity. Similarly, other works of fiction about Spaniards in the United States where the theme of Spanish migration is not relevant, such as *Llámame Brooklyn* (2006), by Eduardo Lago, have not been included in this study. *It is important to consider* that, with the exception of *Las hijas del capitán* (2018), the other five texts were originally written in English. As a result, language will be a fundamental element when analyzing the stories as well as the interactions in Spanish and English that take place in these narratives and that outline the cultural identity of the characters of these works and their authors. The choice of Dueñas's novel, being the only one written in the twenty-first century and not by an immigrant, is deliberate, since Dueñas interviewed the last survivors and witnesses of that period, some of whom I had the honor to meet. She also used the original archives of the Spanish Benevolent Society, dating back to 1889, which I was also able to use in my research, to recount her story.[2] Therefore, *Las hijas del Capitán* represents the result that the phenomenon of collective memory and literature written by writers of Spanish origin has had on later authors such as Dueñas. The author decides to revisit the spaces described by other writers, thus creating literature inspired by real historical facts but whose main characters are fictional.

To understand these narratives, I will combine the theoretical framework with the historical background before focusing on the phenomenon of the cultural transformation and coexistence of the cultures represented in these stories. *It is important to consider* that, again, except for Dueñas's *Las hijas del Capitán*, the novels are written by first-generation Spanish immigrants (Alfau) or second-generation Spaniards who were raised in one of the Spanish communities (de Pereda, González) in the United States. The case of Morell is especially interesting because, although he migrated to America with his parents, he was only eleven months old, so he could be included in both groups, but especially in the second one, as he lived in the American country until he became an adult. Furthermore, the historical background will focus on the history of the Spanish immigrants in the United States, especially in New York City, between the 1840s and the 1950s, although other centers of Spanish migration will also be mentioned when the waves of Spaniards who arrived in the States were more significant and constituted the basis of the Spanish communities.

I will also delve into the cultural hybridization of the characters between their Spanish culture of origin and the Anglo-American culture of reception, represented through topics such as family, religion, tradition, and the interpersonal relationships among the characters. Scholars such as Homi Bhabha, Edward Said, Gustavo Pérez Firmat, and Mary Louise Pratt have examined the effects of hybridity, colonization, biculturalism, and transculturation

2 La Nacional. 2018. Spanish Benevolent Society of New York Archive. New York City, New York.

and have shown that migration creates cultural conflicts between groups, producing multicultural situations where the clash of cultures plays a major role, thus giving way to new realities and identities. The importance of the use of language, memory, and observation to create an image of the past will also be examined to decipher the complex and contradictory reality of the Spanish immigrants represented in these books. The clash of the dominant and the dominated culture is depicted, and the possibilities of the interaction between them entail a wide variety of possibilities: cultural death or cultural evolution, the non-assimilation of the first generation, the assimilation of the 1.5 and the second generation—who are integrated but also keep their culture of origin—and the following generations, who are more susceptible to losing their culture. This book aims to analyze how the characters evolve and are changed by the interaction between their culture of origin and their culture of reception using the notion of transculturation and biculturalism and examining how a new hybrid self is created when they engage in the process of constructing a new culture. I will use concepts such as acculturation, deculturation, and neoculturation to study the complex transitions between the Spanish and the American cultures and to analyze the effects of these changes in the characters portrayed by González, de Pereda, Morell, Alfau, and Dueñas.

Another element to highlight in the literary description of Spanish immigration in the United States between 1900 and 1950 in the selected texts is the varied representation of the different origins of these Spanish immigrants. Among them are Andalusians, like Dueñas's protagonists Victoria, Mona, and Luz Arenas, from Málaga, or the family described by de Pereda in *Windmills in Brooklyn*. There are Basques, like those described by Alfau in *Chromos*; Galicians, like de Pereda's Agapito López; Valencians, like Claude Morell himself and his family; Asturians, like the community of Spaniards living in Gonzalez's West Virginia; and Castilians, like Ros Varona, who flies to his hometown of Mozares in the province of Burgos.

My claim is that these immigrants did not erase their Spanish identity but rather evolved when mixing the culture of origin with the one of reception, thereby creating a new hybrid self. In all six stories, the main characters negotiate their identity through biculturalism and the transculturation phenomenon, the cultural transition that Spanish immigrants experienced after their arrival to the States, a new context where the representation of their identity blurs as the characters are assimilated into American society. This transition is represented by a wide range of features, such as displacement, bilingualism, nostalgia, and so on, creating a broad spectrum of possibilities for an examination and analysis of how Spanish immigration literature represents and replicates their idea of Spain in the United States, a place where "the exile aspires to reproduce, rather than recast, native traditions" (Pérez Firmat 1996, 8). As a result, the people that inhabit these texts exemplify the negotiation of the identity that Spanish immigrants were forced to face. Consequently, the particularities of each story help to better understand these narratives as the phenomenon of emigration prompts the characters' negotiation of their self, which transforms depending on the time and space where they and their descendants are displaced from their original culture.

The characters embody the concept of transculturation, coined and defined by the Cuban anthropologist Fernando Ortiz in 1940 in his work *Cuban counterpoint, tobacco and sugar*, and its different stages (acculturation, deculturation, and neoculturation), as the transition from a Spanish to a Spanish-American identity. They contribute to providing a picture of Spanish immigration in the United States that can complete the space created by mainstream history and literature. The use of the characters and their interactions with other Spaniards around them is essential to see the diversity of the Spanish community and to understand the different approaches that they use to succeed in the American nation while negotiating their identity. Additionally, the space that these invisible immigrants hold in their new country has to do with the importance of the when and the where, the time and the place where these communities were constructed.

The monograph will be organizationally structured in the following format. Chapter 1, "Of Theory and Migration," provides an academic response to the concepts that will be used for the analysis of these texts. Section one, "Approaches to the Concept of Culture," will focus on terms such as culture,[3] transculturation, biculturalism, hybridism, and the Third Space. They will be examined to understand the concept of community and how Spanish immigrants negotiated their identity in the United States,

3 As a compendium of beliefs, knowledges, and behaviors of a group of people.

creating their own representation of their motherland based on their idea of Spain, their region, and their traditions, and connecting their memories to the construction of their community on the other side of the Atlantic. The term "transculturation," coined by Ortiz to define the mix of cultures, and the concept of hybridity, which refers to the result of this merging in the creation of a new individual, and the postcolonial sociolinguistic theory of identity of the Third Space developed by the critical theorist Homi K. Bhabha, will be later used to examine both the characters and the literature where they appear. I will demonstrate that the texts analyzed are essential to understanding the construction of the memory of Spanish immigrants in the United States during the first half of the twentieth century, as literature represents a valuable weapon in the arsenal of the portrayal and witnessing of the past.

The second section, "Identity and Culture," focuses on other concepts that can sometimes be confused with culture but are not, and yet are part of the individual. It begins by pointing out that terms such as race, blood, soil, and ethnicity cannot be understood as culture, as sometimes the boundaries between what culture is and what it is not seem to blur under the wide range of studies around the topic. The third section, "The Process of Transculturation"; the fourth section, "The Question of Mestizaje"; and the fifth section, "The Character of Hybridity Discourse," present a theoretical framework of the concepts related to transculturation, biculturalism, and hybridism that the characters of the Spanish immigrants will experience. The third section will introduce the postcolonial theory of the Third Space using the works of Benedict Anderson and his *magnum opus*, *Imagined Communities*, and Homi Bhabha's *The Location of Culture* in order to approach the topic of what communities are and how the individuals who live in these communities move in-between cultures.

Chapter 2, "Spaniards in the Melting Pot: A Historical Background," provides a historical context for future analyses of the texts. The chapter will be divided into two major sections: "Origins" and "Building Spanish Communities in the New World." The phenomenon of Spanish emigration to the United States has always been a residual topic in the studies relating to migration from Spain to America, focusing more on the migratory flows that took place from the Iberian Peninsula to the countries in South America (Gómez 1962; Azancot, Vega and Oyamburu 1992; Redondo

Carrero 2017). In fact, it was not until the last decade of the twentieth century that it was conscientiously studied by historian Germán Rueda Hernanz in works such as *La emigración contemporánea de españoles a Estados Unidos. 1820–1950. De "dons" a "misters"* (1993) and *Españoles emigrantes en América (Siglos XVI–XX)* (2000). Rueda Hernanz focused his work on quantifying and delving deeper into Spanish immigration in the United States using archival data and testimonies to create a conceptual map of the distribution of Spanish immigration in the American country in the period spanning from the early nineteenth to the mid-twentieth century when this migration was most relevant. As a historiographical work, Rueda Hernanz presents the results of his research in an objective and concise manner, avoiding a subjective analysis of the data and creating very useful bibliographical material to illustrate the context of Spanish migration for over a hundred years.

However, it was not until the beginning of the twenty-first century that academia began to pay attention to the phenomenon of Spanish migration in the United States with the creation of its corresponding communities. Thanks to works of Professor James D. Fernández such as *Facing Facism: New York and the Spanish Civil War* (2007) and *La Colonia: A Photo Album of Spanish Immigrants in New York, 1898–1945* (2011), the phenomenon of Spanish immigration[4] in the United States once again took hold in the debate around aspects of that migration and the context of how the successive waves transformed the lives of those Spaniards who arrived on the shores of their new country from the mid-nineteenth century onward. Fernández's contribution to the study of Spanish migration has been essential to understanding its role in the United States, producing a literary boost that reached one of its high points in 2018 with the publication of the novel *Las hijas del Capitán* by Spanish writer María Dueñas, partially inspired by Fernández's research, which uses the life in the Spanish

4 Immigration: moving permanently to another country. Emigration: the action of leaving one's own country to live in another one. Migration: movement of people from one place to another. In this book, the term immigration will be used when talking about the Spaniards who arrived in the United States of America during this time period.

communities established in New York City during the early twentieth century as a background for her story.

Chapter 3, "Spanish Memory and Migration," is divided into four sections. Section one, titled "The Construction of Collective Identity," offers a brief approach to the history of the study of memory and witnessing. The question of memory in literature as a reconstructive tool of the history of the Spanish immigration in the United States is essential to understand the importance of recollection to (re)create a past drawn on the testimonies and the fiction (albeit based on reality) used to create a time and a space that would otherwise be impossible to represent and remember for future generations. The second section, "Literary Representation of Spanish Immigration in the United States," includes a summary of the books that revolve around this topic. The third section, "*Morriña*: The Return to the Imagined Spain," begins with the idea of remembering and the recollection of past events, underlining the importance of witnessing and testimony through history to understand the past. Section four, "Spanish Communities and Societies," offers a brief overview of the oldest representation of the construction and growth of the Spanish community in the metropolis; with it, I wanted to supply a quick view of New York's most important neighborhoods and societies that are represented in one way or another in the selected works, places where Spaniards negotiated their portrayal of their country, in which memory, nostalgia, and community are entangled, defining the new roles of the Spanish immigrants operating at different levels of cultural transformation.

Chapter 4, "The Representation of Linguistic Hybridization," is divided into five parts, corresponding to the five authors of the six selected works. It offers a closer view of their use of language. It will also focus on the hybridization in the texts themselves and how the identities of the characters are transformed in the different settings presented, along with the mixing of cultures and, as a result, the mixing of languages that will manifest in the use of code-switching. I believe that the readings included in this book represent a good example of the different approaches that Spaniards took when they arrived in the United States. It is therefore essential to analyze the linguistic hybridization that occurs in order to understand the cultural changes experienced by the protagonists of the stories and even by the authors, who often inhabit the space of the narrator and of the characters themselves. Thus, for example, the first section, "Prudencio de Pereda's Portrayal of Spanish Immigration," is divided into three parts. The first is dedicated to *teverianos*, cigar sellers whose origins date back to the Spanish immigration to Cuba. The second, "From Andalusia to Brooklyn," focuses on the use of language in *Windmills in Brooklyn*, and the third and final part, "The Tragedy at Mozares," is about de Pereda's linguistic work in his novel *Fiesta*. The following four sections, "Claude Morell's The Lower East Side Kid That Made It Good," "Gavin W. González's Kinnick Hill, An American Story," "María Dueñas's Calle 14," and "Felipe Alfau's *Chromos*: The Spanish New York City Novel," will also focus on the use of languages in the authors' works.

The fifth and last chapter, "Cultural Hybridization and the Creation of the Americaniard," revolves around the result of the process of cultural clash experienced by the protagonists of these texts. This will be a conceptual approach to the notion of transculturation as a question of identity and how these new immigrants have their own role as new American citizens in the City of Lights. First, in the acculturation stage, I will examine how some of the characters acquire elements of the American culture. Second, in the deculturation phase, I will analyze whether they lose part of their Spanish culture, now mixed with the American culture. Third and finally, in the neoculturation phase, I will evaluate the characters' evolution to see if a new identity has been created due to the mixing of the Spanish and American cultures. The characters under study here are a perfect example of the literary representation of transculturation in twentieth-century Spanish immigrants, as they faced new challenges in the new country. In this sense, the novels are a good example of how the Spanish and American concepts of womanhood have changed. As Professor María del Pilar Cagiao Vila, an expert in the History of the Americas, points out, "el hecho de ser mujer mediatizó la decisión de emigrar, la manera de hacerlo y hasta la elección del destino" (2007, 161).[5] As a result, Spanish immigrant women represent a duality of identities and how the patterns of female interaction among

5 This book uses bilingual quotes: "the fact of being a woman mediated the decision to emigrate, the way of doing so and even the choice of destination." Unless otherwise specified, all translations are mine.

themselves and also with men become an opportunity to grow and develop their personalities. This chapter closes with the completion of the transcultural circle when the identity of the Spanish immigrant has been transformed and they are fully or partially assimilated into American society.

Chapter 1: Of Theory and Migration

1.1. Approaches to the Concept of Culture

In 1492, the era of migratory movements to America began. Initially, it was the controlled movement of people to colonies and overseas territories by nations such as Spain, Portugal, France, England, the Netherlands, and Germany (Horn and Morgan 2005, 21–22). Until that time, no Western culture had permanently settled in the Americas, and the Spanish were the first ones. This means that, for more than five hundred years, Spanish culture has been present on the continent, converging with other cultures as people from both sides of the Atlantic went back and forth between America and Spain. Consequently, one cannot understand the history of Spain without America and the history of America without Spain.[6] However, to comprehend the effects of one culture on another and vice versa, it is essential to address the notion of culture since its definition is open to many interpretations.

In *Theories of Culture* (1974), the linguist and anthropologist Roger M. Keesing describes two different theories to approach culture from an anthropological point of view: those authors who consider cultures as adaptive systems and those who see cultures as ideational systems. Keesing argues that there is not only one definition for "culture" but different interpretations depending on how we see it. He asserts that

> "culture" does not have some true and sacred and eternal meaning we are trying to discover; but that like other symbols, it means whatever we use it to mean; and that as with other analytical concepts, human users must carve out—and try to partially agree on—a class of natural phenomena it can most strategically label (1974, 73).

Therefore, there is no single definition of culture, but different interpretations of what culture means depending on the branch to which scholars belong, whether it is anthropological, literary, historical, or any other.

6 The two-way relationship between Spain and America has been as positive as it has been conflictive and, in many contexts, it continues to be so.

If we consider the etymology of the word "culture," "comes from the Latin *cultus*, which means 'care,' and from the French *colere* which means 'to till' as in 'till the ground' " (Berger 2000). Although it is true that there is no consensus on the best way to define the concept of "culture," authors have theorized about its definition and come very close to what could be considered a consensus. Two articles with the same title, "What is culture?" by George F. MacDonald (1991) and "What is culture?" by Yamini Krishnamurti (1993), offer two relevant definitions of culture. MacDonald links the concept of culture to the idea of a museum, as culture, he writes, "is not something that belongs purely to the past; it is an integral and inalienable part of what we are today and will become tomorrow" (MacDonald 1991, 9). On the other hand, Krishnamurti refers to culture from a less theoretical perspective, leaving aside the sociological or psychological point of view, as she considers that culture "relates to ideas which enables us to see the world... Culture is in the realm of ideas as it helps us see the world through the 'higher algebra of metaphors' " (Krishnamurti 1993, 74).

Other authors, such as Keesing (1974), prefer to embrace a more theoretical perspective and point out "cultural adaptationists" as a set of culture theories that agree that "cultures are systems (of socially transmitted behavior patterns) that serve to relate human communities to their ecological settings" (1974, 75). According to this definition, a culture is, therefore, a structure that serves to transmit patterns of human actions that connect people to their environment. Contrarily, the German Anthropologist and Professor Dr. Emeritus Thomas Bargatzky considers that this "adaptation" of culture creates an antagonistic position between sociocultural systems, a theoretical construct where people interact using their culture and the environment (Bargatzky *et al.* 1984, 405).

The way of life of these communities encompasses settlement patterns and territorial distribution, including their political, religious, and economic organization. In other words, everything that has to do with the way human beings live in a community. However, Keesing underlines that "cultures are viewed broadly as behavior systems characteristic of populations, extending, and permitting somatic givens, whether we consider them to be patterns *of* or patterns *for* behavior is a secondary question" (Keesing 1974, 75). Each culture is a way of socially transmitting the behavioral characteristics of each of the communities. These characteristics may include elements such as their religious beliefs, their economic model, even the way they organize themselves as a social community, and how they relate to other ones.

In opposition to "cultural adaptationists," there are different branches of ideational theories of culture. Each branch has its own interpretation of culture, where theorists define the term depending on how they see culture as a system of ideas. There are scholars who see cultures as cognitive systems, a "system of knowledge" (Keesing, 77). According to other anthropologists, like Ward Goodenough, "A society's culture consists of whatever it is one has to know or believe in order to operate in a manner acceptable to its members" (Goodenough 1957, 167). Goodenough's culture is not a material phenomenon, as it does not refer to emotions, behavior, things, or people but to how these things are organized. On the contrary, authors such as Laura Nader consider that Goodenough is optimistic in his perspective of anthropology and, therefore, of his definition of culture since he leaves the inevitable political and procedural nature of the discipline uncovered (Nader 2002, 441).

According to Goodenough's optimistic view, culture is the "form of things that people have in mind, their models for perceiving, relating, and otherwise interpreting them" (Goodenough 1957, 167); thus, it is a view of things from their own personal prism. "As such, the things people say and do, their social arrangements and events, are products or by-products of their culture as they apply it to the task of perceiving and dealing with their circumstances" (167). Their culture is the result of their circumstances, and, as a result, daily living and events are also cultural forms representations. Goodenough defines culture as cognition. Culture becomes an ideational system, a set of ideas that individuals have as members of a community in relation to the meaning of things, their behavior, emotions, and relations with other people. Goodenough's cultural cognition hypothesis establishes that human beings determine their cultural identity based on their psychological perception of the world.

Another approach to culture as a system of ideas is the continental structuralist system of authors like the French anthropologist and ethnologist Claude Lévi-Strauss. According to Lévi-Strauss's structuralism, culture is what the British anthropologist Edward B. Tylor defined in his work *Primitive Culture* (1920) as, taken in its wide ethnographic sense, that complex whole which includes knowledge, belief, art, morals, law, custom, and any other capabilities and habits acquired by an individual as a member of society (1920, 1). The condition of culture among the various societies of humankind, insofar as it is capable of being investigated on general principles, is a subject apt for the study of laws of human thought and action. Lévi-Strauss agrees with Tylor's definition of culture but adds that mind and culture follow a structural system. Additionally, he considers that culture is a symbolic system, "a fragment of humanity which, from the point of view of the research at hand and of the scale on which the latter is carried out, presents significant discontinuities in relation to the rest of humanity" (Lévi-Strauss 1963, 295). Therefore, this system is a part of human beings that represents important variations when compared to other human beings.

This conception of culture is essential to understanding the evolution of the term that will later help to define transculturation. For Lévi-Strauss, culture is cumulative and depends on many contexts. Individuals can be analyzed from different cultural contexts depending on the size of the group they belong to, as well as other elements such as their language, religion, profession, art, family structure, and so on. He further characterizes his definition of culture through the representation of "cultural units" and uses an example to explain these discontinuities. In his opinion, if we wanted to know what the most relevant discontinuities are between, for example, North America and Europe, we would be talking about different cultures. However, if we refer to the discontinuities between, for example, New York and Chicago, we can speak of these two groups as different cultural "units." Some of these discontinuities may not vary according to what Lévi-Strauss is the goal of structural analysis. Culture can be, then, an objective reality and a function of the type of research conducted. As a result, context is fundamental to understanding the culture of a people, a community, and an individual. The more connections it has, the bigger its culture and, therefore, the greater its complexity (Lévi-Strauss 1963).

However, these are not the only definitions of culture. Edward B. Tylor and Franz Boas are considered two of anthropology's founding fathers. According to Boas, anthropology must focus on creating a framework in which the growth of human culture is considered, taking into consideration both the progress of the civilization of antiquity and the cultures of our own times (1898). If Tylor developed his concept of culture in his work *Primitive*

Culture, Boas challenged Tylor's definition of culture by providing context to the term and explaining the importance of studying the field before developing it. Boas did not provide a specific definition of culture but, instead, focused on the importance of the plurality of the concept and helped to establish the pillars of future interpretations of the definition. Later, the American anthropologist-linguist Edward Sapir, one of Boas's students, provided a clear definition based on Boas's studies of culture, indicating that it is "the spiritual possessions of the group rather than of the individual... those general attitudes, views of life, and specific manifestations of civilization that give a particular people its distinctive place in the world" (Sapir 2013, 2). In this respect, Sapir provides a much more holistic definition than his mentor, focusing on culture as the result of the community more than just one subject, a culture of collective individuals.

Boas's influence on the definition of culture did not stop there. In *Culture: A Critical Review of Concepts and Definitions*, the American anthropologists Clyde Kluckhohn and Alfred L. Kroeber, Boas's first PhD students (Lentz 2017, 188), formulated a new definition of culture as

> patterns, explicit and implicit, of and for behavior acquired and transmitted by symbols, constituting the distinctive achievement of human groups, including their embodiments in artifacts; the essential core of culture consists of traditional (i.e., historically derived and selected) ideas and especially their attached values; culture systems may, on the one hand, be considered as products of action, on the other as conditioning elements of further action (Kluckhohn and Kroeber 1952, 181).

According to Kluckhohn and Kroeber's definition, culture consists of traditions and behaviors acquired and transmitted through signs and symbols that represent the achievements of the community. This culture is based on their perception of life and the values that regulate their lives, while culture systems are the result of practice and experience of continuous action over time. Nonetheless, according to other authors like Carola Lentz, Sapir's concept of culture is open to interpretation by other theorists, allowing one to understand the concept as "the spiritual foundation of a community of values" (Lentz 2017, 186), far from the approach of theorists more focused on ideational theories of culture, such as Goodenough's cultural cognition hypothesis.

However, Goodenough's approach is not the only one when attempting to define culture as a system of ideas. The anthropologist and social system theorist James Clifford has a close but slightly different explanation to define cultures as symbolic systems. In *The Predicament of Culture: Twentieth-Century Ethnography, Literature, and Art* (1988), Clifford explores the meaning of culture and indicates that its construction is directly connected to the West, where "expectations of wholeness, continuity, and essence have long been built into the linked Western ideas of culture and art" (1988, 233). He explains that culture is like an organism: "Culture is enduring, traditional, structural (rather than contingent, syncretic, historical). Culture is a process of ordering, not of disruption. It changes and develops like a living organism. It does not normally 'survive' abrupt alterations" (235). This organism can change, mutate, and adapt to different encounters with other cultures but can also disappear if it gets in contact with an aggressive, dominant culture. His view understands culture as an organism that is always changing but also as a fragile structure that cannot survive extreme hybridizations.

Clifford concludes that the concept of culture accommodates internal diversity and an "organic" division of roles but not sharp contradictions, mutations, or emergences. It sees tribal "traditionalists" and "moderns" as representing aspects of linear development, one looking back, the other forward. It cannot see them as contending or alternating futures (338). This means that while culture is malleable and can accommodate different elements when in contact with other cultures, it cannot be fragmented, as survival is tied to several characteristics that shape its concept of native culture in its community and the identity of its members: groups negotiating their identity in contexts of domination and exchange persist, patching themselves together in ways different from a living organism. A community, unlike a body, can lose a central "organ" and not die. All the critical elements of identity are in specific conditions replaceable: language, land, blood, leadership, and religion. Recognized, viable tribes exist in which any or even most of these elements are missing, replaced, or largely transformed (338). While it is true that the dominated culture is the one that tends to lose its language, religion, or traditions, it is also true that the dominant culture may undergo changes when in contact with it, and the absorption of the former into the latter may mean the survival of the community as hybrids. In this regard, Clifford points out that identity is "conjunctural, not essential" (11), and although culture and identity are not the same, they are interconnected. Therefore, there cannot be an identity without a culture, nor a culture without a collective identity.

Clifford treats cultures as a system of meanings and symbols. In *Interpretation of Cultures* (1973), he claims that "[the] cutting of the culture concept down to size, therefore actually ensuring its continued importance rather than undermining it... for a narrowed, specialized, and, so I imagine, theoretically more powerful concept of culture" (Clifford 1973, 4) has been the objective of many scholars. He also considers that there are many interpretations for the term and defines culture in his own words as "an historically transmitted pattern of meanings embodied in symbols, a system of inherited conceptions expressed in symbolic forms by means of which men communicate, perpetuate, and develop their knowledge about and attitudes toward life" (89). Clifford understands Lévi-Strauss's ethnographic and structural approach but considers that context is important to analyze culture. Similarly, he considers Goodenough's cognitive system as simplistic and far from his own vision of culture as a collection of signs.

Other social system theorists, like the German sociologist Max Weber, did not define "culture" *per se* but understood the social functions of culture as it

> possesses *motivational or utopian functions* through its ability to influence the way people lead their lives following extra-ordinary or utopian principles, for "all historical experience confirms the fact that man would never achieve what is possible were he not to forever strive, in his world, toward the impossible" (cit. in Jäger and Wiskind 1991, 118).

For Weber, "culture" is given and maintained by the community through symbolic systems that reinforce the values of its "culture." In this respect, one of the social system theorists who support the definition of cultures as symbolic systems is the American anthropologist David Murray Schneider. He defines the term "culture" at the beginning of *American Kinship: A Cultural Account* (1980), applying the same concept of units used by Lévi-Strauss:

> A particular culture, American culture for instance, consists of a system of units (or parts) which are defined in certain ways, and which are differentiated according to certain criteria. These units define the world or the universe, the way

the things in it relate to each other, and what these things should be and do (1980, 1).

Schneider's definition of "culture" is much more abstract than that of other authors, but it indicates that he agrees that culture is a system of symbols where the categories that comprise what we know as culture are represented by a set of rules or units independent of the behavior of individuals.

In 1984, the American cultural anthropologist Sherry Ortner published "Theory in Anthropology since the Sixties," where she condemned the debate among symbolic anthropologists like Clifford and the evolution of the concept of culture during the last two decades. Ortner points out that culture has been viewed as an objective reality; however, it is fundamental to understand how culture is created and replicated "through human intention and action" (Ortner 1984, 158). According to Lentz (2017), the evolution of the concept of culture that Ortner predicted has not "materialized," and theorists like Roger Keesing and Adam Kuper agree that "the classical conception of culture is irredeemably reified, serves problematic purposes in discourses outside the academy, is no longer useful as an analytic concept, and thus needs to be abandoned" (Lentz 2017, 194). Kuper, for example, published *Culture: The Anthropologist's Account* (1999), where he stated that to define culture, it must be analyzed closely, separating from each other elements such as moral values, religious beliefs, language, knowledge, and so on, and studying the changes in which these elements are related to each other (Kuper 1999, 245). This does not mean that the definitions of culture mentioned before should not be considered, but, on the contrary, they should be used to understand that the concept of culture is broad and difficult, as theorists have been studying and working on it for decades without a consensus due to its different interpretations and meanings.

To distinguish modern society from traditional forms of social organization, Weber created his own dualistic terminology of "charismatic or traditional versus legal and routinized forms of authority" (2005, 72). According to Friedrich Jäger and Ora Wiskind, when distinguishing between the idea of culture and society, *it is important to consider* cultural history, as it understands culture as a process of integrating society by internalizing the necessary traditions. Jäger and Wiskind highlight that routinization is a historical prerequisite for knowing more about culture-based everyday behavior. This culture has a pre-established meaning, as it is concerned with the spread of knowledge collected in the "lifeworld" in order to orientate it (Jäger and Wiskind 1991, 117). For them, culture is understood as a process of social integration through tradition. The behaviors of the community are based on the experience of the behavioral routines of everyday life. This daily life has a meaning, and this meaning is transmitted through tradition. The transmission of knowledge creates a culture that integrates the community and represents what we understand today as culture.

On the other hand, the concept of "culture" from the point of view of sociology and psychology has provided diverse definitions. One of the most popular ones is sociologist Paul DiMaggio's. He explains that sociology views culture as "complex rule-like structures that constitute resources that can be put to strategic use" (DiMaggio 1997, 265). DiMaggio's review of culture from a sociological perspective portrays a term much more difficult to define, as culture evolves in the same way as human communities evolve. In his approach, to understand the concept of culture from a sociological point of view, *it is important to understand* that culture is a variable, and therefore it changes over time. As for the psychological perspective of the term culture, DiMaggio stresses that psychologists connect culture with memory, as they "have rejected behaviorism, accepted and demonstrated the existence of mental structures used to perceive, process, and retrieve information, and found ways to make inferences about such struct" 265). As a result, psychology establishes that memory is a fundamental part of the construction of culture not only by the individual but by the whole community. DiMaggio continues by underlining that "just as sociological research has demonstrated culture's complexity and fragmentation, psychological research has demonstrated the complexity of memory and provided glimpses of the partitioning of mental structures by domain" (265). In other words, the individual's mental structures have helped to establish memory as an element without which culture is not possible.

People use their memory to establish their culture, but they do not use all the knowledge that they have to assert it, as they consider all the knowledge connected to their culture to be true: "Our heads are full of images, opinions, and information, untagged as to truth value, to which we are inclined to attribute accuracy and plausibility" (267). DiMaggio indicates that information, including false information, "passes into memory without being 'tagged' as to source or credibility, and that active inference is required to identify the source of the information when it is recalled" (267). As a result, knowledge and memory are intertwined as two indispensable elements in establishing the culture of the individual. Besides, he states that there are several interferences to be considered regarding how culture is created, as people retain "almost every image or idea with which they have come into contact," making "intelligible otherwise anomalous research findings about inconsistency in expressions of attitudes across time, cultural volatility in periods of rapid change" (268). In other words, interference goes beyond the ability of individuals to be in a single culture, as they are influenced by everything around them, as well as by other cultures. As DiMaggio points out, "the research explains the capacity of individuals to participate in multiple cultural traditions, even when those traditions contain inconsistent elements" (268). Besides, this "establishes the capacity of people to maintain distinctive and inconsistent action frames, which can be invoked in response to particular contextual cues" (268). This is especially interesting if we consider that human beings can interact with more than one culture; that is, the individual has the capacity to be multicultural and, therefore, to adapt to different environments even outside his or her community and culture.

As we have seen, the definitions of "culture" are varied and depend on the branch of knowledge that defines it. From anthropology to sociology and psychology, the term "culture" has had varied interpretations, turning this concept into one of the most abstract and complex to interpret. However, *it is important to note* that not everything counts when defining the concept of "culture," as we will further see when examining philosopher Lawrence E. Cahoone's work, essential to narrowing down its meaning and excluding those terms that, although similar, do not mean "culture."

1.2. Identity and Culture

As we have seen, the definition of culture is broad and debatable. Scholars in anthropology, sociology, or psychology have their own axioms regarding the term, and each author has their own explanation for the concept. However, not everything can be considered culture. Being an abstract concept, the idea of culture can often be confused with other notions, such as ethnicity, race, or blood. These elements, although related to the term, are not synonyms and should be used with caution. In *Cultural Revolutions: Reason Versus Culture in Philosophy, Politics, and Jihad* (2005), the philosopher Lawrence E. Cahoone examines the concept of culture in Chapter 2, "Who is culture?" where he analyzes what can be considered as culture and what cannot. According to Cahoone, culture is not just *whats* and *hows*, but *whos*; in other words, it is not only what it is regarded as culture and how it is perceived as such, but who represents those cultures. As a result of this approach, he raises two questions: "What are the criteria for deciding what counts as a particular culture, and what constitutes cultural membership and identity?" (Cahoone 2005, 56). The first question refers to the conditions of what culture means, and the second connects to the issue of what it means to be a people. For Cahoone, these connections are not easy to study because of the ambiguity of the words that make the term "culture" be misinterpreted on many occasions.

Culture is, according to the author, a question of perception. He explains that when people identify themselves as members of a culture, this "self-acknowledgement of membership is prima facie sufficient, if fallible, condition for cultural identification" (Cahoone 2005, 57). As soon as an individual identifies him/herself as part of a culture, he/she considers that there is a cultural association between them as individuals and, therefore gives birth to "a system of judgmental endogamy, the boundaries of a lifeworld of socially compelling expectations and norms" (57). However, *it is important to remember* that this set of behaviors, rules, beliefs, and traditions is also flexible and pluralistic within groups of human beings.

Another major fact regarding the term is, according to Cahoone, the level of cultural phenomena. At the lowest level, "everyday social behaviour, society and culture *must* merge" (57). He points out that in polycultural societies, different cultures tend to overlap, as "individuals or groups who bear distinct rites, icons, and metanarratives may yet function together under common norms of intelligibility and property on the everyday level in public and restrict the nonoverlapping portions of their cultures to privacy" (57). This is especially relevant in a polycultural society like the American society, which has been a melting pot of cultures and diversity since its foundation, a space where, at the beginning of the twentieth century, Spanish immigrants hid their Spanish culture on many occasions and only shared it with their Spanish family, their friends, and their neighborhood.

In *Acquired Alterity: Migration, Identity, and Literary Nationalism* (2022), there is a chapter, "Culture: Samurai, Spies, and Serialized Fiction," by Edward Mack, that considers that there are two similar but, at the same time, different definitions of the concept of culture. According to the author, there is a broad definition of culture, which he defines as "all the shared daily practices that are presumed to make one community of individuals different from another" (Mack 2022, 41), which includes all the traditions, customs, religious practices, and ways of life of a community, and a narrow definition of culture that can include literature: "the shared creative (in this case literary) products that (putatively) both reveal and reproduce the particular genius of that community" (41). This second definition of culture is not considered by Cahoone but can be very useful when considering the representation of culture in a community like the ones created by Spanish immigrants in the United States, especially if it is taken into account that this description can include the texts selected in this study to analyze the representation of culture and hybridity of these communities.

On the other hand, one of the most relevant things related to culture is to understand the meaning of acquiring one. It can be argued that being Spanish, for example, is not only a "body of values, or history, or civic institutions" (Cahoone 2005, 58), but also having a set of traditions (religious or not) and speaking the Spanish language. However, the cultural variety of a country like Spain, where each region, province, and municipality has its own intrinsic characteristics, makes us cautious in this respect. In that sense, other languages are spoken in the country, such as Galician, Catalan, or Basque, and, at the same time, "a matter of acquiring conceptual competence in handling the prevailing cultural language" (Parekh 1991, 203) seems to be relevant enough to be part of a culture. Besides, the distinction between language and culture is also *important*. In that sense, Cahoone indicates that

> the "having" of many languages is possible precisely because it does not make the demands on the self that cultural membership makes. A culture is not merely a competence, it is a social group. Having a culture is not like having a language, it is more like having a family, regarding which *having* it entails *being had by it*.

> Here having is belonging, I'm belonging constraints individuality while constituting it (Cahoone 2005, 59).

As a result, this idea of culture through language would be understood as 'cultural familiarity' but not 'cultural identity.' In the case of Spain, it could be argued that Spanish culture encompasses regional cultures such as those found in Asturias, Andalusia, or Castile and that, at the same time, they are all part of a bigger picture.

Managing to know and use Spanish culture is not equivalent to being Spanish. Accordingly, it could be argued that acquiring a culture requires broad experience based on living with the social group of the culture in question. The best way to possess this culture would be through birth and nurture, in this case, having been born and raised in Spain. This, according to Cahoone, distinguishes "knowing" a culture from "belonging" to a culture, or cultural *facility* from cultural *identity*" (2005, 58). Thus, first-generation Spaniards in New York City could love American culture, speak the English language, even adopt American values, and yet not identify themselves as Americans. This is very interesting, as it would only happen in the first generation, while the following ones would already be considered, as in this case, members of two cultures.

In his paper, "Language, Culture, and National Identity" (1996), Eric Hobsbawn focuses on languages in cultures and the subject of multiculturalism related to them. In his opinion, today, there is a new element of political language creation, the systematic regionalization of states, which could assimilate regions without special characteristics, whether they be linguistic, ethnic, cultural, or otherwise. That is, new region-states could be created, which is what Benedict Anderson would call a new imagined community, under a language uniting a group of people living within a common geographical framework but without a common culture, ethnicity, or language (Hobsbawn 1996, 1078). According to Hobsbawn, then, even first-generation immigrants could belong, as any native national, to a country of reception, creating a new nation based on the former, even without changing the political status of the country and regardless of whether the immigrants spoke Spanish rather than English and regardless of whether their culture, let us say Latina, cohabited with an Anglo-Saxon culture plus different ethnicities. The creation of this new imaginary community would be possible as long as a language was accepted to unite them all, one that would unify this multiculturalism and could be maintained, or not, but always within the parameters established by the dominant language to govern them all.

But then, what should *not* be considered culture? Cahoone describes four different human groupings "through which the *who* of culture has been understood" (Cahoone 2005, 59). These forms of human association or identity are race, blood, soil, and ethnicity. He makes it clear that these four elements are not culture *per se*. On the contrary, they are characteristics that may have an *important* cultural component but are not determinative in and of themselves. The author defines race as "a set of morphological traits that are inherited" that has "functioned in many places and times as a sign for social, psychological, and cultural differences" (59). However, he points out that this morphology is not a sufficient marker, as, according to his definition, there are fewer races than cultures in the world. It can be argued then that race is "*contingently* correlated with some sociocultural traits" (59), although the morphological distinctiveness does not justify the belonging of a person to a particular culture.

The second human grouping is blood: it is "in one *sense* narrower and in another sense broader than race. For blood means *descent*, and descent is a complex matter. It first refers to nationality and parentage. It is partially genetic" (62). Professor Werner Sollors, in his introduction to *Beyond Ethnicity. Consent and Descent in America* (1986) develops Cahoone's view of blood as a *descent* connected to culture but in no way part of culture as such. Sollors explains that "Descent relations are those defined by anthropologists as relations of 'substance' (by blood or nature); consent relations describe those of 'law' or 'marriage'" (Sollors 1986, 6). But Cahoone underlines that blood is "also partly social and legal, given that nonincentuous parents are not close blood relatives" (Cahoone 2005, 63). From this follows the interesting fact about blood that it can create connections with people that do not share it, as "descent generates non-descent ties" (63). Significantly, Cahoone concludes that in the case of political manifestation, blood is not related to ethnic or racial politics but clan politics because "under normal conditions even a small segmentary society cannot be constituted by a single clan, unless marriage partners are regularly imported from outside" (63), a fact that is not usual, at least in Western societies and most of the world.

Another term related to blood is "tribalism." He defines it as something completely different from "nationalism," "racialism," or "ethnocentrism" and talks about the tribe as supralocal and subethnic, covering several clans living in the region. Interestingly, this definition of tribe confirms that there is a clear connection between blood and culture but indicates that blood "relates to the *who* that teaches me a culture and to the *where* they taught me, in short, my *natal-maturational world*" (63). This is in keeping with what the Canadian anthropologist and museum director George F. MacDonald calls culture as something that does not belong "purely to the past; it is an integral and inalienable part of what we are today and will become tomorrow" as "individuals and institutions constantly create and re-create culture" (MacDonald 1991, 9). The importance of location for human beings is essential to understand the relevance of emigration as a compelling phenomenon that changes forever those involved in the process of relocation.

The third and fourth human groupings that Cahoone defines and differentiates from culture are "soil" and "ethnicity." The concept of soil would refer to the idea of the land of the community, while the term ethnicity is sometimes used as a synonym for nationality. As an example, he compares premodern societies, where soil and blood could be considered equivalent to ethnicity, to modern societies, where this is not contradictory because "rather than blood and place becoming supralocal, they simply decline in public significance altogether" (Cahoone 2005, 67). This example is especially significant, as it shows how the definitions of ethnicity, soil, and blood have changed over the centuries, and the idea that we can have of culture, location, and heritage nowadays has nothing to do with the one our ancestors had. Cahoone adds that the meaning of "ethnicity" is connected to the etymology of the English word "ethnic." He points out that "ethnic" comes from "the Greek *ethnikos*, which referred to a foreign people, normally in a somewhat disparaging way, like 'heathen.' This holds true also for the roots of 'nation,' which in Roman times meant non-Italianate peoples ruled by Rome" (67). He continues, indicating that

> although the connotations of the terms differ—*ethnikos* was linked both to *éthos*, character, and *ethos*, custom, while "nation" derives from *nasci*, to be born, hence refers to descent—their referent is the same: *a people*: understood either through the reproductive isolation or distinctive character. Unfortunately,

> he stresses that for people in general the word "nation" has been overtaken by the term national*ism*, hence sovereignty and states. As a result, in his opinion, the term "nationality" is used for "the political mobilisation of a people" and "ethnicity" "for the more fundamental condition of being *a people*" (67–68).

However, who is *a people*? The author answers that in the "ideal type" of people, it would be easy to find "*the identity of society and culture,*" as "being a social member and being a cultural member would not be distinguished" (68). On this occasion, it can be understood how social and cultural members are equivalent because the culture that these utopian people

> may of course specify distinctive roles and norms in each, and there may well be interclan conflict. But as long as all social members regard themselves as one "people," their forms of family life will be continuous with the social order (68–69).

In other words, if all members maintain the cultural and social forms, the order established by the community will also be maintained.

Other authors, such as Joane Nagel, maintain the importance of culture and identity as part of ethnicity. Nagel considers both elements as essential building blocks in the construction of ethnicity as both "are fundamental to the central projects of ethnicity: the construction of boundaries and the production of meaning" (Nagel 1994, 153). She does not consider directly that culture is ethnicity but part of it, in opposition to Cahoone's perspective that isolates the concepts as something completely different and not connected to each other. As a result, Nagel partly collides in the meaning that Cahoone wants to give to the concept of culture by separating it completely from ethnicity. For Nagel, ethnicity is something more dynamic than culture, as it is evolving constantly. Therefore, she also underlines that "the interplay between pre-existing cultural forms and the new uses to which they are put in the ethnic movement" (167) is fundamental to understanding both, and Cahoone's position would imply an independence of the two terms that would not correspond to that expounded by Nagel.

Due to the connection that Cahoone creates between social and cultural members, we may better understand his final definition of culture, where the cultural life of the perfect society, the "shared culture," will be "adequate to the determination of the sense and significance of human life" (Cahoone 2005, 69). He indicates that "*a people*" could be "formed by a *descent society* = *culture*, a group that subsists in the homogeneous condition, in which social and cultural membership are indistinct, and both acquired by descent or birth". However, he also points out that this is not the proximal meaning of it anymore, as we can also use the term "ethnicity" to "*claim descent from* a group that *is claimed to have at one time subsisted in the homogeneous condition of society = culture*". Nevertheless, he points out that this definition does not have to be completely true as our ancestors may "have lived in relatively modern societies that were no longer homogenous" (71).

It is in this approach that the political scientist Benedict Anderson claims that "ethnicity" or "nation" is imagined and constructed, because the individuals "of even the smallest nation will never know most of their fellow-members, meet them, or even hear of them, yet in the minds of each lives the image of their communion," as "communities are to be distinguished, not by their falsity/genuineness, but by the style in which they are imagined" (Anderson 2006, 6). The concept of "imagined communities" will be expanded on later, but it is relevant to mention it here, as it is fundamental in the construction of societies anywhere in the world. The idea of a homogeneous society = culture, for example, as in Spanish society, is easily proven wrong if we think about the social and cultural diversity of the Spanish regions, their languages, and the Spanish ancestors who, "in a premodern and prenationalistic age, may have regarded each other as competing" kingdoms and territories with an entangled cultural and historical background, with different characteristics according to their premodern particularities and morphology (Cahoone 2005, 71).

Cahoone concludes by indicating that if we refer to someone's identity as an ethnicity where there is modern meaning for behavior, two conditions must be considered: first, people must "*continue to exist* in some form, although not necessarily in the homogenous condition," because ethnicity only matters in the present day "if there is a community in some place that shares the ethnicity". In other words, if there is no such community, there can be no such ethnicity. And second, ethnic membership must be "relevant" when there is a problematic social circumstance (72). As can be seen, the concept of culture and its different definitions depend very much on the science that studies it and the time when the concept is established. As a result, the term "culture" and what we mean by it, as well as the cultures that define it, are constantly changing.

1.3. The Process of Transculturation

The scholar Lars Allolio-Näcke in *Encyclopedia of Critical Psychology* (2014) indicates that the concept of "transculturation" was coined in 1940 by the Cuban anthropologist Fernando Ortiz in his work *Cuban counterpoint, tobacco and sugar,* improved in 1963 with 200 extra pages (Santí 2002, 17). Ortiz indicates that transculturation is "the different phases of the process of transition from one culture to another" (2012, 132) through cultural exchange in three different phases: acculturation, deculturation, and neoculturation. According to Ortiz, transculturation can be defined as

> the different phases of the process of transition from one culture to another because this does not consist merely in acquiring another culture, which is what the English word acculturation really implies, but the process also necessarily involves the loss or uprooting of a previous culture, which could be defined as deculturation. In addition, it carries the idea of the consequent creation of new cultural phenomena, which could be called neoculturation. (2012, 132)

In his definition, Ortiz explains what he means by "transculturation"—the "transition from one culture to another"—but also by "acculturation"—"acquiring another culture"—, "deculturation"—"the loss or uprooting of a previous culture"—, and "neoculturation"—"the consequent creation of new cultural phenomena". These concepts denote Ortiz's pioneering vision and offer a guide to understanding the insights on the complex issue of Spanish culture in the United States. It can also help to clarify our understanding of the "Third Space" as a social and cultural space where the subjects, in this case Spanish immigrants, develop their hybrid selves, combining the culture's first space represented by their country of origin, Spain, and the one from the country of reception, the United States of America. This is a new liminal space created by the Spanish community and its interaction with the American Anglo-Saxon culture, whose memory is represented in literature as members of a cultural minority.

In *Cuban counterpoint, tobacco and sugar*, Ortiz underlines that there are different types of transculturation in Cuba and compares such a process between communities of Spanish and African origins where the culture shock was clearly different. His work reflects the author's "cubanidad" through the two most emblematic and world-renowned crops in Cuba: tobacco and sugar. This "cubanidad" is nothing more than the hybridism resulting from the process of transculturation that has taken place in Cuba over the last five hundred years, exemplified by Ortiz through the figures of tobacco and sugar: these two plants are now from the same country, from the same culture, and Ortiz uses their characteristics to analyze their permanent antagonistic parallelism: "Tobacco is born, sugar is made" (2012, 30), as these two natural riches go through the origin of cultivation, care, exploitation, processing, and trade. Ortiz uses the example of tobacco and sugar as a metaphor for the transculturation that takes place in Cuba between communities of Indigenous, African, and European (mainly Spanish) origin. For Ortiz, the result is the twentieth-century Cuban, a hybrid that blends the culture of the three continents. In addition, both tobacco and sugar have the peculiarity that they do not originate from Cuba, although it is true that tobacco comes from the American continent, while sugar comes from Asia. To Ortiz, it is important to explain the process of transculturation through examples in Cuba because he thinks that this process provoked the historical evolution of Cuban culture as the first American case of transculturation and hybridization on the continent (159).

The arrival of these Spanish immigrants to the United States and their subsequent literary production creates spaces where their lived experiences need to be told, hence the importance of the Third Space as a hybrid place where authors develop novels based on the lives of Spanish immigrants in places like New York. I will analyze this Third Space to focus on the main features of the literary representation of Spanish immigration. To understand the "Third Space" theory, it is essential to refer to two works: *Imagined Communities* (2006) by Benedict Anderson and *The Location of Culture* (2004) by Homi Bhabha. Anderson explains in his theory the origin of nationalism and how countries are a cultural construct, while he rejects the idea that nations are natural constructs. He defines all communities as "imagined" because "the members of even the smallest nation will never know most of their fellow-members, meet them, or even hear of them, yet in the minds of each lives the image of their communion" (Anderson 2006, 6).

On the other hand, Bhabha theorizes both about the "Third Space" and hybridity. To Bhabha, the borderline work of culture is found in the "in-between" space that revitalizes the colonial past while it disrupts the postcolonial present. This interruption of the postcolonial present by the colonial past introduces the concept of the "Third Space." As Bhabha points out,

> The theoretical recognition of the split-space of enunciation may open the way to conceptualizing an *international* culture, based not on the exoticism of multi-culturalism or the *diversity* of cultures, but on the inscription and articulation of culture's *hybridity*. To that end we should remember that it is the "inter"—the cutting edge of translation and negotiation, the *inbetween* space—that carries the burden of the meaning of culture. It makes it possible to begin envisaging national, anti-nationalist histories of the "people". And by exploring this Third Space, we may elude the politics of polarity and emerge as the others of our selves. (Bhabha 2004, 56)

Bhabha speaks about a new product. A hybrid space where cultures can intermingle in a single individual. According to this postulation, the articulation of hybridity is characterized by the representation of a postcolonial community where the individual manifests his or her uniqueness through a new space between past and present. However, in the case of Spanish immigrants, it would be difficult to speak of a post-colonial community in the United States, as they have been completely assimilated into American society; also, the evolution of the United States of America from an English colony to an independent nation has not experienced a proper process of decolonization, as the colonizers established a dominant European culture and expelled the Native Americans from the construction of the new American country. If we accept Anderson's theory about the construction of "imagined communities," it is essential to examine the texts selected to understand the history of the Spanish community in the United States. To follow a historical narrative of the lives of these Spaniards, the novels will be discussed in the chronological order in which the author places them, regardless of their date of publication. However, before starting this analysis of the novels, it is necessary to clarify the historical background of these works, as it is connected to the "Third Space" in the process of hybridity of the characters.

However, there are authors such as the historian Xosé Manoel Núñez Seixas who believe the opposite and consider that in the case of the first stage of transculturation, acculturation, the older the migrant is when they meet the dominant culture, the greater their resistance to idealizing their country and culture of origin. He thinks that, when we talk about migration,

> la ausencia del país de origen se convierte en un recuerdo idealizado, en el que confluye la memoria de la propia infancia y juventud, de la familia y de la comunidad, con una idea recibida y transportada de la nación de pertenencia. Esa

idea recibe cambios a través del tiempo, y deviene una representación híbrida, mezcla de imágenes del pasado—y, por lo tanto, no actualizadas y a veces arcaicas—y de proyecciones de las vivencias e intereses presentes. (Núñez Seixas 2007, 15)[7]

According to Núñez Seixas, this would explain the resistance of many immigrants during the process of acculturation to the new dominant culture of the country of reception and the representation of the new "Third Space" between the culture of the domain in the United States and that of the Spanish immigrants in the texts analyzed.

Characters such as Don José, little Prudencio's grandfather,[8] in *Windmills in Brooklyn*, or Remedios, the mother of the sisters Arenas, in *Las hijas del Capitán*, could represent those immigrants who, due to their age, social and cultural circumstances, rejected American culture while idealizing their Spanish culture of origin. In this sense, in his article "Los modelos de aculturación e intervención psicosocial en la inmigración" (2001),[9] Claudio Vicente Villanueva López describes the immigrant experience with four different levels of acculturation when arriving in a new country. These four levels of acculturation between the cultures, regarding the preservation of the cultural identity and the traditions of the immigrants are the following: a) integration, when the identity and traditions are preserved by the immigrants while in contact in harmony with the country of reception; b) assimilation, when this identity and traditions are left behind by the immigrants in order to embrace only the new one; c) segregation, when there is no contact with the new country or community of reception while keeping the immigrant's identity and traditions; and d) exclusion when the

7 "The absence of the country of origin becomes an idealized memory, in which the memory of one's own childhood and youth, family and community converges with a received and transported idea of the nation to which one belongs. This idea undergoes changes over time, and becomes a hybrid representation, a mixture of images from the past—and, as a result, outdated and sometimes archaic—and projections of present experiences and interests."

8 Although the name of the narrator and protagonist of *Windmills in Brooklyn* is never revealed in the story, the fact that it is an autobiographical novel and for practical purposes in the description of the protagonist, his family, and his friends, the author's first name has been used to differentiate it from de Pereda's as the writer of this work and of *Fiesta*.

9 Models of acculturation and psychosocial intervention in immigration

immigrants leave behind their culture of origin and tradition but also alienated from the country of reception . In the case of those Spanish immigrants who arrived during and after the Spanish Cuban-American war, Fernández and Argeo highlight that "by the end of World War II, with their home country in shambles, many Spanish immigrants—and, particularly, their children—by then were well on the way down the path of assimilation" into the culture of the domain (Fernández and Argeo 2014, 221). In other words, the process of transculturation began taking place from the moment that the Spanish immigrants settled in the United States, but this circumstance affected especially the younger ones, who did not have such a strong cultural reference as the older ones in Spain and its culture.

At the beginning of her essay "Transculturing Transculturation" (1991), Diana Taylor points out that concepts like acculturation, deculturation, neoculturation, and transculturation "have been used by anthropologists and literary theorists alike to describe the impact of one culture on another" (1991, 90). In a clear allusion, among others, to Ortiz's work *Cuban counterpoint, tobacco and sugar*, Taylor considers that *it is important to underline* that transculturation is "not a theatrical phenomenon but a social one," and, as a result, it touches a whole culture, as it includes a change of sociopolitical borders while modifying both the collective and the individual identity (Taylor 1991, 90–91). For Taylor, transculturation encompasses the totality of social and cultural changes those human beings experience as active and passive subjects, both as part of a community and on a personal level.

The discussion above is even more relevant as, in his *magnum opus Cuban counterpoint, tobacco and sugar*, Ortiz concludes that the arrival of tobacco in the Old Continent was a surprising example of transculturation and clear assimilation due to the speed with which it was carried out and the social revolution that the passage from one culture to another entailed. The origin of the use of tobacco and its discoverer is unknown, as has happened throughout history with so many other discoveries and inventions: agriculture, fire, the wheel, clothing, and writing; but in addition to the what, as in the case of tobacco, it is necessary to know the society that developed it, the who, and of that there are indeed traces and testimonies: the Native Americans. Ortiz recounts that tobacco was able to penetrate Africa from Portugal during the first half of the sixteenth century and spread along the Mediterranean coast to its most eastern part thanks to traders and merchants. He found that the Native American and African transmigration is reflected in the different ways of taking up tobacco. The first one is based on the techniques used by the islanders of Cuba itself, and the second one originated in some areas of Central Africa and Ethiopia, which Ortiz points out would be very similar to those used by the Native Americans: tobacco powder, twisting the leaves of the plant, collective smoking pipes, and so on (2012, 236). As Ortiz highlights, this transculturation also had its contribution in the opposite direction, from Africa to America.

At the end of his work, Ortiz indicates that the cultural transition of tobacco to Europe was made through Spain. It was in the mid-sixteenth century when tobacco became a commodity and began to be grown in Europe, probably because its small seeds could travel in the hands of sailors, merchants, clergymen, and crown officials when its use in Spain was already standardized and became part of its culture. It is known that, at the end of the sixteenth century, Cuban tobacco was very popular in England, where it was smoked rather than grown, and different versions are told about its dissemination. Some support the idea that English soldiers spread it throughout Bohemia during the Thirty Years' War and that English sailors introduced it to Turkey. Others point to Turkish and Moorish smugglers in contact with southern Spain and Portugal, organized by Jewish merchants, who would spread it around the Mediterranean and the Black Sea (Ortiz 2012, 236).

The constant conflicts between France and Spain seem to have made it impossible for tobacco to enter through what would be its natural route. Therefore, it is attributed to the work of the renegade friar A. Thévet, who claimed to have brought it from Brazil to France, and the doctor Juan Nicot, who would become its great propagator in the court of Catalina de Médicis, in the form of rapé or snuff, and gave it its name, from which the word nicotine is derived (Ortiz 2012, 290). In Italy, the use of tobacco would enter the regions that belonged to the Spanish crown: Sicily, Naples, Milan, and the Papal States through the action of the cardinals. Thus, kings and clerics smoked the best tobacco in Havana without fear of heresy, making peace with the devil and money (297–98). In this way, the process of transculturation of tobacco took place not only among the cultures that lived and coexisted in Cuba but also among the European cultures in which tobacco settled when it was exported as assimilation became a fact.

The Cuban culture brought to the United States by Spanish migrants was characterized by the hybridism and the assimilation of three cultures: the Spanish, the Native American, and the African. However, this fact seems to have been forgotten. Nevertheless, elements such as making and selling cigars and communities of Spanish origin, both from the Iberian Peninsula and Cuba, living and working together in jobs related to tobacco will be present in several of the stories used in this research. Ortiz indicates that from its arrival on the island, tobacco became the main element of transculturation from the pre-Columbian Cuban culture to the Spanish one. Havana was linked to Spain through their culture and trade, while the Havana cigar turned into a symbol of social prosperity as it spread through Europe. When Spanish-Cuban immigrants arrived in the United States, they brought with them the hybridism of tobacco culture. The Spaniards' assimilation of tobacco characterized the creation of Spanish communities in states such as Florida and New York, where tobacco became one of the main sources of income. In this new country, the production and distribution of tobacco were connected to the Spaniards, who had been trading it for centuries. As a result, the figures of the Spanish *teveriano*[10] became the epitome of the Spanish worker in many cities of the United States, as we will see in the figure of Don José and Agapito in Prudencio de Pereda's *Windmills in Brooklyn*.

As Bronislaw Malinowski indicates in the preface to *Cuban counterpoint, tobacco and sugar*, Ortiz introduced the term "transculturation" "to replace various expressions in use such as cultural exchange, acculturation, diffusion, migration or osmosis of culture, and similar ones that he considered inadequate" (Ortiz 2012, 8). Malinowski endorsed Ortiz's new term as he agreed with Ortiz, who wanted to make sure that the word was specifically used to indicate the cultural transition phenomena taking place between two cultural systems. In Malinowski's introduction, he establishes his own definition of transculturation:

> It is a process in which both parts of the equation are modified, a process from which a new reality emerges, transformed and complex, a reality that is not a mechanical agglomeration of traits, nor even a mosaic, but a new phenomenon, original and independent. To describe this process the word *trans-culturation*,

10 Spanish cigar street vendors

> stemming from Latin roots, provides us with a term that does not contain the implication of one certain culture toward which the other must tend, but an exchange between two cultures, both active, both contributing their share, and both co-operating to bring about a new reality of civilization. (Ortiz 2012, 9)

In the case of the Anglo-Saxon American culture, this would also imply a change, as this was the dominant culture. However, in the case of the Spanish emigrants, their culture did not affect the American culture in a relevant way; rather, the Spaniards assimilated the American culture, with no real effect on both cultures. According to Malinowski, in the process of transculturation, both cultures are affected by this phenomenon. However, it was only the Spanish immigrants who were experimenting with what Malinowski called "culture contact" and what Ortiz would develop as "transculturation," in opposition to the term "acculturation." Other scholars like Pérez Firmat have pointed out that Ortiz's "acculturation stresses the acquisition of culture; transculturation calls attention to the passage from one culture to another" (Pérez Firmat 1996, 5), and therefore, this transculturation would become a transition toward a new cultural reality based on the elements of an individual's own culture and those that in this case the migrant borrows from the culture of reception.

There is another term, "biculturation," not mentioned by Ortiz but used by Pérez Firmat "to designate the type of blending that is specific, or at least characteristic, of the one-and-a-half generation" (1996, 5). Pérez Firmat's biculturation can be considered to examine the texts selected for this study, but transculturation seems more adequate as it can apply to the transition that Spanish immigrants in the United States of America experienced from a Spanish to a Spanish-American identity, where both cultures coexist, creating a new hybrid individual. Ortiz's definition seems more appropriate for analyzing these works than Perez Firmat's precisely because of the bidirectionality in the transfer from one culture to another, as is the case of Spanish immigration to the United States of America. While Perez Firmat's definition may be useful in those cases where there is multiculturalism, as in the case of Cuba, the term "transculturation" is also useful in the Spanish case because it helps to describe the situation of hybridism of the first generation and the assimilation of the later generations together with the scarce impact of the dominated culture on the dominant one; in this case, those Spanish immigrants who arrived between their childhood and older age, that is, young immigrants who kept their Spanish roots and were eager to become part of their country of reception.

The characters, as members of the Spanish community in the United States, experience a clash of cultures while seeking their social identity, where "ethnic cultures are constantly trying to negotiate between the contradictory imperatives of tradition and translation" (Pérez Firmat 1996, 3). Pérez Firmat considers both tradition and translation essential in the construction of the new hybrid person. He explains that tradition "designates convergence and continuity, a gathering together of elements according to underlying affinities or shared concerns" (3); it indicates confluence, the coming together of components based on interests. On the other hand, translation "is not a homing device but a distancing mechanism…; implicit in the concept is the suggestion that to move is to transmute, that any linguistic or cultural displacement necessarily entails some mutilation of the original" (Pérez Firmat 1996, 3). In other words, any change is a transition, a change that disfigures the primordial one.

Pérez Firmat's work focuses on "the achievement of biculturalism, that is, from a Cuban to a Cuban American identity" (López 2012, 60), and his analysis can be extrapolated to the Spaniards who arrived in the American nation and their transition from a Spanish to a Spanish-American identity, but not as easily to their descendants who, through Ortiz's transculturation, can create a new cultural phenomenon: neoculturation. Pérez Firmat says that in this case, "the interstitial placement of the one-and-a-half generation" results in "having two cultures" and belonging "wholly to neither one" (7), and thus, there is no creation of a hybrid space where both cultures can coexist. Years after the publication of Ortiz's first definition of "transculturation," the Cuban author improved his term by highlighting the importance of the mixture of cultures, of the culture hybridity to understand the relevance of its meaning:

> Synthesis of two phases occurring simultaneously, one being a de-culturalization of the past with a métissage with the present. This new reinventing of the new common culture is therefore based on the meeting and the intermingling of the different peoples and cultures. In other words one's identity is not strictly one dimensional (the self) but is now defined and more importantly recognized in rapport with the other. In other words one's identity is not singular but multiple. (Ortiz, qtd. in Cuccioletta, 2002, 8)

There are other relevant definitions of transculturation, such as Alfonso de Toro's. In *Transculturation, Mestizaje and Hybridism. (Teoría y crítica de la cultura y literatura)* (2006), there is a chapter written by de Toro, "Figuras de la hibridez: Ortiz: transculturación—Paz: hibridismo—Fernández Retamar: Calibán" (2006), where the Chilean-German Romanist uses the definition of transculturation as the merging of cultures that goes back and forth, while deculturation responds to the loss of the previous culture, and as a result, the creation of a new one, neoculturation (de Toro 2006, 24). While Pérez Firmat's insights are very helpful, as he considers that for bidirectionality to happen, there must be an exchange between the two cultures, Ortiz's concept of transculturation with its cross-culturality seems more adequate when analyzing the representation in literature of the Spanish community in the United States in *Chromos* (1948), by Felipe Alfau; *Windmills in Brooklyn* (1954) and *Fiesta: A Novel of Modern Spain* (1960), by Prudencio de Pereda; *Las hijas del Capitán* (2018), by María Dueñas; *Pinnick Kinnick Hill: An American Story* (2003), by Gain W. González; and *The Lower East Side Kid That Made It Good: The Autobiography of Claude Morell* (2008), by Claude Morell.

Besides his definition of biculturation, the other relevant contribution of Pérez Firmat to this research can be found in his study on Cuban Americans and immigration in *Life on the Hyphen: The Cuban American Way* (1996), where he refers to the 1.5 generation, drawing on Cuban American sociologist Rubén Rumbaut's definition of the one-and-a-half generation:

> Children who were born abroad but are being educated and come of age in the United States are what may be called the "1.5" generation. These refugee youth must cope with two crisis-producing and identity-defining transitions: (1) adolescence and the task of managing the transition from childhood to adulthood, and (2) acculturation and the task of managing the transition from one sociocultural environment to another. The "first" generation of their parents, who are fully part of the "old" world, face only the latter; the "second" generation of children now being born and reared in the United States, who as such become fully part of the "new" world, will need to confront only the former. But members of the "1.5" generation form a distinctive cohort in that in many ways they are marginal to both the old and the new worlds and are fully part of neither of them. (Rumbaut 1991, 61)

Rumbaut labeled the 1.75 generation (2004, 1167) as young immigrants who transit from youth to adulthood as "their intercultural placement makes them more likely to undertake the negotiations on compromises that produce ethnic culture" (Pérez Firmat 1996, 4). Just as what occurs with second-generation immigrants, the 1.5 and 1.75 generations are also between two worlds, in a hybrid place, a "Third Space" where the culture of origin and the culture of reception intermingle, going through all the phases of the cultural transformation process. Subsequent studies by Cuban American sociologists Alejandro Portes and Rubén Rumbaut (2001) themselves reinforce these labels, while other academics such as Mark and Jamie Goodwin-White support the 1.5 classification in their article "1.5 Generation Internal Migration in the U.S.: Dispersion from States of Immigration?" (2006), stating that the 1.5 immigrants are those who entered the United States before they were around ten years old, and the foreign-born are those immigrants who arrived later in life, during their teenage years, as Ellis and Goodwin-White point out (Ellis and Goodwin-White 2006, 906). They thus underline the importance of differentiating the 1.5-generation population from the rest of the foreign-born population by age at arrival. On the other hand, Joel Perlmann and Roger Waldinger, in "Second Generation Decline? Children of Immigrants, Past and Present" (1997), write about second-generation immigrants' assimilation and their culture loss in the United States, pointing out how second-generation's conditions are determined by their level of transculturation.

According to Richard A. Rogers (2006, 474), transculturation establishes culture as a "relational phenomenon constituted by acts of appropriation, not an entity that merely participates in appropriation." In other words, this appropriation constitutes a circumstance where the individual evolves according to his or her relationship with the environment. Rogers identifies four categories of cultural appropriation and classifies them according to economic, social, historical, political, and cultural conditions as follows:

1. Cultural exchange: the reciprocal exchange of symbols, artifacts, genres, rituals, and/or technologies between cultures with symmetrical power. Examples include the reciprocal borrowing of linguistic words and phrases, mutual influence on religious beliefs and practices, technological exchange, and two-way flows of music and visual arts. In its ideal form, cultural exchange involves a balance of this reciprocal flow. Appropriation of this type is generally voluntary, with the "choices" involved being individual and/or cultural. (2006, 478)

2. Cultural dominance: the use of elements of a dominant culture by members of a subordinated culture in a context in which the dominant culture has been imposed onto the subordinated culture, including appropriations that enact resistance (477). Cultural dominance refers to a condition characterized by the unidirectional imposition of elements of a dominant culture onto a subordinate (marginalized, colonized) culture. (479)
3. Cultural exploitation: the appropriation of elements of a subordinated culture by a dominant culture without substantive reciprocity, permission, and/or compensation (477). In the literature of critical/cultural studies, cultural appropriation has most commonly been used to reference acts in which aspects of marginalized colonized cultures are used by a dominant/colonizing culture in such a way as to serve the interests of the dominant. (486)
4. Transculturation: cultural elements created from/by multiple cultures, such that identification of a single originating culture, is problematic, for example, multiple cultural appropriations structured in the dynamics of globalization and transnational capitalism creating hybrid forms. (477)

These four categories are essential to understanding the evolution of the clash of cultures experienced by the Spanish immigrants as individuals and their struggle between the dominant and the dominated culture in the texts analyzed. Authors like Gayatri Spivak (1988) have pointed out the role of dominance and globalization in the creation of subjects or subalterns based on the experience of Anglo-Saxon dominant cultures in countries like India, where the postcolonial circumstances have created a prolific source of literature regarding the members of the dominated culture. For example, Spivak points out that, in the case of India, what may make one culture dominate another does not necessarily work in all cultures, as each situation is different and depends on many factors, such as language, the social structure of the community, economic development, and so on. She understands that

> the same class or element which was dominant in one area... could be among the dominated in another. This could and did create many ambiguities and contradictions in attitudes and alliances, especially among the lowest strata of the rural gentry, impoverished landlords, rich peasants and upper-middle peasants all of whom belonged, ideally speaking, to the category of "people" or "subaltern classes." (Spivak 1988, 79–80)

In this respect, when referring to cultural dominance, Rogers (2006, 480) differentiates five different tactics or strategies used by members of the dominated or subordinated culture to negotiate their relationship to the "the dominant or imposed culture"). These tactics are defined as follows: the first strategy of cultural domination is "assimilation," and it implies

> internalization of the imposed culture, including reformation of identity, values, and ideologies. Assimilation involves the displacement of the subordinated/native culture by the colonizing culture, which necessarily involves the appropriation (broadly speaking) of the dominant culture by a member of a subordinate culture. (481)

"Assimilation" becomes one of the most successful strategies of resistance, as the dominant culture is in control over the native culture; however, it is the subject of the subordinated culture who chooses to appropriate the dominant culture, leaving some margin for the preservation of the native culture and a sense of control.

The second strategy described by Rogers to negotiate their relationship with the dominant culture is "integration." "Integration" entails

> internalization of some or all the imposed culture without (complete) displacement or erasure of native culture and identity. Integration can involve the operation of two distinct cultures within an individual or a group or the fusion of aspects of each into a single culture and identity. (481)

This second strategy keeps some independence of the colonized culture, as the combination of both cultures creates a new self where the dominant culture leaves room for some previous manifestation of the native culture.

The third tactic is "intransigence," which "involves overt resistance: a refusal to appropriate the imposed culture or other overt means of opposing its imposition, individually or collectively… This strategy involves refusal to appropriate the imposed elements" (481). This tactic is one of the most straightforward among those employed by members of the subordinated culture in order to deal with the dominant culture. The imposed culture is confronted by the native culture to reject any element that might be appropriated. The fourth strategy is "mimicry." It implies

> "going through the motions" without internalising the imposed culture. If performed successfully, it will appear to the dominant group that assimilation or integration has been achieved. Here, appropriation involves an intentional

> performance design to negotiate structures of power while maintaining once native culture and thereby begins to demonstrate the active nature of appropriations under the conditions of cultural dominance and hence of the crucial role of agency. (481)

This strategy involves a kind of equilibrium between the imposed culture and the subordinated culture, where both negotiate their position of power and identity. If performed successfully, it provides one of the best ways to maintain the native culture while making the dominant culture believe that dominance has been achieved.

The last tactic employed to negotiate with the imposed culture is "resistance." It "involves more covered opposition: the adoption of aspects of the imposed culture in such a way as to maintain a native culture and/or resist culture domination, often without the awareness of the colonising culture" (481). This strategy is a disguised form of intransigence, as the dominant culture is unaware of the opposition offered by the native culture in negotiating its power relations. During this cultural resistance, the term "cultural appropriation" can also be used to define "the use of elements of a dominant culture by members of subordinated cultures to resist that dominant culture" (483). Rogers indicates that transculturation and hybridity are an inevitable condition of contemporary culture (493). Cultural appropriation is key to understanding today's postcolonial and globalized world, and thus, the last phase of cultural appropriation: "transculturation." Rogers defines "transculturation" as "cultural elements created through appropriation from and by multiple cultures such that identification of a single originating culture is problematic. Transculturation involves ongoing, circular appropriations of elements between multiple cultures, including elements that are themselves transcultural" (491). In other words, transculturation itself appropriates elements from different cultures, which in turn may be original to the native culture or the product of previous transculturation. Lull defines transculturation as "a process whereby culture forms literally move time and space where they interact with other cultures' forms... and change the cultural setting" (Lull 1990, 242). He explains that "transculturation produces cultural hybrids—the fusing of cultural forms" (243), though he understands that "hybrids such as these never develop from 'pure' culture forms in the first place" (245), but are a further step in the process of transculturation of the individual between two or more cultures.

1.4. The Question of *Mestizaje*

The process of transculturation in Cuba between people from Africa, Europe, and Native America was the first in the continent, but it was not the only one. The anthropologist Néstor García Canclini (2005) supports the use of Ortiz's idea of hybridization:

> Occasional mention will be made of the terms syncretism, mestizaje, and others used to designate processes of hybridization. I prefer this last term because it includes diverse intercultural mixtures—not only the racial ones to which mestizaje tends to be limited—and because it permits the inclusion of the modern forms of hybridization better than does "syncretism," a term that almost always refers to religious fusions or traditional symbolic movements. (2005, 11)

García Canclini clarifies in his introduction that hybridization must be hierarchized in connection to concepts such as transculturation, mestizaje, syncretism, creolization, and so on (29).

In the case of transculturation and hybridization, this connection is always present in Ortiz's work, and Ortiz himself later explains why he has coined the term transculturation:

> I have chosen the word *transculturation* to express the highly varied phenomena that have come about in Cuba as a result of the extremely complex transmutations of culture that have taken place here, and without a knowledge of which it is impossible to understand the evolution of the Cuban folk, either in the economic or in the institutional, legal, ethical, religious, artistic, linguistic, psychological, sexual, or other aspects of its life. (2012, 127)

According to him, the cultural diversity of the immigrants who arrived in Cuba influenced both the native culture of reception and the one coming from overseas. As a result, from the end of the fifteenth century, a cultural transformation began that continues to this day. Ortiz refers to these cultures and the process of transculturation when he speaks of the Europeans who arrived not only in Cuba but also in the rest of America: with their traditions, their music, their ideas, and, of course, their language.

In 1976, the Peruvian anthropologist and ethnographer José María Arguedas published *Formación de una cultura nacional indoamericana*, where he developed the concept of transculturation and stressed the survival of the Native American culture from Peru in contact with the Spanish Western culture. Arguedas introduced the concept of *mestizo* because of transculturation. He considers that the Peruvian *mestizo* is a hybrid of two cultures, the Native American culture and the Spanish culture. He adds that this hybridism has managed to preserve the best of both worlds as a new hybrid culture unites its members. At the same time, he highlights the figure of the *mestizo* as a cultural phenomenon; Arguedas leaves aside the idea of race (1976, 2) because, for him, race is not as relevant as other elements in this scenario. He speaks of the *mestizo* in terms of culture as something positive. For him, the result of this hybridization has been the resistance of the Native American culture while connected to the dominant Spanish culture. He considers the *mestizo* to be the triumph of this balance between the two cultures, regardless of race, with the behavior and tradition of the new Peruvians being more *important*. Arguedas claims that the mixture of both cultures is positive since the exchange of customs and traditions has created new behaviors that he considers more valuable due to their *mestizaje* and multiculturalism. He praises the Peruvian native culture, underlying that it has been able to assimilate foreign elements through a process of transculturation since the time of the Spanish Conquest, maintaining itself as a valuable hybrid Peruvian culture.

Some authors, like Diane Taylor (1991), have pointed out that "the Peruvian culture Arguedas studied, like most of the inhabitants of Peru themselves, was neither 'pure' Indian nor 'pure' Spanish, but a mixture of both and hence, differentiated from both" (1991). As a result, "uni-cultural paradigms set up to analyze their *mestizo* culture either by Eurocentric standards or by a historic indigenous ones were bound to misunderstand the hybrid nature of the phenomenon" (92). Arguedas distinguished the original native culture of pre-Columbian Peru from the culture brought by the Spaniards, and the result of that transculturation as a new hybrid product that became the new hallmark of the identity of Peru, creating a unique new person as the *mestizo*. However, according to Mark Millington (2007), *it is important to point out* that *mestizaje* and hybridization are not the same:

> Though, by no means exactly synonymous, the nexus of terms from transculturation and hybridisation to heterogeneity and *mestizaje* all manifest the will to subvert, transgress, undermine, oppose or obstruct the workings of metropolitan and internal elite power and authority. But my point is that these terms acquire their own authority; sooner or later all of them come to obey a logic that consolidates their impact into the domesticated authority of a now mainstream cultural studies, however much qualified as postcolonial. (2007, 257)

Millington argues that *mestizaje* is a fundamental part of the process of transculturation and hybridity but underlines that the term has become a way of referring to racial mixing, creating a parallelism with syncretism, which had a more encompassing use but today is mainly employed to define the fusion between religions. Therefore, he prefers the terms transculturation and hybridization when referring to the process of transition between cultures and the final product of that procedure. Millington also explains that the idea of transculturation is the best definition of a process toward cultural mixing. While on the other hand, hybridization, in addition to that process, also defines a state with the individual as a hybrid, which is the result of that blending (2007, 257–258).

Millington continues by underlining the importance of differentiating these concepts, as "the degree to which hybridity and hybrid are seen as static and hybridization as dynamic could spark an interesting debate: given that objects are in use, it is unlikely that a hybrid object is ever simply static" (258). However, one must keep in mind that Millington thinks that hybridization is a term that, unlike the concept of transculturation, has a global reference, and it can be easily associated with post-structuralist postcolonialism (258). Here, he defines two terms according to his parameters, yet, as we can see, there are difficulties in using some terms due to the interpretation that different authors can give to the meanings of their own definitions.

The term *mestizaje* has been studied by many authors, including the American scholar of Chicana cultural theory, Gloria Anzaldúa. In her work, *Borderlands/La Frontera: The New Mestiza*, especially in Chapter 7, "*La conciencia de la mestiza/Hacia una nueva conciencia*" (2016), Anzaldúa explains that the hybridism of the offspring is like a crossbreeding of races, ideologies, cultures, and biology itself, based on José Vasconcelos' concept of cosmic race, "una conciencia de las Borderlands" (2016, 133).[11] She points out that the duplicity resulting from the clash of voices leads to mental and emotional states of inner struggles generating insecurities in the immigrants, which can make the construction of hybridity within the

11 "an awareness of the Borderlands."

"Third Space" complex (134). The multiple personality that the immigrant develops when arriving at a new place and speaking a new language can make them feel insecure, as they lack self-confidence. The immigrant, like the *mestiza* described by Anzaldúa, whether aware of it or not, transfers their cultural values to a new group.

Besides, she underlines that, on many occasions, as in the case of the Spanish immigrant in the United States, this cultural transfer may be tricultural, monolingual, bilingual, or multilingual, as the immigrant and the *mestiza* may be trapped between cultures. Both the immigrant and the *mestiza* can suffer an interior borderline struggle, considering that their perception of reality is shaped by their culture of origin and the clash with the new dominant culture of reception. Immigrant communities and individual subjects who live in contact with more than one culture can receive multiple messages, sometimes contradictory and sometimes consistent but incompatible (Anzaldúa 2016, 134), and it is then when the cultural clash occurs. Arthur Koestler, in his work *The Act of Creation* (1964), called this encounter of two frames of reference, a real bisociation. Koestler coined the term bisociation as a blending of concepts from different contexts that are "unrelated, often conflicting, information in a new way" (1964). Information that combines data that may be contradictory or belong to different backgrounds. This is essentially what happens to the Spanish immigrants in the United States.

This struggle between the dominant and the dominated establishes an internal struggle in the immigrant, thus generating antagonistic positions. The authority of the culture of reception creates a confrontation between the oppressor and the oppressed that can never end for the first-generation immigrant. This fight will evolve, and the following generations will move toward the culture of the domain (Anzaldúa 2016, 135) as the influence of the community and culture of origin diminishes. Like the *mestiza* who, when perceiving conflicting information, is subject to a saturation of her psychological boundaries, the immigrant who arrives in a new country suffers the contradictions of the borderlands as they discover that reality has different interpretations depending on their culture. The *mestiza*/immigrant realizes that they cannot contain ideas, while they are supposed to keep out undesirable ideas, habits, and ingrained behavior patterns (135). These patterns change as the immigrant moves from one culture to another and between them, creating a new, increasingly complex, and contradictory hybrid person.

Both the *mestiza* and the immigrant must be flexible. They must adapt to new ways of thinking, move toward divergent thinking, and adopt an inclusive rather than an exclusive perspective (136). In 1948, the Spanish-American writer Felipe Alfau finished his *opus magna*: *Chromos*. In its pages, he coined the term "Americaniard" to identify the Spanish immigrants who settled in the United States and evolved toward Spanish-American biculturalism. Like the *mestiza*, the Spanish immigrant in New York City must learn to be Spanish in the Spanish community and to be an "Americaniard" in an Anglo cultural dominated metropolis. In her article, "Latina or Americaniard?," Professor Debra Castillo (2005) shows her concern about Spanish-born authors like Alfau who write in English about the United States as if they were Americans:

> Authors, texts, and ideas have always moved across international borders; yet to the degree that they confound monolingual and nationally-based literary projects, such crossings and meditations have been insufficiently studied even by an academic audience that prides itself on its border-crossing analytic abilities (2005, 47).

However, it would be at least debatable to consider Alfau as a uniquely Spanish author and not a Spanish-American or an "Americaniard," as the author himself states in his novel *Chromos*, if we consider that since he settled in New York at the age of fourteen, he has maintained both cultures, described by Pérez Firmat as biculturalism, a two-way Spanish-American identity which allowed him to write his only two novels, *A Comedy of Gestures* (1936) and *Chromos* (1948), and a book of children's stories, *Old Tales from Spain* (1929) in English, a language that he mastered, while his work *La poesía cursi*, written between 1923 and 1987, was written entirely and published for the first time in 1988 in Spanish, his mother tongue.

Pérez Firmat's biculturation becomes true if both cultures are separated, but this does not seem to be the case for Alfau. The culture or cultures of the protagonists of the texts analyzed seem to be one hybrid culture formed by two different ones. It is not two cultures that one person can switch from one to the other but a mixture of both. As the transition occurred, these Spaniards and their descendants evolved from a native Spanish culture of origin to a Spanish-American identity where both cultures mingled but the former was ultimately dominated by the latter, thus creating a hybrid individual, Alfau's "Americaniard." Spanish immigrants in the United States combine their cultures as the *mestiza*, using a dual personality so that they not only sustain contradictions but also turn ambivalence into something else (Anzaldúa 2016, 136). However, this plurality is not always stable, and, as a result, the emotional stability of the immigrant depends on the mental development of the subject as a new individual who evolves from a "foreigner" to an assimilated subject of the dominant culture. As a result, the immigrant develops, like the *mestiza*, a new consciousness, a *mestiza* consciousness, a hybrid consciousness, and a new paradigm (136). In this sense, Anzaldúa's idea of the *mestiza* consciousness has some similarities with Bhabha's concept of hybridity (2006). To fulfill this cultural transition, the Spanish immigrant needs to live between two cultures: the Spanish and the American, the Catholic and the Protestant, the Latino and the Anglo. This transition is a change in the way reality is perceived (Anzaldúa 2016, 137), a new conscience created by the immigrant, a leap forward in this clash of cultures due to a "mestizaje cultural" (138). Anzaldúa highlights that it is difficult to distinguish those cultural elements that were inherited from those that were acquired and from those that were imposed, as the cultural transition transforms the subject into a new individual, a hybrid individual.

Just like Arguedas, the Uruguayan literary critic Ángel Rama (2012) expanded the concept of transculturation, considering the process of transculturation as constant change, always transforming and always in motion. Rama uses the term "narrative transculturation" in his *Transculturación narrativa en América Latina (Writing across Cultures: Narrative Transculturation in Latin America)*, where he leaves aside sociological theories to focus on the phenomenon of transculturation in literary studies. Rama points out that there are three moments where Ortiz's definition must be adjusted before it can be applied to literary works:

> The first moment involves varying degrees of "partial deculturation," which can affect different aspects of both culture and literary production, though it always entails a loss of elements considered obsolete. The second involves the incorporation of elements from the foreign culture. In the third, there is an effort at mending culture, using both surviving elements from the original culture and elements from outside it. This schema pays insufficient attention to the criteria of selection and inventiveness that must always be part of the mix in any case of

> cultural plasticity, for such a state testifies to the energy and creativity of a cultural community. (Rama 2012, 22)

According to Rama, the loss of elements of the native culture leads to a partial and gradual deculturation. Then, there is an acquisition of elements of the dominant culture that implies an attempt to fix the culture, using those elements of the native culture that have survived this process in combination with others from the dominant culture. Rama's position, like Pérez Firmat's, seeks a broader definition that allows for bidirectional assimilation to be adapted or not, depending on the type of transculturation experienced by the dominated culture of the subject. As a result, to Rama, the structure presented by Ortiz has no bearing on the judgments employed for this "cultural plasticity" and therefore no bearing on the importance of the original cultural community. Before this clarification, Rama underlines that a country's traditional culture is not passive, while Ortiz's definition "resists considering the country's own traditional culture as if it were passive, inferior to the foreign culture that would modify it, destined for great losses, and lacking any means to respond creatively" (Rama 2012, 19).

The plasticity of Rama's culture is active in its contact with the dominant culture, while Ortiz's culture would be passive and dependent on this same dominant culture. This is especially important for Rama, as he highlights that

> If the community is alive, it will carry out that act of selection, both on itself and on the introduced foreign elements, and it will necessarily invent new things through a combinatory system that matches the cultural system's own autonomy. (Ortiz 2012, 22)

That is, the community of the native culture has the capacity to choose and resist certain elements of the dominant culture so that the result of the combination of both cultures and its hybrid outcome depends not only on the strength with which the foreign culture imposes itself but also on the resistance and the capacity to choose of the dominated culture.

Ethnographers have used the concept of transculturation to illustrate how dominated cultures choose elements transferred by a dominant culture. Besides García Canclini, scholars such as Homi Bhabha, Edward Said, and Mary Louise Pratt have examined the effects of hybridity, colonization, and transculturation and have shown that migration creates cultural conflicts between groups, producing multicultural situations where transculturation plays a major role in the creation of new realities and identities. In *Imperial Eyes: Studies in Travel Writing and Transculturation* (2007), Mary Louise Pratt analyzes the connections between traveling and transculturation during the era of the empires and colonization since the 1700s. Pratt's work focuses on the study of travel literature and postcolonial criticism, exposing how travel books created a distorted image of the dominated cultures by describing them from the eyes of empires/dominant cultures. In *Imperial Eyes*, Pratt shows the Eurocentric perspective of the colonial endeavor through writing, using the constructed image that transculturation left during the clash between the European dominant culture and the Latin American and African subjugated cultures.

Pratt defines the concept of transculturation as "a phenomenon of the contact zone" where "while subjugated peoples cannot readily control what the dominant culture visits upon them, they do determine to varying extents what they absorb into their own, how they use it, and what they make it mean" (Pratt 2007, 7). She defines contact zones as "social spaces where disparate cultures meet, clash, and grapple with each other, often in highly asymmetrical relations of domination and subordination" (7), which is the essence of the beginning of the transculturation process. In these contact zones, the dominated culture and the dominant culture enter a relationship in which the native culture is transformed by the contact and asymmetrical power relations with the foreign culture, and the process of transculturation begins. Although they are subject to the same process of transculturation, the cases commented on by Pratt are not the same as those of the Spanish immigration during the first half of the twentieth century, since she speaks of "native culture," of dominated (colonized) peoples who have not moved, while in the case under analysis, it is the Spanish immigrants who move and encounter the dominant culture.

Pratt also uses the term contact zones to "refer to the space of imperial encounters, the space in which peoples geographically and historically separated come into contact with each other and establish ongoing relations, usually involving conditions of coercion, radical inequality, and intractable conflict" (8). At the same time, she indicates that the term is frequently used in her book as a synonym of "colonial frontier," but considers that "while the latter term is grounded within a European expansionist perspective (the frontier is a frontier only with respect to Europe), 'contact zone' shifts the centre of gravity and the point of view" (8). This is especially interesting in the case of the United States and Spain because although the former nation has a large part of its culture based on cultures from Europe, it is in turn a new culture and the result of a centuries-long process of transculturation.

However, the culture of the United States is an Anglo-American culture that imposes itself not as an empire that imposes its culture when it arrives in new territories, but as a dominant culture that imposes itself after the arrival of immigrant waves such as the Spanish, whose European culture becomes the dominated culture when they arrive in the host country and in the different states and cities where they settle. In the case of the texts analyzed, Harrison County and the metropolis of New York influenced the Spanish culture of the immigrants and inhabitants, giving meaning to the definition of transculturation that other authors like Ashcroft, Griffiths, and Tiffin have already given to the term. Ashcroft himself is keen to highlight postcolonial literature as the best illustration of transculturation:

> As post-colonial literature has revealed time and again, appropriating the dominant technologies of representation to communicate the reality of the colonized world can also transform the cultural bases of that representative process. This is possibly the most profound demonstration of "transculturation"—that mutual alteration which occurs when two cultures come into contact. (Ashcroft 2001, 122)

Pratt is not the only author who has studied transculturation through literature. This is also the case of Professor Ana de Zaballa Beascoechea, who in *Transculturación y misión en Nueva España* (1990) makes a historical-doctrinal study of Bernardino de Sahagún's *Libro de los Coloquios*, written around 1564. Bernardino de Sahagún was a Franciscan friar from León (Spain), considered the creator of the modern ethnographic method, who promoted the study of indigenous languages. He was a historian of pre-Columbian religions, as well as an educator among the Aztecs. Sahagún wrote his *Libro de los Coloquios* in Spanish and Nahuatl as a testimony of the customs and mentalities of the Anahuac.[12] In her book, de Zaballa analyzes the representation of transculturation in Sahagún's work and

12 The inhabitants of the Valley of Mexico

demonstrates his ability to show the American reality from the point of view of the dominant culture and his adaptation to it.

However, it was in *Writing across Cultures: Narrative Transculturation in Latin America* (2012) that Rama highlights that Ortiz's idea of transculturation is not specific enough regarding the plasticity of a cultural community and coined the term "narrative transculturation" when analyzing the process of transculturation deployed in literature. Rama's concept has been applied to the analysis of literary texts of writers as relevant as Gabriel García Márquez, José María Arguedas, Augusto Roa Bastos, and Juan Rulfo (Arnedo-Gómez 2007, 9), while other intellectuals, such as Tan Chye Sing, Sobia A. Khan, Bharatender Sheoran, and Kanak Lata Tiwari, have studied "the multicultural circumstances" in several literary texts and indicated that the circumstances caused by this multiculturalism have provoked the loss of the identity and culture of certain ethnic groups (Ng, Mani, and Yahya 2016, 1).

Other authors like Víctor Silva and Rodrigo Browne have pointed out that Rama combined Ortiz's idea of "acculturation" with part of the analysis created by Gonzalo Aguirre Beltrán in his work *El proceso de aculturación* (2011) to affirm that "ad-culturation" means union or contact among cultures, "ab-culturation" means separation of cultures, and "trans-culturation" means transference from one culture to another (2011, 89). According to Aguirre Beltrán, transculturation

> at first, was only limited to Cuba due to the very complex cultural transmutations that took place on the island. The history of Cuba is that of a crossroads of transculturations that go from "el indio del paleolítico"[13] to "la cultura castellana." (2011, 89)

However, there was a transculturation of successive waves of Spanish immigrants who came from different regions and transferred their traditions to America, adjusting them to the new living conditions.

13 Silva, Víctor, and Rodrigo Browne. 2011. " 'Transculturación literaria' y 'elogio del mestizaje' en La ciudad letrada los intersticios en las escrituras de José María Arguedas y de Ángel Rama."

1.5. The Character of Hybridity Discourse

Old societies like those belonging to the Sumerians, Greeks, and Romans encouraged the incorporation of ideas, technology, and philosophies from abroad. As a result, these ancient civilizations practiced and created their own hybrid cultures. However, it was not until 1837 when the English naturalist Charles Darwin used the term "hybridity" for the first time to define "cross fertilization in plants" (Acheaïou 2011, 87). During the twentieth century, and especially the last decades of the millennium, the concept of hybridity was linked to "cultural studies and social sciences," where scholars have been using it in areas such as economics and politics, creating "a scramble for hybridity and the Third Space" (87). Scholars such as Edward Said, Homi Bhabha, and Gayatri Spivak have deepened the study of hybridity, developing a postcolonial theory led by Said's analysis of colonialism in his works *Orientalism* (1978) and *Culture and Imperialism* (1993); or Bhabha in *The Location of Culture* (1994) about the theory of hybridity and the "Third Space" (Acheaïou 2011, 90), supported by Spivak's analysis of postcolonialism in *A Critique of Postcolonial Reason* (1999), where she explains the role of subaltern subjects in postcolonialism.

At the beginning of *The Location of Culture*, Bhabha focuses on the idea of postcolonialism as a reminder of the new interactions between the former colonizers and colonized and how these interactions shape the construction of cultures and identities:

> Postcoloniality, for its part, is a salutary reminder of the persistent "neo-colonial" relations within the "new" world order and the multinational division of labour. Such a perspective enables the authentication of histories of exploitation and the evolution of strategies of resistance. Beyond this, however, postcolonial critique bears witness to those countries and communities—in the North and the South, urban and rural—constituted, if I may coin a phrase, "otherwise than modernity." Such cultures of a postcolonial contra-modernity may be contingent to modernity, discontinuous or in contention with it, resistant to its oppressive, assimilationist technologies; but they also deploy the cultural hybridity of their borderline conditions to "translate," and therefore reinscribe, the social imaginary of both metropolis and modernity. (Bhabha 2004, 9)

For Bhabha, postcolonialism stands as a reminder of the colonial past and the new division created during this new neo-colonialism. The new countries and communities that emerged during this period constitute an example of the hybrid cultures that can be created under conditions of counter-modernity, where the metropolis is the result of colonial transculturation. Bhabha resorts to the concept of "in-between" space. One can speak of postcolonialism in the United States in relative terms since there was "colonialism" by a multitude of groups over the territory. But, on the other hand, it also occupies a special position because it was not colonized in terms of other countries, such as Africa, India, and so on. For instance, while the assimilation of other cultures by the dominant Anglo-American culture in the United States occurs, except for Native Americans, when people, in this case, immigrants from other parts of the globe, come to the American country, in the case of India, it was the dominant Anglo-Saxon culture that went to the Asian country to impose its culture on the native Indians. For Bhabha, the encounter with a new culture must be independent of the past and present of the individuals who have confronted the physical and mental frontier of the new dominant culture:

> The borderline work of culture demands an encounter with "newness" that is not part of the continuum of past and present. It creates a sense of the new as an insurgent act of cultural translation. Such art does not merely recall the past as social cause or aesthetic precedent; it renews the past, refiguring it as a contingent "in-between" space, that innovates and interrupts the performance of the present. The "past–present" becomes part of the necessity, not the nostalgia, of living. (Bhabha 2004, 10)

As a result, the borderline becomes an in-between space that, once overcome in the present by the individuals, does not allow them to return. Furthermore, the present and the past of these subjects become dependent on each other since for the hybrid person to prevail, they must be conscious of their past and culture of origin while embracing the union with the new dominant culture in the present.

Postcolonial literary theory was born to study the literary production of authors from formerly colonized countries. This theory has also been used to analyze literature produced by the new inhabitants who live in those new independent nations due to migration. Within the branches of postcolonial literary theory, one of the most popular theories of the last decades is the postcolonial sociolinguistic theory of the "Third Space." In this sense, Bhabha indicates that

> all forms of culture are continually in a process of hybridity. But for me the importance of hybridity is not to be able to trace two original moments from which the third emerges, rather hybridity to me is the "Third Space" which enables other positions to emerge... The process of cultural hybridity gives rise to something different, something new and unrecognizable, a new area of negotiation of meaning and representation. (1990, 211)

This theory, which focuses on the nature of the new hybrid individual between cultures, is also useful for examining the construction of post-colonial individuals such as the Spanish immigrants in the United States. Spaniards are in-between spaces, placed between the dominant culture of reception and their culture of origin. As a result, the "Third Space" theory will be crucial to understanding the process of hybridity developed in the six novels selected for study. This theoretical framework will help to comprehend how the authors experience the process of hybridity as depicted by the characters in their works, the experiences narrated, and the use of the language. Vince Marotta's view on hybridity complements Bhabha's theory:

> There has been a long tradition in anthropology and sociology of studying the attitudes and characteristics of cultural hybrids or "in-between subjects"... This tradition continues in contemporary conceptualisations of multicultural, intercultural and transcultural identities. Initially these categories might seem to be mutually exclusive, but a closer inspection demonstrates that what binds them together is the notion of the "in-between" cultural subject. These three categories have been utilised to firstly delineate an ontological state and a mode of being with otherness and secondly, in their more radical manifestations, as interpretative positions which move beyond essentialist practices. (Marotta 2014, 1)

In other words, "in-between cultural subjects" can be studied through the current concepts of multicultural, intercultural, and transcultural identities as hybrid subjects and how they relate to each other and to the world around them. Other authors, such as the sociologist Yasmin Gunaratnam, consider that Bhabha's "Third Space" is "one within which novel meanings and subject positions can be manufactured and performed in the communication and interpretation of meaning" (2014, 6-7) and, therefore, may serve to interpret transculturation and the result of this hybridism in the characters of the texts selected.

At the beginning of Chapter 10 of *The World, the Text and the Critic* (1983), Edward Said analyzes the question of "whether by virtue of having moved from one place and time to another an idea or a theory gains or loses in strength, and whether a theory in one historical period and national culture becomes altogether different for another period or situation" (1983, 226). This idea is applicable in the case of the "Third Space" and the hybridism that Spanish immigrants experienced in the United States because the period when they arrived in the country can be said to be postcolonial, but their situation as well as their tradition and national culture are not encompassed in that of a country that has experienced decolonization. When mentioning the importance of tradition and discourse in *Orientalism* (1979), Said assumes a "hybrid view," as he points out that "my hybrid perspective is broadly historical and 'anthropological,' given that I believe all texts to be worldly and circumstantial in (of course) ways that vary from genre to genre, and from historical period to historical period" (1979, 23). For Said, the vision of the hybrid interweaves anthropology and history, culture, and tradition, allowing for a broader analysis of the real meaning of the process of transculturation and hybridization of the characters depicted in the selected novels. In *Culture and Imperialism* (1994), he points out the construction of boundaries around a culture:

> In time, culture comes to be associated, often aggressively, with the nation or the state; this differentiates "us" from "them," almost always with some degree of xenophobia. Culture in this sense is a source of identity, and a rather combative one at that, as we can see in recent "returns" to culture and tradition. These "returns" accompany rigorous codes of intellectual and moral behaviour that are opposed to the permissiveness associated with such relatively liberal philosophies as multiculturalism and hybridity. (Said 1994, xiv)

Said provides his own opinion about multiculturalism and hybridity and considers them philosophies dominated cultures "othered" by the dominant culture (1979). However, in this case, Said's perception of hybridity does not take into account the fact that the dominated culture of the immigrant is the one that moves toward the colonizing and dominating one. As a result, there is a heterogeneous view on the concept of hybridity with positive and negative interpretations depending on the scholars' approach to the circumstances of hybridity. In the case of the Spanish migration in the United States, the reconstruction of the life and process of hybridity of this invisibilized community was made possible by the recognition of the discursive currents that have focused on their immigration and the figure of the Spanish migrant in the States in the recent decades thanks to scholars such as Rueda Hernanz and Fernández and authors like de Pereda, Morell, Alfau, González, and Dueñas.

The descriptions of the Spanish communities in New York City provided by Konrad Bercovici in *Around the World in New York* (1924) and Julio Camba's *La ciudad automática* (1932), although relevant, are found in travel books and therefore do not provide characters where the effects of transculturation, biculturalism, and the Third Space can be examined. In the six selected texts, the characters represent/embody the phenomenon of hybridity. All these works contain the hybrid figure of the "Americaniards," the Spanish migrants who arrived in the United States and established themselves in it, developing an identity in-between their Spanish culture of origin and the Anglo-American culture of reception. There is a Third Space both in New York City and in Harrison County (in the case of *Pinnick Kinnick Hill*). Except for María Dueñas's fictional *Las hijas del Capitán* (2018), in five of these six texts—*Fiesta* (1954) and *Windmills in Brooklyn* (1960), by Prudencio de Pereda; *Chromos* (1990), by Felipe Alfau; *Pinnick Kinnick Hill* (2003), by G. W. González; and *The Lower East Side Kid That Made It Good* (2007), by Claude Morell—the authors inhabit the Third Space of their own stories, both as narrators and/or protagonists. The author's introduction into the narrative also complicates their binary presence in their works, which explains why these hybrid Spanish-American individuals decided to write these stories using English as their main language.

To understand the Third Space, *it is important to define* the meaning of the other two previous spaces. The "first space" refers to the country of origin: the motherland. In the case of the Spanish immigrants in the United States, the concept of first space refers to their cultural framework of origin and homeland: Spain, or what authors like the Anglo-Irish historian and political scientist Benedict Anderson in *Imagined Communities* (1983) call "the nation." According to Anderson, in a community, everybody must know each other. If that is not possible, then it is not a community but an *imagined community*, where it is presupposed that a communion is shared. As a result, he considers that the idea of "nation" is a cultural construction, a fiction created to artificially group together the inhabitants of a territory. A "nation" is then an imagined political and social construct because the members of this given country do not know each other, and what they think they share may be only in their minds. Additionally, Anderson also points out the importance of *langue* when building a nation as one of the core elements of its construction.

As to the "second space," it is the binary representation of the "Other." It is therefore the opposite of the "first space" for the Spanish immigrant, in this case, the American culture. Finally, there is the place between them, the "Third Space," a space where hybridity takes place and where the "Americaniards" of these texts experience the process of transculturation. "Americaniard," as the concept of "Europeanness" used by Rosi Braidotti in *Nomadic Subjects: Embodiment and Difference in Contemporary Feminist Theory* (2011) to write about her own experience as an immigrant in Australia, stands opposed to the Anglo attitude that was hegemonic during the last decades of the nineteenth century and the first half of the twentieth century, the time when Spanish immigrants arrived in the United States (2011, 32). In her book, Braidotti explores the construction of the nomadic subject as a "multicultural individual, a migrant who turned nomadic" (21). The Spanish immigrants during this period were also nomads. Rueda Hernanz (1993) explains that it was common for many Spaniards to immigrate to America to work as seasonal workers. This type of migration was known as "emigración golondrina" (*swallow emigration*) since at the end of the season the Spaniards returned to their country.

The nomadic character of the Spaniards who came to the United States can also be seen in the fact that many of those who arrived there between the late nineteenth and early twentieth centuries did so not only from the Iberian Peninsula but also from other American countries, as many continued a migration path that had been initiated by their parents or grandparents when they took them first to places like Cuba or Puerto Rico, before bringing them to the United States, especially after 1898, when the "disaster" of the Spanish-American War gave rise to a new migration of Spaniards from overseas to places such as California, Florida, or New York.

The concept of a nomadic subject is represented by two essential elements: language and the frontier. In the case of these Spanish emigrants in the United States, learning English made them not only bilingual, since many of them came from regions of Spain where more than one language was spoken, but also polyglots, which, according to Braidotti (2011, 29), transformed them into linguistic nomads. The other aspect is the frontier, "points of transition across the multiple geographical, ethnic, and linguistic dividing lines" (31). The Spanish migrants crossed the geographical borders that separated them from the United States by sea, with a Spanish culture with its regional idiosyncrasies and a language that was very different from the dominant English north of the Rio Grande.

Braidotti underlines that there are three crucial notions that should be considered regarding frontiers. First, that territories are powerful locations. In her opinion, the location of a region contributes to its geopolitical relevance. Secondly, she points out that all communities are imaginary constructions, and communities are material structures that brand their inhabitants. And lastly, the third aspect of this nomadic subject is passage (2011, 31-32). Spanish immigrants in the United States are marked by these three aspects: when the Spanish immigrants would arrive in New York City, they were sent to Ellis Island. There, they were classified according to their origin, and once in the city, they regrouped in small communities with people from the same country, province, city, or village. This shows the importance of the territory as a powerful location for Spaniards abroad, although it does not show whether this construction is artificial or not.

Braidotti also states that "*European* also refers to a special brand of historic political memory that, however aware it may be of colonialism, cannot easily share the claims of a postcolonial condition" (2011, 33). This is the case of Spanish immigration to the United States. The origin of the United States of America is the result of the independence of the Thirteen British Colonies; however, the inhabitants of the territories who became independent from the British Empire were not the Native Americans or slaves of African origin, but mainly a population of European ancestry from the Anglo-Germanic world. They were mainly from the British Isles, with around 85% of them of English, Irish, Scottish, and Welsh origin (Smith 1972). This fact conditioned that those arriving in later migratory flows were dominated by a culture imposed by the inhabitants of the new American country and not by the new settlers. Thus, the people who came from Europe, among whom were the Spaniards, did not have the status of subjects under a foreign colonizer or experienced postcolonialism as such.

This chapter has analyzed the concept of "culture," its definitions according to different branches of knowledge, and what can and cannot be considered as such. Likewise, I have examined the term transculturation, coined by Fernando Ortiz to describe how cultures mix and the processes into which this phenomenon is divided (acculturation, deculturation, and neoculturation) in order to understand the phases of change that an individual experiences when they come into direct contact with a culture that is not their own on a permanent basis. This section has also briefly explored the phenomenon of transculturation of tobacco as dealt with by Fernando Ortiz, as it will be essential to understand the hybrid figure of the *teverianos* in some of the stories under study. Additionally, I have also approached the question of biculturalism and *mestizaje* to apprehend its meaning and differentiate it from hybridity.

Finally, I have explored the postcolonial sociolinguistic theory of the "Third Space," identifying the "first" and the "second" spaces to comprehend the position of the culture of origin and the culture of reception as dominated and dominant in a framework of postcolonial and migrant culture that will certainly help in the analysis of the development of the hybrid subject in the literary space represented in the chosen works. The culture of the Spanish immigrant has been established as a result, in a situation of subjugation to the domination of the Anglo-American culture, a situation which will be reflected in the literary works of Morell, Alfau, de Pereda, González, and Dueñas. These stories have become the voice of those Spanish communities living in the United States under the control of a dominant Anglo-American culture that has been assimilating all the peoples arriving on its shores for centuries.

Chapter 2: Spaniards in the Melting Pot: A Historical Background

> I walked through the Rumanian section, a corner of the Austro-Polish section, the Austrian, touched the German section, edged the French one, and and then arrived into Spain. Which only means that I went from Fourth Street to Eighth Street on foot, then walked along Second Avenue to Twenty-third Street, and followed Twenty-third Street to Seventh Avenue, the edge of the Spanish district. It extends from there southward to Abingdon Square and encompasses all that lies between Seventh and Eighth avenues.
>
> — *Konrad Bercovici, Around the World on New York*

2.1. Origins

The history of migration in a country like the United States of America is as diverse as its people. The movements of human beings to this territory have produced an enormous number of publications dedicated to the study and analysis of the political, social, and economic causes of immigration over the last two centuries. However, not all immigration processes have attracted the same attention from scholars. Even in a country with a vast racial and ethnic landscape like the United States, most of the research carried out focuses on its Anglo-Saxon, Eastern European, Asian, and continental migration, leaving in the background most of the Southern European migration, except for that from Italy. However, there is a numerical explanation for this: between 1830 and 1930, more than 52 million Europeans migrated to America, 72.8% of whom went to the United States (Liñares Giraut *et al.* 2007a, 40).

Despite being a minority and never becoming as relevant as other European immigration groups, between 1850 and 1914, Spaniards joined the Age of Mass Migration, when about 30 million immigrants arrived from Europe in the American country (Hatton and Williamson 1998). As Fernández and Argeo (2014) explain, this period of Spanish history and the following decades until the 1950s "está definido por enormes reajustes" globales: la agonía del Imperio Español; la guerra entre España y EE.UU. por Cuba y la posterior aparición de algo así como un Imperio Americano; las dos guerras mundiales y, entre ellas, la brutal Guerra Civil española (1936–39) (Fernández and Argeo 2014, 223).[14] During these years, more Spanish immigrants arrived in the United States than during all previous centuries, creating *important* Spanish settlements in places such as New York, California, Ohio, or Florida (Fernández and Argeo 2014). However, as Professor Carmen González López-Briones explains in her article "Windmills in Brooklyn: A Story of the Spanish Immigrants in New York" (2019), "The Spaniards, however, never having arrived in New York in large numbers, had been far less studied than other national groups" (2019, 119). The case of New York is not the only one, since other states where the number of Spaniards was also relevant, such as Florida or West Virginia, have not received much attention from most scholars.

According to Sallé *et al.*, "el fenómeno migratorio debe tener en cuenta cuatro elementos: las fuerzas estructurales que promueven la emigración; las fuerzas estructurales que atraen inmigrantes; las motivaciones, objetivos y aspiraciones de quienes responden a estas fuerzas estructurales; y la consideración de las estructuras sociales, económicas y culturales, que surgen para conectar las causas producidas en el origen y en el destino" (2009, 8).[15] If in 1492 the migratory movements from Europe to America began, it was after 1776, with the emancipation of the thirteen American colonies, when a big migration occurred, as people felt encouraged to look for the American dream, make a fortune, or achieve a better life. There was also the social phenomenon derived from wars: voluntary exile or flight to neutral countries or countries not involved in war, which led to territories bordering the belligerent countries becoming security corridors to safe and sometimes distant destinations (Dolan 2010).

In "Settlers and Slaves: European and African Migrations to Early Modern British America" (2005), James Horn and Philip D. Morgan

14 "is defined by huge global realignments: the agony of the Spanish Empire; the war between Spain and the US over Cuba, and the subsequent emergence of something like an American Empire; the two world wars and, between them, the brutal Spanish Civil War (1936–39)."

15 "the migration phenomenon must take into account four elements: the structural forces that encourage emigration; the structural forces that attract immigrants; the motivations, objectives and aspirations of those who respond to these structural forces; and the consideration of the social, economic and cultural structures that arise to connect the causes produced at origin and destination."

analyze the evolution of European migration to the Americas between 1500 and 1820. Focusing on a total of six European countries (Spain, Portugal, Britain, France, the Netherlands, and Germany), the authors indicate the number of European immigrants arriving on American shores in five different periods: 1) from 1500 to 1580, coinciding with Spain's "discovery" of America by Spain, the beginning of the Spanish conquest, the arrival of the Portuguese in the territories of what would eventually become Brazil and the first British settlements on the East Coast; 2) from 1580 to 1640, referred to the Iberian Union of the Kingdoms of Spain and Portugal and the arrival of new immigrants from France and Holland; 3) from 1640 to 1700, from the beginning of the decline of the Spanish Empire and the final establishment and growth of the thirteen British colonies that would become the origin of the United States of America; 4) from 1700 to 1760, with the arrival of the first significant flows of immigrants of German origin and the pre-revolutionary period; and 5) from 1760 to 1820, coinciding with the American Revolution and most of the Spanish-American wars of independence.

Despite the increase of Spanish immigrants, their number remained low in comparison to other European groups (Dolan, 2010). Spanish immigration never became as relevant as the Anglo-Germanic immigration at first, or the immigration from other parts of Europe, Africa, Asia, and America soon after. As Anderson (2006) points out, the big "European migration to the Americas took place on an astonishing scale" (2006, 188) during the seventeenth, eighteenth, and nineteenth centuries; however, there were a few Spaniards. As a result, "by the end of the eighteenth century there were no less than 3,200,000 "whites" (including no more than 150,000 *peninsulares*) within the 16,900,000 population of the Western empire of the Spanish Bourbons" (189).[16] Most of the Spanish immigration to the Americas during the nineteenth and twentieth centuries went to Latin America due to the lack of a language barrier and the ease of integrating into those societies. This fact made the United States of America a less appealing destination compared to countries south of Río Grande. If we compare,

16 "White" is a term used by Anderson and borrowed from Lynch (1973) and not exempt of controversy.

Table 1. European migration to the Americas, 1500–1820 (Horn and Morgan 2005, 21–22)

1500–1580	
Spain	100,000
Portugal	90,000
England, Scotland, Wales	0
Total	190,000
1580–1640	
Spain	90,000
Portugal	110,000
England, Scotland, Wales	50,000
France	4,000
Netherlands	2,000
Total	256,000
1640–1700	
Spain	70,000
Portugal	50,000
England, Scotland, Wales	303,000
France	45,000
Netherlands	13,000
Total	481,000
1700–1760	
Spain	90,000
Portugal	250,000
Britain	289,000
France	51,000
Netherlands	5,000
Germany	97,000
Total	782,000
1760–1820	
Spain	70,000
Portugal	105,000
Britain	615,000
France	20,000
Netherlands	5,000
Germany	51,000
Other	5,000
Total	871,000

1500–1820	
Spain	420,000
Portugal	605,000
Britain	1,257,000
France	120,000
Netherlands	25,000
Germany	148,000
Other	5,000
Total	2,580,000

for example, the great period of European migration to the United States between 1850 and 1930, studies show that more than 200,000 Spaniards arrived in the American country, but if we compare them to the number of other European immigrants from the same period—Irish (4.5 million), German (5 million), or British (3.5 million)—that is a relatively small number (Dolan 2010, 67–83). This invisibility was a constant trend during the nineteenth and twentieth centuries, even during periods when Spanish immigration to the United States was higher due to the intense turmoil of the years of the Spanish-American War (1898), the War with Morocco (1920–1926), the Spanish Second Republic (1931–1939), the Spanish Civil War (1936–1939), and the dictatorship of General Franco (1939–1975). As González López-Briones explains:

> The reasons behind the decision to emigrate are several. On the one hand, there are "pushing" reasons, as poor economic expectations. And to avoid conscription and thus the Spanish-Moroccan War. And during the mid-1930s and early 40s, to escape the Spanish Civil War, and subsequent exile. There were also «pulling» reasons, such as the call of relatives, friends and neighbors, and the attraction the United States had as a land of opportunity, and the expectations for improving their lives. (1997, 20)

However, this migration never reached large numbers. One of the main reasons why the Spanish community in the United States was so small can be found in the Immigration Act of 1903 and the subsequent laws of 1907 and 1910, but especially in the Emergency Quota Act, also known as the Emergency Immigration Act of 1921 (Rueda Hernanz 1993, 50–53). This law, as Rueda Hernanz states, "asignaba a cada país un porcentaje anual equivalente a un 3% de inmigrantes a contar a partir de los que ya vivían en Estados Unidos en 1910. En 1924 se tomó como base el censo de 1890 y se disminuyó la base porcentual al 2%. De esa manera, los españoles vieron muy limitadas sus posibilidades de emigrar" (1993, 53).[17] The Spanish historian Rosendo A. Gómez (1962, 60) estimates that between 1882 and 1947, the number of Spanish migrants who left the country to cross the Atlantic was around five million. At the same time, if one compares the number of Spaniards who decided to return to Spain, this figure rises to 3.8 million returnees. As a result, the number of migrants who traveled to and stayed in America during this period could be around 1.2 million people, mainly between 1900 and 1924. More than half, some 600,000 Spaniards according to some sources (Gómez 1962), and up to 60% according to others, went to Argentina, and around 300,000, around 25%, went to Cuba, and 15% were unevenly spread between the United States, Brazil, Mexico, and other countries. Gómez (1962, 61) also provides a pattern of movements to and from Spain between 1882 and 1947:

1882–1898: Heavy net emigration to Argentina and Cuba
1899–1900: Decline (Spanish-American War)
1901–1913: Heavy net emigration; beginning of substantial movement to the U.S.
1914–1918: Net immigration (World War I)
1919–1930: Heavy net emigration but virtual disappearance of emigration to the U.S. after 1921
1931–1947: Decline; net immigration 1931–1934 (depression); followed by Civil
War, World War II

---

17 "assigned each country an annual percentage equivalent to 3% of immigrants to be counted from those already living in the United States in 1910. In 1924, the 1890 census was taken as the basis and the percentage base was lowered to 2%. As a result, Spaniards' possibilities to emigrate became severely limited."

On the other hand, clandestine migration was very common among Spanish immigrants during this period. The harbors of Bordeaux in France and Gibraltar were the most used for this type of illegal emigration, due to their location in the north and south of the Peninsula (Gómez 1962, 68). This migration was possible thanks to customs agents who facilitated the emigrants' passage upon payment of the amount of money previously stipulated by a contract agreement. This meant that there was no official registration when these migrants embarked. As a result, it is estimated that, for example, between 1911 and 1915, the number of clandestine immigrants who arrived in the United States could be around 25% of the total number of departures, while during other years this figure could go up to 40% (68–69). According to Professor Rueda Hernanz, between 1875 and 1900, 75% of the Spaniards who emigrated to the United States arrived in New York City. He also seems to share the same numbers that Professor Morell Moll used in her work, but he goes even further. According to R. A. Gómez (1962, 68),

> clandestine emigration was very common. One form of this centered on departure from a foreign port. Gibraltar and Bordeaux, convenient to the south and north respectively, were very extensively used for that purpose. Agents were very important to this procedure since one had to make passage connections through a distant port in a foreign country. The emigrant, choosing this route, simply left Spain as a temporary visitor and boarded ship under the general direction of the agent, and without bothering to clear through any officialdom. This was occasionally begun as a contract arrangement, the agents in these negotiations often being paid so much per head.

However, this clandestine migration did not favor the visibility of Spanish immigrants in the United States, whose numbers seemed to be lower than those really arriving. This explanation is supported by the data about Spanish immigration from the U.S. Department of Justice published in 1996: the Statistical Yearbook of the Immigration and Naturalization Service indicated that between 1869 and 1940, officially only 153,233 Spanish immigrants arrived on the coasts of the United States:

Years	Number
1869–1870	3,090
1871–1880	8,221
1881–1890	21,528
1891–1900	25,553
1901–1910	44,211
1911–1920	25,158
1921–1930	15,901
1931–1940	9,571
TOTAL	153.233

Source: U.S. Department of Justice 1996.

Another element to consider is the Spanish immigration from the Caribbean to the United States, especially from Cuba, which increased since the "Ten Years War" from 1868 to 1878 (Fernández and Argeo 2014, 221) and after the disaster of 1898. In the case of the Spanish-Cuban migration to the United States, this wave was higher between 1891 and 1930, "mostly as a result of political and economic turmoil on the island," as Jorge Duany indicates in "Cuban communities in the United States: Migration Waves, Settlement Patterns and Socioeconomic Diversity" (1999), where he explains that this migration established colonies in Key West, Tampa, New York City, and New Orleans (1999, 74). Although the flow of Cubans of Spanish origin who continued to migrate to the United States remained stable until 1959, it is impossible to measure the real number of those who made it to the Northern American country. In the year of the Cuban Revolution, many Spaniards emigrated from Cuba and other Caribbean countries to the United States. This migration brought a hybrid Spanish-Caribbean—but especially—Cuban hybrid culture whose maximum representation can be found in the figure of tobacco, especially the *teverianos*, as was the case in cities like Tampa and New York City.

Spanish migration in the United States was invisibilized during the nineteenth and twentieth centuries, even during the periods when it was higher (Powell 2005). As mentioned before, although studies about American migration have been constant during the last and the present century, Spanish immigration in the United States did not gain any relevance until 1993, when the Spanish professor and historian Rueda Hernanz published *Españoles emigrantes en América (Siglos XVI–XX)* (2000) and *La emigración contemporánea de españoles a Estados Unidos. 1820–1950. De «Dons» a «Misters»* (1993), where he analyzes Spanish migration in the United States in depth. However, he is not the only author who speaks about this flow of Spaniards to the United States.

For over a decade, Professor James D. Fernández, from New York University, has published numerous articles, book chapters, and books focused on Spanish immigration in the United States. In *Invisible Immigrants: Spaniards in the US (1868–1945)*, he focuses on the under-representation of Spanish immigration by using documents and pictures to portray their life and integration in the country. However, this kind of research is the exception, not the rule. Enric Bou (quoted in Faber and Martínez Carazo 2010) uses intellectuals to show the parallelism between the Spanish migration and that from other European countries to explain why Spaniards have never been perceived as *important*, even when they arrived by the thousands in the United States:

> El exilio español en los EE.UU. tuvo la (mala) suerte de coincidir con una migración masiva de intelectuales europeos, en gran parte alemanes, algunos italianos y muchos de otros países europeos. El carácter masivo de esta otra emigración de intelectuales europeos, en competencia lingüística y numérica, ha hecho mucho por borrar los rastros de la presencia de españoles en este movimiento migratorio. (Faber and Martínez Carazo 2010, 31)[18]

Since the sixteenth century, relations between the Hispanic and Anglo-Saxon worlds in the Americas have been indivisibly intertwined due to the great contrast between these cultures in matters of religion, the distribution of their inhabitants throughout the American territory, their treatment of the Indigenous population, and the different waves of immigrants that have populated the continent. The creation of new nations, especially during the nineteenth century, and the establishment of new borders with the

18 "The Spanish exile in the US had the (bad) luck to coincide with a massive migration of European intellectuals, largely German, some Italian and many from other European countries. The massive flow this other emigration consisting of European intellectuals, in linguistic and numerical competence, has done much to erase the traces of the presence of Spaniards in this migratory movement."

intention of defending these new states have been the cause of wars and all kinds of international conflicts for more than three hundred years. During the twentieth century, the lack of political stability beyond the Rio Grande and the constant irregular immigration from South and Central America to the United States have overshadowed much of the European immigration, such as Irish, Italian, or even Spanish immigration, with a lower number of immigrants.

At the same time, it was not until the second half of the nineteenth century and the first half of the twentieth century when more Spaniards migrated to the United States than during all the previous centuries, creating an *important* Spanish diaspora in places like New York, California, Ohio, or Florida (Fernández and Argeo 2014, 10, 46, 47). Núñez Seixas (2007) asserts that "el éxodo masivo de españoles hacia diferentes destinos desde mediados del siglo XIX, primero hacia América y después, hacia otros países de Europa, constituye un laboratorio ideal para observar esos procesos de mutación e imaginación de identidades" (2007, 18),[19] that is, a laboratory like the United States where the identities of Spanish immigrants became a hybrid product of the dominant culture of reception and the dominated culture of origin. As Bou points out based on Azancot's research,

> la emigración más importante desde España hacia las Américas se produjo a finales del siglo XIX. Más de tres millones y medio de españoles se trasladaron a través del Atlántico. Los principales destinos fueron Cuba (34%) y Argentina (48%) y solo 2% a los EE. UU. Estos no eran sólo viajes de ida, sino que para muchos significó el de vuelta, al cabo de pocos años, y no siempre con éxito. (1992, 180, 183)[20]

The 2% quoted above is equivalent to over 70,000 Spanish immigrants arriving in the United States in the latter part of the nineteenth century,

19 "the massive exodus of Spaniards to different destinations since the mid-19th century, first to America and later to other European countries, constitutes an ideal laboratory for observing these processes of mutation and imagination of identities."

20 "The most important emigration from Spain to the Americas took place at the end of the 19th century. More than three and a half million Spaniards moved across the Atlantic. The main destinations were Cuba (34%) and Argentina (48%) and only 2% to the USA. These were not only one-way journeys but for many it meant a return journey, after a few years, and not always successfully."

many of them settling in New York City. Thus, 2% may seem a relatively small number compared to the total of immigrants but is nonetheless a rather large number of immigrants for Spain at the time, whose population at the beginning of the twentieth century was under 19 million (INE 2001). This immigration was especially significant in the metropolis, where, according to some studies, it is estimated that more than 30,000 Spaniards went during these years to work and live there, most of them Galicians but also Asturians, Basques, Valencians, or Andalusians. However, the number could be even higher if we consider that, according to University of Alicante Professor Teresa Morell Moll (2017), between 1904 and 1924, 15,000 Valencians arrived in New York following the footsteps of other Spaniards, many of them Valencians too, like the architect and artist Rafael Guastavino Moreno, creator of the City Hall Loop and the tile vaulting at the Grand Central Terminal in New York City. The number of Valencians was so high that in 1928, a few years after their arrival, they founded El Círculo Valenciano de Nueva York. Among them was painter José Segrelles, who joined them in 1929 (Ferrer Álvarez 2016) and lived in New York City from 1929 to 1932, before returning to Spain.

Morell Moll's study includes a detailed analysis of the ports of departure of the Spanish immigrants and the number of Spaniards who arrived in the United States between 1820 and 1949. According to her study, during those three decades, the official number of Spaniards who arrived at Ellis Island was 240,642 (Moll 2017). Many of them decided to stay initially in the Lower East Side of Manhattan, but many others chose to continue their trip with the intention of working in Waterbury, Connecticut, and Bridgeport, Shelton, and New Britain, which also offered good working opportunities. A comparison of Moll's figures from 2011 with those of Professor Ana Varela-Lago's from 2008 shows serious discrepancies. Moll did her research a few years after Varela-Lago, so it seems that her data are more reliable because they are more up to date. Their results only seem to coincide for the period between 1881 and 1890. Because of this, a further review of their sources is necessary:

YEAR	Number of Spaniards who emigrated to the United States of America according to Morell Moll	Number of Spaniards who emigrated to the United States of America according to Varela-Lago
1881–1890	4,419	4,419
1891–1900	6,662	8,731
1901–1910	48,944	27,937
1911–1920	102,954	68,611
1921–1930	41,954	28,958
1931–1940	4,945	3,258
1941–1949	3,287	2,898
Total (1881–1949)	**213,162**	**144,794**

Sources: Morell and Moll 2008, Varela-Lago 2008, 153

Regardless of the discrepancies between the two studies, it can be affirmed that between 144,794 and 213,162 Spanish immigrants arrived in the United States between 1881 and 1949. As Rueda Hernanz points out, from 1820 to 1977, roughly 320,000 Spaniards officially arrived in the United States, approximately 250,000 before 1950 (1993, 74). However, *it is important to consider* that the official statistics about Spanish migration from the Instituto Geográfico y Estadístico began in 1882, and historians agree that they do not reflect the real numbers (Álvarez Gila *et al.* 2007, 40–41). Most of these new migrants stayed in the country, but, according to the United States' official statistics, between 1907 and 1940, around 70,000 Spaniards returned to their homeland. Contemporary literature of the time also emphasizes the fact that one of the returning waves of Spaniards might have been produced owing to the recruiting process that the United States had to establish in 1917 after their entry into the Great War, as can be read in "Spaniards in the United States," in *The Literary Digest* (March 22, 1919), in its section about "Education in Americanism, Lessons in Patriotism prepared for and especially designed for High School Use":

> Despite the fact that many of the workers in war-industries were gaining from seven to twelve dollars per day a great return movement to Spain began with the inauguration of the compulsory military service law after the United States had become involved in the world conflict. The spirit of the law, Spanish authorities

> admit, was "very magnanimous," but the interpretation as practised by some agents of the Government confounded a host of Spanish laborers who did not understand English, either to speak or to read, sufficiently to assure them of their rights. The result was that many of these workers simply ignored the law, basing their decision on the fact that they were not American, but Spanish citizens. Naturally, many of them were taken into custody by the agents of the Government. But the United States Government fairly met the problem by appointing a military exemption board at the service of the Union Benefica Española, the chief Spanish benevolent association in this country. The appraisers on this board, lawyers who know Spanish and American law equally, served, as American lawyers all did, without remuneration, and voluntarily. It is in the records of the Union Benefica Española that it retrieved two thousand men who were drafted mistakenly. (1919, 40)

This returning movement is known as "emigración 'golondrina'," [21] which Rueda Hernanz indicates might have been caused by the Wall Street Crash of 1929 after World War I (1993, 77). In the same article, this type of migration is already mentioned as the desired one by the United States, not only because Spanish immigrants were considered hard workers but also because most of them wanted to return to Spain after making some money: "Here we are interested solely in the assimilation of Spaniards from Spain, who have immigrated to the United States to settle here for good, or merely to earn a livelihood during a certain fixed period and thereafter to return to their homeland" (1919, 40). Gómez (1962) adds a complementary explanation to the Spanish migration to America, but especially to Argentina:

> The seasonal character of agricultural employment aroused desires to seek employment elsewhere for part of the year. Thus arose the fantastic golondrina movement by means of which thousands of Spaniards annually attempted to gain the advantages of working in two growing seasons: one in the spring-summer of Spain and another in the spring-summer of South America, mainly Argentina, where the warm season extended from November to April. The golondrinas were not, properly speaking, emigrants, but they were so recorded in the official records of embarkation. (1962, 64)

Spanish "golondrina" immigrants and those who decided to stay permanently in New York City, both single and married, used to send money, *remesas*, to their families, as we can see in de Pereda's *Windmills in Brooklyn* (1960). In general, Spanish immigrants to the United States were

---

21 "swallow emigration."

young, single men (Rueda Hernanz 1993, 181–82). As Rueda Hernanz highlights, at least initially this immigration was not family migration. He identifies three types of family situations: the first is comprised of those who remained single their whole lives: “Han llegado solteros a Estados Unidos y permanecen solteros de por vida lo que ocurre en una proporción algo mayor de lo corriente en España en todo caso, no era lo común” (1993, 182).[22] This is certainly a very significant fact; if we consider that this meant that these people did not form a family, they very likely did not have children, and, therefore, their transculturation into American society would be very limited, and there would be no next-generation assimilation, as they had no offspring.

The second group is those who had a family: “Emigran desde el principio con la mujer y los hijos, si los tienen. Una emigración familiar poco frecuente. Lo más común era que dejaran a su mujer y a sus hijos en España” (182).[23] This is the case of the Arenas family before they moved to New York. Emilio Arenas gained vast experience moving around after leaving his family in Spain: “Estibador en los puertos de Marsella y Barcelona, camarero en la plaza Independencia de Montevideo, vendedor callejero en Manila, pinche de cocina en un carguero holandés” (Dueñas 2018, 17).[24] This situation makes immigrants return to their homes eventually, “una auténtica emigración golondrina” (Rueda Hernanz 1993, 182),[25] but not for long before they decide to go on their next trip and leave their families in Spain. As Gómez (1962) underlines,

> many were the Spaniards who emigrated to Argentina, Cuba, or the United States only long enough to gain sufficient savings at general skilled labor or mercantile activity, after which one lived in Spain at a rather higher level than before the venture. Indeed, there were Spaniards who “commuted” between Spain and

---

22 “They have come to the United States single and remain single for life, which is at least a somewhat higher rate than is common in Spain but was not common.”

23 “They migrate from the beginning with their wives and children if they have them. This family emigration is unfrequent. Most commonly, they left their wives and children in Spain.”

24 “Stevedore in the ports of Marseille and Barcelona, waiter in Montevideo’s Plaza Independencia, street vendor in Manila, kitchen assistant on a Dutch cargo ship.”

25 “a real swallow migration.”

> somewhere in the Americas over a long period of years, usually maintaining a principal household in Spain. (Gómez 1962, 64)

As a result, a Spanish immigrant like Emilio Arenas would sooner or later return to Spain "o bien estabiliza su situación en Estados Unidos, lo que supone la emigración de la familia hasta diez o veinte años después del primer viaje, con la consiguiente dificultad de crear una relación familiar nueva después de años de vida tan diferentes y distantes" (Rueda Hernanz 1993, 182).[26] As the reader notices at the beginning of the novel, Emilio's family arrives in the City of Lights when he is already an experienced traveler: "Tras esfumarse de un remolcador del canal de Panamá, Emilio Arenas había recalado en Nueva York a principios de 1929"[27] (Dueñas 2018, 18). Emilio is already old and tired when he buys a bar in 1935 and decides to bring his family from Spain. In this case, the fact that the family was already settled at home before migrating to the United States meant that their cultural transition depended on whether the children were born either in Spain or in the United States and their age when they arrived in the United States if they had been born in Spain. In the case of little Prudencio in *Windmills in Brooklyn*, it was the children, raised in a hybrid environment, who helped their elders to assimilate into the new society better: "Going to Grandmother's had some responsibility, for there were always parents to be done and I would often have to act as a translator. My grandmother spoke only about 10 words of English, and my Grandfather just a few more" (De Pereda 1960, 5).

The final group is made up of those who got married in the United States: "La mayoría de estos se casan con cónyuges de nacionalidad española. Así se desprende de los libros de matrimonios de la Iglesia de Nuestra Señora de Guadalupe en Nueva York o del Spanish Mission en

26 "or he stabilises his situation in the United States, which means that the family emigrates up to ten or twenty years after his first trip, with the subsequent difficulty of creating a new family relationship after so many different and distant years of life."

27 "After slipping off a Panama Canal tugboat, Emilio Arenas landed in New York in the early 1929."

San Luis" (Rueda Hernanz 1993, 182).[28] This would be the case of Emilio's oldest daughter, Victoria, who married the Spanish widower Luciano Barona at the Church of Our Lady of Guadalupe on 14th Street. This group of young Spanish migrants who marry in the United States is the one who would have a better chance of adapting to and integrating into American society. By creating a family and starting a new phase in their lives in the same spot where they had moved to, they felt more connected to it than to their country of origin, thus constructing a new hybrid identity as a Spanish American couple.

Because of this constant movement of regular immigrants, of their families, and of *golondrina* workers going from Spain to the United States and vice versa, it is difficult to know the real size of Spanish migration at this time. In the case of New York City, Rueda Hernanz mentions that at least 24% of the Spanish immigrants in the United States have lived in the metropolis since 1880. Between 1897 and 1944, for example, around one-third of the Spaniards decided to stay in the city, and during the following decades, New York became not only a place where most Spanish immigrants resided but also a place of transit where thousands of them decided to stay provisionally before continuing their exodus or temporary migration toward other destinations in the state of New York or even outside of it.

2.2. Building Spanish Communities in the New World

The encounter between Spanish immigrants and New York City was a culture shock that influenced the customs, political life, economy, and society of the time. It is in the metropolis, a space where the Anglo-American culture stands as the culture of domination, where the Spanish identity is constructed or, in Benedict Anderson's terms, imagined. The first element for the creation of this new identity is the family. The Spanish family constituted the core from where these immigrants built the Spanish community in the city and nurtured the next generations in what these families

---

28 "Most of them marry in the United States with spouses of Spanish nationality. This is evident from the marriage books of the Church of Our Lady of Guadalupe in New York or the Spanish Mission in St. Louis."

considered were the Spanish values, cultural traditions, religious beliefs, and even atavisms.

The second element that helped to shape the new settlers was the local societies. According to Vicente Peña Saavedra, these could be divided into three different categories depending on regional organization: "El primero corresponde a las sociedades de cobertura *macroterritorial*, que agrupan a los emigrantes por comunidades regionales. El segundo acoge a las entidades de alcance *microterritorial* o local, con gradaciones internas desde la aldea hasta la comarca. Y el tercero, intermedio entre estos dos, es el propio de las instituciones de dominio mesoterritorial o provincial" (Liñares Giraut et al. 2007a, 79).[29] These societies began to spread during the second half of the nineteenth century, as Spanish immigration continued to increase, becoming centers of life in the areas where Spaniards resided. They were found in all Spanish immigrant communities and in states such as California, Florida, Hawaii, Idaho, Illinois, Indiana, Louisiana, Massachusetts, Michigan, Missouri, Nevada, New Jersey, New Mexico, Ohio, Pennsylvania, Rhode Island, Vermont, and even Washington D.C. (Rueda Hernanz 1993, 231–37). New York City was no exception:

> Like other immigrant groups arriving to the US before the New Deal, the Spaniards landed in a country in which there was no such thing as a safety net: no unemployment insurance, no health benefits, no social security. They responded to this predicament with an astounding spirit of entrepreneurship and solidarity. Wherever they settled, they organize an impressive number and range of organizations to take care of each other. They formed associations based on their home regions or even towns, they established sports, cultural and social clubs, mutual aid societies, an even, in the case of Tampa, Florida, two state-of-the-art hospitals built by and for the city's Spanish colony. Sports competitions, performances and picnics, there marked the rhythm of the colonia's calendar. (Fernández and Argeo 2014, 162)

While the historical documentation of this period is limited, it nevertheless constitutes a unique source of historical information that provides

29 "The first corresponds to societies with macro-territorial coverage, grouping migrants by regional communities. The second is for micro-territorial or local entities, with internal gradations from the village to the county. And the third, intermediate between these two, is that made of meso-territorial or provincial institutions."

transcendence to the history of countries like the United States and Spain and to the cultural heritage that Spanish immigration contributed to the American "melting pot." Chelsea and Hell's Kitchen, on the Middle West Side of Manhattan, are fine examples of this melting pot where Spanish immigrants experimented with their cultural transformation in the neighborhood where the community of Little Spain was established:

> Ethnically the section is a typical metropolitan melange. Since the late 1840's, the Irish have been the predominant group in Chelsea and Hell's Kitchen. Not so numerous perhaps, but constituting a sizable minority in each of these localities, are the Italians. The northern part of the Hell's Kitchen district also contains small French, German, and Negro groups, while Chelsea also houses Spanish, Puerto Rican, Greek, and Balkan colonies. On the whole, however, the long process of assimilation, accelerated by immigration restrictions, is rapidly transforming the Middle West Side into a native American community. According to the 1930 census, native- born residents of the district outnumbered the foreign born by nearly two to one. (Federal Writer's Project 1939, 145)

In the case of Spanish immigration in New York City, this cultural heritage is an indispensable source of information to understand the changes and development not only of the metropolis but also of Spain during the 1800s and 1900s. New York City is dominated by the Anglo-American culture. Therefore, Spaniards who lived there decided to create their own spaces to preserve their identity. As Núñez Seixas points out regarding the role of the Spanish communities in America and how they helped their country by taking economic initiatives, "fue en este apartado donde la *otra* España imaginada por los emigrantes más influyó sobre la evolución de la España *real*. Sobre todo, entre las colectividades españolas en América, y con especial incidencia colectivos como los emigrantes gallegos y asturianos, se registró una multiplicidad de iniciativas tendentes a articular la sociedad civil" (Liñares Giraut et al. 2007a, 26).[30]

The clash of cultures in the metropolis and the desire to construct an identity where their Spanish roots were preserved was not easy for these

---

30 "It was in this section that the *other* Spain imagined by the emigrants most influenced the evolution of the *real* Spain. Above all, among the Spanish communities in America, and especially among groups of Galician and Asturian emigrants, there was a multiplicity of initiatives aimed at articulating the civil society of the country."

new American citizens: "A partir de 1905 y, sobre todo, durante los cuatro lustros que preceden a los años 30, el asociacionismo *microterritorial* se propagó a un ritmo creciente en los entornos donde recalaba nuestra emigración" (Liñares Giraut et al. 2007a, 80).[31] In those societies, education, tradition, and culture were used as useful instruments to encourage the preservantion of the local heritage of the Spaniards, creating "sistemas de enseñanza 'étnicos' que asegurasen la transmisión de la identidad nacional de los padres extranjeros a sus hijos ya americanos" (Liñares Giraut et al. 2007a, 47).[32]

Several of the Spanish immigrant communities acted as small neighborhoods within the city of New York. There were many communities that represented regions of Spain, such as Galicia, Asturias, Andalusia, Valencia, and so on., usually accompanied by people from other Spanish-speaking countries of Latin America, mainly Mexicans, Puerto Ricans, and Cubans, with whom they shared the language and similar cultures. These groups mainly covered the island of Manhattan from the south to the north of Central Park, from Downtown to its upper part, around 110th Street, where Hispanic Harlem is located, but there were also surrounding communities such as Brooklyn, Queens, the Bronx, and State Island. Rueda Hernanz (1993) indicates that there are four areas where Spanish immigrants settled and resided and where these local societies could be found:

1) The Southeast of Manhattan in the neighborhood of Cherry and Roosevelt Street. According to Rueda Hernanz, in 1926 there were between 25,000 and 30,000 Spaniards who lived in an area of thirty blocks (Rueda Hernanz 1993, 87). By the 1930s this area had become the heart of Spanish immigration with many Spanish societies like the Círculo Valenciano at 104 Madison Street, the Centro Vasco Americano at 48 Cherry Street, the Sociedad Cultural Gallega at 26 Cherry Street, Bergondo and its surroundings at 94 James Street, Socorros Mutuos Muradanos, Unión Cultural Bueu, and Beluso and its surroundings at

31 "From 1905 onward, and especially during the two decades preceding the 1930s, micro-territorial associationism spread at an increasing rate in the areas where our emigration was settling."

32 "Ethnic' education systems that ensured the transmission of national identity from the foreign parents to their already American children."

39 Cherry Street. A little bit further south, at 311 Water Street, was Sociedad Cultural Deportiva y Recreativa Sada and its surroundings (Memoria Casa Galicia 1962, 19). Many of these societies and their members eventually became part of La Nacional-Spanish Benevolent Society or la Unidad Gallega (Rueda Hernanz 1993, 87). According to Liñares Giraut, "las sociedades de Beneficencia… intentaron ayudar al inmigrante en el país de acogida, para hacer frente a situaciones de enfermedad…, falta de trabajo, desgracias económicas y atenciones fúnebres" (Liñares Giraut 2007c, 129).[33]

2) During the 1930s, the area of West Side Manhattan, between the neighborhoods of Chelsea and the West Village, had around 15,000 Spaniards located between Christopher Street and West 23rd. Many Spanish immigrants in New York City were concentrated around West 14th Street in Manhattan, between the Eighth and Seventh Avenues, in an area known as Little Spain (Fernández and Argeo 2014, 58). The community evolved rapidly between the late 1890s and the 1960s as a result of the constant arrival of Spanish immigrants in the American metropolis wishing to establish themselves in the area:

> Among the immigrants were Spaniards, who gathered in the vicinity of Fourteenth Street . . ., bodegas (grocery stores), carnicerias (butcher shops), Spanish benefit societies, the SPANISH-AMERICAN WORKERS ALLIANCE at 349 West Fourteenth Street, and the SPANISH CHURCH OF OUR LADY OF GUADALUPE at 229 West Fourteenth Street still preserve the Iberian flavor. (Federal Writer's Project 1939, 151)

Between the last decades of the nineteenth century and the first half of the twentieth century, thousands of Spaniards arrived in New York City as a consequence of different Spanish economic crises, wars, and the high level of unemployment in most regions of Spain. The area of West 14th Street, also known as Little Spain, *La España Chica*, or simply *La Catorce*, was the second largest area of Spaniards. There were two Catholic churches in New York: Nuestra Señora de Guadalupe, at 229 West 14th Street and the Church N°2 of San Francisco Javier, at Church N° 1 46 West 16th Street, with a parish school in Seventeenth Street; El Centro Español: Sociedad Española de Beneficencia (merged

33 the Charity Societies… tried to help the immigrant in the host country to cope with situations of illness… unemployment, economic misfortunes, and funerals.

years later with La Nacional of Brooklyn) at 239 West 14th Street; the Casa Galicia in the 16th; and the Club Juvenil El Sada in the 11th Street (Rueda Hernanz 1993, 89). The Centro Montañés was at 219 East 28th Street, and the Centro Asturiano moved from Brooklyn to 245 West 14th Street. Other societies in the area were the Sociedad Naturista Hispana at 26 West 15th Street, with a Spanish Camp in Annadale, Staten Island (Memoria Casa Galicia 1962, 20) and the Alianza Republicana Socialista Española de N.Y. at 239 West 14th Street (1993, 89).

3) In the 1930s, around 6,000 Spanish immigrants lived in Brooklyn Willow Place, Columbia Place, and Henry Street, creating the third Spanish neighborhood in the metropolis. For many years, societies like La Nacional, the Centro Andaluz at 59 Henry Street, or the Ateneo were also there. There was another community around Atlantic Avenue, where the Ateneo Español, derived from the Centro Español, was located. There were other societies, like Las Sociedades Españolas Confederadas and the Club El Segura. The Centro Asturiano was at 50 Willow Street during the early 1930s (1993, 89–90). The number of Spaniards became so high in the area that, during the 1940s, two schools were founded under the name of Juventudes Escolares Españolas (1993, 90). The Salmerón Group made up mainly of immigrants from Almería, was also in the neighborhood (Rueda Hernanz 1993, 89–90), at 123 5th Avenue, Brooklyn (Amate 2011, 94).
4) The fourth area where the Spanish immigrants lived, especially since the beginning of 1927, was Astoria in Queens. From 1934, the number of Spaniards began to grow there, and a Centro Español was founded. Many Spaniards decided to settle next to people coming from the same regions, or even villages, creating homogeneous communities (Rueda Hernanz 1993, 90).

There is a fifth area not included by Rueda Hernanz but mentioned by Fernández: El Barrio. Spanish Harlem, East Harlem, or El Barrio, as it is also known, occupies the northeast part of Manhattan, between Fifth Avenue and the East River. Originally a Dutch settlement founded in 1658, it took its name of New Harlem in honor of the Dutch city of the same name, Harlem:

> Nieuw Haarlem was established in 1658 by Director Peter Stuyvesant in the lush bottomland between Harlem River and Morningside Heights. The village was

> named for the old Dutch city, in all probability by the director himself. A few Hollanders, French Huguenots, Danes, Swedes, and Germans developed rich farms there and gave them such idyllic names as Quiet Vale and Happy Valley. New Harlem was about ten miles from the little town of New Amsterdam on the island's southern tip, and was connected with it by a road built "by the [Dutch West India] Company's negroes" on an Indian trail, now part of Broadway. (Federal Writer's Project 1939, 254).

Both the name and the area evolved to the present day through various waves of immigration: Italians, Africans, and Puerto Ricans for the most part, who gave the neighborhood its unique idiosyncrasy (Federal Writer's Project 1939, 264–65). At the heart of the area is 116th Street, and its life in 1936 is described in *Las hijas del Capitán* as follows: "Había gente por la calle, olor a arroz con gandules y chicharrón frito, corrillos de viejos que fumaban mientras parlamentaban y reían con pocos dientes" (Dueñas 2018, 392).[34] Through Adela, Tony's friend, we are given a close view of the everyday lives of Puerto Rican families where there is room for parents, children, grandparents, nephews, nieces, nephews, and other relatives who at any moment would arrive in the USA from their country of origin. Thanks to Adela, Mona, and Luz undergo a sophisticated physical change. In the same neighborhood, on 110th Street, there is the music shop Tay-Tay (a239), where she drops in on Frank Kruzan, Luz's manager, and a dance studio on 109th, where the aspiring artist receives her dance lessons from Revuelta, her Cuban teacher (333).

Although the South Village is not strictly speaking a Spanish community, some Spanish families live there. It also deserves to be mentioned because it was here that events of great relevance to the Arenas family took place. Located in Manhattan, the South Village is part of the authentic Greenwich Village: "Beginning in the 1880's Greenwich Village was occupied by the Irish and Negroes, and later by Italians. At approximately the same time, the Germans and Irish of the Lower East Side were supplanted by Italians, Russians, Poles, and to an even greater extent by East European Jews, who, despite poverty, filth, and overcrowding retained their native gaiety and

34 "There were people in the street, the smell of rice with *gandules* and fried pork rinds, clusters of old men smoking as they chatted and laughed with their few teeth."

hope" (Federal Writer's Project 1939, 60). Between the end of the nineteenth century and the beginning of the twentieth century, the area became an *important* center for Italian immigrants, and their influence was reflected in the aesthetics of its buildings and in its churches, particularly in that of Nuestra Señora de Pompeya, "un referente entre los inmigrantes italianos del barrio" (Dueñas 2018, 517).[35] It is there, in the Italian South Village, where Dueñas places the office of the lawyer Fabrizio Mazza, a stereotypical mafioso character who does not measure up to his handicapped uncle Marcelo, founder of the firm. Mazza will do anything to get his hands on the case that the Arenas family brings against the Compañía Trasatlántica Española.

According to Rueda Hernanz (1993, 91), the cultural assimilation of those Spanish immigrants made up of professionals, intellectuals, businessmen, and financiers who were integrated into Anglo-Saxon society was quicker as they lost contact with their Spanish community and their roots. This facilitated their oblivion on both sides of the Atlantic. As Cagiao Vila points out, these communities began to grow faster thanks to women: "muchas esposas, madres o hijas de emigrados, deseosas de reunirse con ellos, tomaron el camino de la emigración guiadas en muchas ocasiones por la intención de mantener su papel aglutinador en el grupo familiar" (in Liñares Giraut et al. 2007b, 161).[36] Rueda Hernanz (1993) uses the testimony of one of those intellectuals as an example:

> Los intelectuales, salvo casos aislados, se separaron antes de la colonia española, si alguna vez estuvieron integrados. Emilio González López, una de las excepciones, llegó a Nueva York en 1939. En España, Oviedo, era profesor de Derecho penal. Debido a las dificultades de adaptación de su profesión al derecho norteamericano, se especializó en Lengua, Literatura e Historia, a lo que dedicó un año. Fue a Panamá en 1941 y 1942, donde trabajó como penalista. Después volvió a Estados Unidos y se dedicó a la docencia universitaria hasta su jubilación en la Universidad de Nueva York. (1993, 91).[37]

---

35 "a place of reference among the Italian immigrants in the neighbourhood."

36 "many wives, mothers, or daughters of emigrants, wishing to join them, took the path of emigration often guided by the intention of maintaining their unifying role in the family."

37 "Intellectuals, except in isolated cases, separated from the Spanish colony earlier, if they ever were integrated. Emilio González López, one of the exceptions, arrived in New York in 1939. In Spain, in Oviedo, he was a professor of

Emilio González López explains that it was not common for Spanish intellectuals to mix with the rest of the Spanish immigrants in any of the neighborhoods where the Spanish communities had settled. As intellectuals belonged to the upper middle class, they did not need to seek the support of their compatriots to find a job, a place to live, or the friendship of someone with the same interests and problems. As a result, their assimilation was almost immediate, although it is true that on most occasions their work was related to the Spanish culture, history, literature, and language: "Quizás con mi excepción y la de un par de ellos (como Eugenio Granell), los intelectuales españoles no se relacionaban con la colonia española, ni la conocían. El profesor español vivía en un mundo profesional, intelectual. En general el profesor español se mantuvo alejado de la colectividad" (Rueda Hernanz 1993, 91).[38]

The Cherry Street area, in Manhattan's Lower East Side, is probably the oldest Spanish settlement. Located at the start of the Manhattan Bridge, it takes its name from a former cherry orchard that occupied this site (Innes 1902, 425). The proximity to the docks made it the most appropriate neighborhood to settle in for the first time. People like Emilio Arenas came to the adventure in search of a better future. And there, in 1929, he rented a small room surrounded by compatriots who worked as stokers, greasers, cooks, and stevedores, people who, as soon as their financial situation improved, called their families to accompany them in this new life. It was a small Spain with its cafés, stores, *colmados*, and so on:

> En La Ideal compraban chuletas, mollejas y morcillas; con el pulpo se hacían donde Chacón; para el jabón, el tabaco y los trajes hechos iban a casa Yvars y Casasin; para los remedios a La Farmacia Española; los tragos y el café los tomaban en el bar Castilla, en el café Galicia o en El Chorrito, donde su dueño,

---

criminal law. Due to the difficulties of adapting his profession to American law, he specialised in Language, Literature and History, to which he devoted a year. He went to Panama in 1941 and 1942, where he worked as a criminal lawyer. He then returned to the United States and devoted himself to university teaching until his retirement from New York University."

38 "Perhaps with the exception of myself and that of a couple more (such as Eugenio Granell), Spanish intellectuals did not mingle with the Spanish colony, nor did they even know it. The Spanish professor lived in a professional, intellectual world. In general, the Spanish professor stayed away from the community."

> el catalán Sebastián Estrada, los atendía con sus más de cien kilos de energía contagiosa y les recordaba un día sí y otro también que la gran Raquel Meyer era clienta asidua cada vez que pisaba la ciudad. El Círculo Valenciano, el Centro Vasco-Americano y algunas sociedades locales gallegas tenían por allí sus cuarteles; había sastres, barberías, fondas y tiendas de comestibles como Llana o La Competidora Española en donde hacerse con garbanzos, habichuelas y pimentón. Había, en definitiva, entrelazando las idiosincrasias regionales, un mullido sentimiento de comunidad. (Dueñas 2018, 19–20)[39]

Spanish immigrants did all kinds of work: "many did jobs… in mines, factories, subways, ship engine rooms… But if the Spanish enclave was large enough, the community itself generated employment for other Spaniards: the bars, restaurants, grocery stores, shoe shops, hardware stores," and, of course, the tobacco companies were some of the most popular places to work in the city (Fernández and Argeo 2014, 28). In 1935, Emilio found employment at La Valenciana, located at 45 Cherry Street, a Spanish business that not only served as a hostelry but also supplied any necessary equipment for the worker (Morell 2017, 20–25) and above all functioned as a center of operations linked to Spain: they translated, managed the purchase of tickets, and acted as an employment agency or as a post office for people with no fixed address who exchanged or transferred money to their places of origin. Today, this old neighborhood has disappeared and is now a large green area with public housing and cooperative buildings (56–57).

Another relevant neighborhood with a Spanish presence was Five Points, near Cherry Street. It owes its name to the intersection of five corners at one point (Anbinder 2001, 444). Although it began as a non-fringe area,

39 "At La Ideal they bought chops, sweetbreads and black pudding; for octopus they went to Chacón's; for soap, tobacco and ready-made suits they went to Yvars and Casasin; for medicines to La Farmacia Española; for drinks and coffee they went to Bar Castilla, Café Galicia or El Chorrito, where the owner, the Catalan Sebastián Estrada, served them with his more than one hundred kilos of contagious energy and reminded them day in and day out that the great Raquel Meyer was a regular customer every time she came to the city. The Círculo Valenciano, the Centro Vasco-Americano and some local Galician societies had their headquarters there; there were tailors, barbers, inns and grocery shops like Llana or La Competidora Española where you could get hold of chickpeas, beans and paprika. There was, in short, by intertwining the regional idiosyncrasies, a soft feeling of community."

the sanitation problems caused by an old sewage pit forced the middle- and upper-middle-class people to leave the area, and it was left to the mercy of poor immigrants and vagrants. It is in this neighborhood that Sister Lito (Dueñas 2018, 116) was born when prostitutes, disease, delinquency, child death, violent crime, and other hardships reigned in its streets. For many, The Five Points is the origin of the genuine American identity, a true example of racial integration and transculturation, for in its streets it was easy to find Germans, French, Irish, Africans, Spanish Bohemians, Russians, Scandinavians, Jews, Chinese, and Italians (Riis 1902, 21). Today its location corresponds to Chinatown, just off Little Italy, and the five corners have given way to Columbus Park (Municipal Archives 1831).

As the years and decades passed, Spanish immigration to the United States decreased, and by the early 1950s, it had practically stopped, with the exception of the almost anecdotal arrival of new Spaniards. During this decade, Spain began to open to the outside world, which made it easier for economic and social development to gradually reach the country. However, although it is true that Spanish immigration slowed its flow toward America, it did not do so toward Europe, where it concentrated in countries such as France, Germany, and Switzerland, countries where Spaniards continued to emigrate steadily until at least the 1970s. With the lack of demographical replacement, the new generations of Spanish Americans, children of the immigrants who had arrived and founded many of the existing communities and societies, began to move away from the places where their parents and grandparents had settled. The assimilation of these new generations caused many of the communities to gradually lose strength, and many of them began to slowly disappear. Some of these communities and the societies created around them chose to merge in an attempt to survive, while others vanished altogether due to economic, demographic, and even urbanistic reasons. In the end, the memory and testimony of these immigrants were captured in academic books and also in literature such as the texts selected for this analysis, which will allow us to examine and discover another history that is not only less aseptic but also different, for it will show the way of life and the process of cultural transformation of the Spanish immigrants who arrived in the United States of America and were witnesses of a past that must be remembered and never be forgotten.

Chapter 3: Spanish Memory and Migration

3.1. The Construction of Collective Identity

> I gave him the cigarette and lighted it for him endeavoring to postpone things—the nadir of abjection—but then the conviction that I was dreaming decided me to sleep the thing through to certain awakening and calmly I inserted a key which I had never expected to use again. As I did this, the last hopeful and irrelevant memory of the Moor's ancestor returning to Granada ran through my mind, but the door opened easily and swung inward without a squeak.
>
> — *Felipe Alfau, Chromos*

When we talk about the Spanish diaspora in the United States, we are referring to those Spanish immigrants who left their former homeland in search of a better life between the end of the nineteenth and the beginning of the twentieth centuries. According to John Strong in "Mobilized and Proletarian Diasporas" (1976), diaspora is "any ethnic collectivity which lacks a territorial base within a given polity, i.e., is a relatively small minority throughout all portions of the polity" (1976, 393). In this case, the immigrants of Spanish origin who arrived in the United States are an example of how this geographical dispersion also led to cultural fragmentation as they spread their wings in the country where they settled, leaving behind their physical homeland, but not the culture that shaped them as a group.

In "Felipe Alfau's Parodisatirical Fiction and the Reconstructive Memory of Spain from the United States" (2018), Professor Cristina Garrigós González analyzes the importance of Alfau's work as part of the literature written to reconstruct the memory of Spaniards in the American country. Memory is a key factor in the construction of the hybrid "Third Space" of the texts. The characters move between the Spanish culture of origin, which no longer exists or which they have never known, and the presence of a dominant culture in the United States that reminds them of their in-between situation as they move towards a new identity, where space and time are different from what they had known theretofore. The authors themselves also transit in this environment by constructing their characters' spaces of interaction based on what they know or think they know of a very limited period of time and place. They share the information they want to be known and experienced by the audience, the reader.

In "Culture is Destiny: A Conversation with Lee Kuan Yew," by Fareed Zakaria, the protagonist Kuan Yew explains that culture changes through time due to social transformation, economic shifts, and technological advances (Zakaria 1994, 126). These cultural changes happen in all societies without exception, and this means that the culture that the immigrants knew in their country of origin is not the same as the one that continued to evolve there during their absence. As a result, the culture of Spanish immigrants in the United States remained static over time. It would only change due to the influence of the Anglo-American dominant culture and other cultures, such as the Spanish one from the other side of the Atlantic, altered by the contact of subsequent Spanish immigrants from their country of origin. What, then, is the connection between culture and memory? Can literature be a continuity of history? Where does history end and memory begin? In "Memory and Literature" (1998), the Mexican American author and academic Ilan Stavans develops his idea about the solid link between memory and literature. Stavans, who speaks Spanish and English, has been studying for years the importance of memory in the production of literature and how it represents a part of history that, on many occasions, cannot be found in academic books about the study of the past.

From the Jewish diaspora study of Yosef Hayim Yerushalmi and his masterpiece *Zakhor: Jewish History and Jewish Memory* to the work of the Holocaust survivor Primo Levi; from the work on memory and literature of Jorge Luis Borges to the writing of Felipe Alfau, Stavans has examined for decades the production of literary works about memory in order to describe the connection between remembering and the portrayal of history. According to Stavans, "the collective identity is linked to this duty of remembering, of stopping time from erasing the details of the past" (1998, 81). He points out that literary writings based on or inspired by memory and the witnessing of true events, such as the texts analyzed here, are a good way to preserve collective memory and maintain the collective identity of a group, such as that of the Spanish immigrants in the United States, that they had in a specific time period. Stavans continues pointing out that "only through remembering, starting with a dialogue between an ancient and primitive past and an unknown but promising future, is it possible to carve a permanent place in history. History, therefore, is the living manifestation of memory" (1998, 81–82). Each immigrant is a witness to their time and space in the historical period in which they live. As generations intermingle with the dominant culture of reception, the memory of the diaspora dissolves, and the weight of their literature increases as a source of remembering, but also as a problematic way to represent history due to its subjectivity, just like memory, when the writer becomes part of history.

The memory of the past tends to idealize what is left behind. Like the homesickness of the native Galicia experienced by the character of Esclavitud in Emilia Pardo Bazán's *Morriña* (1889), a housemaid who works for the widow Doña Aurora and her only son Rogelio. As well as their homesickness of their Galician origin and Esclavitud's longing for her native region, the Spanish immigrants in the United States magnify the memory of their place of provenance, exalting the community of origin while maintaining a feeling of nostalgia. The memory of Spanish immigrants in the United States and the memories they have of both their country of origin and their experience abroad are maintained in three different ways. First, the communities made by the first generation of immigrants when they settled in cities and towns and in neighborhoods where their numbers were larger and they could all support each other in their learning of the dominant language, in finding work, or simply in providing a place to rest and sleep before continuing their individual ways. Second, by creating Spanish associations and societies according to the regional or local origins of these immigrants, as well as emphasizing the cultural elements that united them, such as sports or love of nature. Third, the memory of these Spanish immigrants is maintained through the photographic and written testimonies of the first and second generations, in charge of preserving and transmitting their culture of origin with its traditions, festivals, and customs, which sometimes end up producing texts such as those analyzed in this research. The popular concept of memory comes from Greek philosophy, from Socrates and his notion that

> every man has in his mind a block of wax of various qualities, the gift of Memory, the mother of the Muses; and on this he receives the seal or stamp of those sensations and perceptions which he wishes to remember. That which he succeeds in stamping is remembered and known by him as long as the impression lasts; but

> that, of which the impression is rubbed out or imperfectly made, is forgotten, and not known. (Plato 2008, 1950–51)

A "block of wax" where memories are carved, but when these memories disappear, memory also disappears. One of the characteristics of the texts under study is that, except for Dueñas, who based part of her book on the testimonies of Spanish immigrants of the former communities in the city that she interviewed, each author tells their story according to their experience and memories. The different narratives about the Spanish communities in the American country are based on the memory of their writers and on the historical sources of those who maintained them or rediscovered their past. "Third Space" literature bases much of its production on memory. This memory, which connects the history of a country with the experience of its people, is essential to understand where they come from, why their life is the way it is in their present days, and where they are heading as a community. Memory is a key aspect of hybridity. Five of the six authors have written novelized autobiographies based on recollections of their lives as Spanish immigrants, while the other one, Dueñas, uses a historical background where she mixes actual people with characters inspired by real ones in her novel. For all of them, remembering becomes a way of reflecting on their past, learning from it as they draw lessons for their present and future.

In his novel, *L'écriture ou la vie* (1994), the Spanish writer Jorge Semprún fictionalizes his life as a prisoner at the Nazi concentration camp of Buchenwald, where he was sent after fighting in the French Resistance in occupied France and later denounced and deported to the camp. The main character, also called Jorge, narrates the experiences that he witnessed, replicating what other writers like de Pereda, Alfau, or González had done in their novels to create witnessing narration spaces where they used alter egos, on many occasions even with their same names, to transmit what they went through and still remember about their past. According to Marquart (2011), the readers of these witnessing narratives can give rein to two types of reading: they learn more about the experiences of a particular author's past, "and they believe that a narrative written by a cultural authority… will give them the kind of information that will further their knowledge" (Marquart 2011, 148–49). As a result, stories like the ones selected to analyze Spanish immigration in the United States are a useful way to approach and learn about the lives of migrants in their communities as part of a dominated culture and thus take advantage of the cultural authority that these authors exert in order to understand the process of cultural transition that is portrayed by their characters.

The memory and testimony of Spanish immigrants in the United States analyzed in these texts have two cultural origins. One is the Spanish culture that came directly from the Iberian Peninsula. That is the culture of the different regions and provinces of Spain, united by their common Spanish language, their education, and military service. On the other hand, there was the Spanish-Cuban culture that was brought to the United States by those immigrants who, although of Spanish origin, developed a hybrid culture after living on the Caribbean island. This memory of Cuban culture brought to the Spanish communities in the States, created by the hybridism and the assimilation of Spanish, indigenous, and African cultures, was essential for the construction of the Spanish neighborhoods in New York City, where many of their established Spaniards based their economy on Cuban tobacco-related jobs. This influence is present in several of the stories chosen, such as de Pereda's novel with the characters of the *teverianos* in *Windmills in Brooklyn* and in Dueñas's *Las hijas del Capitán*. These stories include references to cigar businesses in the metropolis as part of the essential history of the Spaniards during the first half of the twentieth century and an inescapable part of the collective memory of the Spaniards in the city.

In *Imagined Communities* (2006), Anderson discusses the beginning of nationalism and the formation of communities from ancient times to the present day. He points out that the construction of an imagined community depends on its group consciousness. In this sense, by the middle of the eighteenth century, the printing of the Greek classics helped to recreate the corpus of the ancient Hellenic myths and civilization, changing the consciousness of the European society of the time (Anderson 2006, 72), and giving more visibility to the idea of memory as illustrated by the classics. Plato continued the ideas of Socrates, pointing toward the concept of memory "like a waxen tablet" held in the mind (Plato 2008, 2544), an idea that was prolonged until the nineteenth century. Unexpectedly, the classics already focused their attention on the theme of remembrance, a fundamental idea in the construction of nations. The collective memory of communities would shape their social and cultural development while the individual would be subordinated to the nature and nurture of their members. Individuals would remember their individual idea of a nation as filtered through the lenses of their respective communities, contributing to their imagined constructions as they became migrants by providing their subjective views on their new communities.

In the nineteenth century, the father of modern memory research, the German psychologist Hermann Ebbinghaus, became the first person to study memory from an experimental point of view, understanding it as something acquired from the outside world that gets inside the human being, producing a series of sensations in the organism and providing a series of outcomes (2011). As a psychologist, he decided to isolate memory by using different candidates or subjects to memorize "separate series" of syllables measuring time and their learning limit (2011, 24–25). These studies proved the limitations of learning; likewise, he observed how the memory of human beings works, noticing that we can remember things learned by repetition (2011, 123). This repetition is also used by a community from generation to generation, so if the community changes locations, but the individuals who make the community remain the same, their descendants could repeat many of the traditions, customs, and rituals of their ancestors in their collective memory and, therefore, in their everyday lives.

During the 1930s, the British psychologist Frederic Bartlett questioned the Ebbinghaus school when he decided to investigate memory and leave aside many of his metaphors by claiming that memory is an active instead of a passive filing cabinet for recollections. Bartlett pointed out that because Ebbinghaus's work focused on memory in isolation, memory retention, and time, it was not as genuine as memory when related to events. However, Bartlett's theory of active memory, which sustained that memory did not remember faithful experiences but imagined them according to the reconstruction process of each individual, brought about many inquiries about the function that passive memory could really have (1995). Consequently, the Greek idea of memory as a wax impression was not plausible because human beings never remember the same event the same way twice, simply because everything that they have learned afterward has been reshaping their own memories, creating connections with their long-term memory and with their previous knowledge. In the case of the novels studied, the authors who act as protagonists have captured in their works the memory of events at a certain point in their lives, as all these stories were written during their adulthood and a number of years, even decades, after the time span of the stories narrated.

Memory is not accurate, and it changes as people grow older. Writers describe events related to their childhoods that have been earlier stored in their subconscious, but all human beings forget most of their past and only remember a few things that are altered over time. In this sense, to Seixas (2007), the construction of the Spanish identity abroad was based on the idea and the memory of Spain that Spanish migrants created from their social surroundings. On most occasions, their families and friends, their municipalities, and maybe their provinces, were all they knew about their country: "Faltos de un proceso de socialización completo en las instancias básicas y clásicas de nacionalización de masas (escuela y milicia, entre otros), la representación de esa comunidad de referencia... podía ser una comunidad local. Y de modo más o menos preciso, podía abarcar también una identidad nacional" (Seixas 2007, 16).[40] As a result, the construction of this "imagined community" in the United States could be unreal to many Spaniards but real to others, since it was a construction made by a few of them: those who were abroad and had their own reality built from what they remembered as their national roots.

These immigrants gathered in Spanish communities with people from the same region, province, and even municipality. At the same time, these groupings led to the creation of regional, provincial, and local societies. These societies or *colectivos* were present in all the Spanish communities of immigrants, and New York City was not an exception: "De las Sociedades de superior alcance territorial y, por lo regular, de más capacidad aglutinante que comienzan a proliferar a partir de la década de los 70 del siglo XIX, los Centros regionales fueron los primeros que asumieron entre sus competencias pragmático-estatutarias la función instructiva" (Liñares

40 "Lacking a complete socialisation process in the basic and classic instances of mass nationalisation (school and military service, among others), the representation of this community of reference... could be a local community. And in more or less precise way, it could also include a national identity."

Giraut et al. 2007c, 80).[41] This concept of human memory helps to understand de Toro's introduction to transculturation in his article "Figuras de la hibridez: Ortiz: transculturación—Paz: hibridismo—Fernández Retamar: Calibán" (2006, 16). According to de Toro, every time a human being discovers a new place, memory accommodates this new environment, rewriting the past and writing the present:

> Estando en un mundo de una comunicación masiva y vertiginosa, donde casi todos los objetos y medios culturales están a disposición, el término de *pasajes* nos parece adecuado para describir fenómenos semióticos, como los culturales, en el sentido de que la cultura siempre se encuentra de paso, recodificándose y reinventándose, como una semiosis de intersecciones, nómada. (Toro 2006, 16)[42]

Human beings construct reality according to their cultural reality and the cultural reality that surrounds them. Thus, for example, the Spanish migrants who came to the United States from the Iberian Peninsula had a different perception of reality than those who came from Cuba or Puerto Rico. However, when they found themselves in New York City, there was an integration between the two groups thanks to the tobacco as a sound source of work and economic benefit. In other words, in some respects, there was an assimilation between the Spaniards from the overseas territories of the Caribbean and those who came from Spain with no distinction between them. Spaniards who arrived in the United States formed hybrid spaces, a new community created and imagined from the memories and the culture of its members, a heterotopia. De Toro indicates that

> el término heterotopía describe el estado híbrido de esos espacios concretos que son territoriales, psicológicos, emocionales, corporales o de otro tipo; espacios donde se juntan y separan los elementos, donde las identidades y el sujeto se fragmentan o se diversifican, en los que la memoria se inscribe,

41 "Out of the Societies of greater territorial scope and, as a rule, of greater binding power, proliferating from the 1870s onward, the regional centres were the first to assume an instructional function among their pragmatic-statutory competencies,"

42 "Being part of a world of massive and vertiginous communication, where almost all cultural objects and media are available, the term *passages* seems adequate to describe semiotic phenomena, such as the cultural ones, in the sense that culture is always in transit, recoding and reinventing itself, as a semiosis of intersections, nomadic."

> el pasado se reescribe y el presente se escribe; son el lugar de la fractura. La transculturalidad indica los procesos de hibridación, las desterritorializaciones y reterritorializaciones culturales, y constituye el lugar de la negociación entre lo ajeno y lo propio. (2006, 16)[43]

Other authors, like the Czech writer Milan Kundera, have stressed the importance for the communities of immigrants to create a new space through memory as they decide to stay together and remember their past, while the process of transculturation transforms them in different ways (2012, 69). There were, of course, a number of Spaniards who decided to assimilate on their own and did not wish to join those communities (Rueda Hernanz 1993, 91), but most of them stayed connected to remember their past, attached to their roots. They were immigrants from the first generation, the 1.5 generation, and even from the second generation. As Pérez Firmat (1996) highlights, "one-and-a-halfers gain in translation. One-and-a-halfers feed on what they lack. Their position as equilibrists gives them the freedom to mix and match pieces from each culture: they are 'equi-libre' " (1996, 7). However, he points out that those who were quickly transformed by neoculturalism tended to forget their origins and were haunted by the ghost of nostalgia due to a lack of memory of their cultural roots. Milan Kundera reflects that

> for memory to function well, it needs constant practice: recollections are not invoked again and again, in conversations with friends, they go. Émigrés gathered in compatriot colonies keep retelling to the point of nausea the same which thereby becomes unforgettable (2000, 33).

Migrants as well as their descendants need to remember their culture in order to negotiate their space of hybridity within the framework of a dominant culture that is not their own but to which they have assimilated and are a part of, regardless of their origin or their individual or collective consciousness. What they do remember is that they have witnessed changes

43 "Thus, the term heterotopia describes the hybrid nature of those specific spaces that are territorial, psychological, emotional, bodily, or otherwise; spaces where their elements come together and separate, where identities and the subject are fragmented or diversified, where memory is inscribed, the past is rewritten, and the present is written; they are the spot of the fracture. *Transculturality* indicates processes of hybridization, cultural deterritorializations and reterritorializations, and constitutes the place of negotiation between foreign and vernacular."

over time. For many years, immigrants are able to recall an event and then share it five, ten, or twenty-five years later only to realize that the event is different from what other immigrants remember. Our brain has the tendency to create its own memories and make people believe something based on their own emotional subjectivity. This truth filters the recollections of the past and constructs a different memory from the present, altering reality and the memory of reconstruction.

It is important to consider that the memory of reconstruction is different and much more complex than the memory of repetition, contemplated as an isolated element by Ebbinghaus. The longer a person has witnessed an event, the more likely that person is to modify their memories if these memories are not written down immediately and kept in the minds of the witnesses for decades. As the American literary critic Shoshana Felman and the psychiatrist Dori Laub argue, "what has been witnessed cannot be made whole and integrated into an authoritative telling" (1992, 171). This subjective narration modifies the reality as described by the witness, creating a point of view of the event that is only partially true.

In *Survival in Auschwitz* (1947), the Holocaust survivor Primo Levi allows the readers to develop their own vision as second-hand witnesses of the tragedy of the Lager camp. To better understand his narrative, Levi uses the action of witnessing with the aim of revealing a closer view of life in concentration camps. The way that he uses language to describe the events and experiences at the concentration camp is essential to understanding his stance as a witness. His writing transforms from friendly conversation between Levi and the reader to an intense work of art where the author tries to transmit his experience as a survivor to the audience. He uses his work to depict the experiences at the concentration camp but also to show how understanding his attitude as a witness allows us to become witnesses. As a result, it is not surprising that Levi seems to struggle to humanize himself as a protagonist. In some chapters, he even employs analytical language as opposed to other occasions in the book when he can reconnect with himself and therefore emerges as a more *human* man.

Levi's representations of the persecution of Jews and non-Jews during this period and his portrayal of concentration camps and the people inside them have become essential to fully comprehend the Holocaust. Levi inhabits the "Third Space" both as a protagonist and as an author. In the same way, de Pereda, Morell, Alfau, and González also inhabit both sides, thus allowing us to understand Spanish immigration in the United States. Except for Dueñas (who uses Fernández's archival research), all the authors are characters and narrators of their stories, presenting a "Third Space" for the characters that they themselves inhabited. The voices of these authors have granted the reader a closer look into the experience of immigration in a country like the United States for several decades of the twentieth century, transmitting a real witnessing and closer understanding of their experiences. This "Third Space" literature becomes this way a humanizing story that, from a historical perspective, could be reduced to a series of figures or statistics, but from a literary representation, it is the written testimony of those communities that occupied a part of the American hybrid space in the last century.

3.2. Literary Representation of Spanish Immigration to the United States

Recalling the history of immigration in a country like the United States is difficult for most of its inhabitants, despite being one of the most discussed topics in the country (Weber 2016; Shukla and Suleyman 2019; Rao 2019). Migration crises in Asia, Africa, Europe, and the Americas have recently produced many publications devoted to the study and analysis of the political, social, and economic causes and consequences that have led to the largest human displacements since the end of World War II (Siegel and Nágy 2018; Barbulescu 2019). In the United States, these studies, initially devoted to the history and social awareness of migratory movements from South and Central America, have evolved toward more rigorous and detailed approaches in the research of new topics such as, for example, legislation and human rights, especially since the early 1980s, with American authors such as Ignatius Bau, responsible for studying Central American refugees and the role of the church as a physical sanctuary (1985), and Robert Tomsho, who authored *American Sanctuary Movement* in 1987. Other authors have developed their studies in other fields of knowledge. This is the case of Ann Crittenden, executive director of the Fund for Investigative Journalism in Washington, D.C., who has focused on the legal effects of these movements (1988), and anthropology Professor Hilary Cunningham, who has analyzed the politicization of immigration and religion in the United States (1995). One of the most recent works on migration, *Deep Dive: Sanctuary Cities*, published in 2017 by Brian Peyton Joyner and Donna Caro, explores how the United States has handled 11 million foreigners residing in the country at the time as undocumented immigrants. All these authors constitute a clear example of the academic approach to the issue of migration in the United States in the last decades with the purpose of unraveling the wide world of immigration in America from a political, historical, and social point of view.

However, not all migration attracts the same attention in the academic world. Research on the origin of most Spanish-speaking migrations to the United States has focused primarily on Latin America (Gutiérrez 1996; Coatsworth and Taylor 1999; Suárez-Orozco 2008; Tienda and Sánchez 2013). Most of the contemporary literature of the late twentieth century and early twenty-first-century centers on the Latino/Hispanic migrant as a universal figure. Despite only studying the past very little, if any, some critical attention has nevertheless been paid, however, to Iberian migration from Spain, Cuba, or Puerto Rico to the United States until the last decades by Professor of Anthropology Jorge Duany, Director of the Cuban Research Institute.[44] Other scholars tend to focus on Spanish migration from a European perspective, when Spaniards had to emigrate to other European countries, such as France, Germany, and Switzerland, with most studies dedicated to Spanish emigration between the years of the Spanish Civil War and the first decades of Francoism (Redondo Carrero 2017, 11).

Immigration from Europe to the United States is rarely connected to Spanish migration, either because it has been obscured by a larger migration wave from other European countries such as England, Ireland, Germany, Italy, or Poland (Dolan 2010), or because the destination of Spanish migrants during their most relevant migratory movements in the nineteenth and twentieth centuries was primarily the countries south of Rio Grande first, such as Argentina, Venezuela, and Mexico, and countries such as

44 Some of his most relevant works include "Nation and Migration: Rethinking Puerto Rican Identity in a Transnational Context" (2007) and "Anthropology in a postcolonial colony: Helen I. Safa's contribution to Puerto Rican ethnography" (2010).

France, Germany, and Switzerland after the Spanish Civil War (Rueda Hernanz 2000). In addition to being one of the least relevant minorities among the immigrant population in the United States, when compared to other groups of Europeans—German, Irish, or British immigrants (Dolan 2010)—, Spaniards who arrived in the country between the second half of the nineteenth century and the first half of the twentieth century represented less than one percent of the total immigrant population (Rueda Hernanz 1993). The restrictions produced by The Emergency Quota Act, also known as the Emergency Immigration Act of 1921 (Rueda Hernanz 1993, 50–53), which favored the immigration of the northern European population to the detriment of those from the south, limited the number of Spaniards allowed to arrive in the United States to almost irrelevant levels. This legal silencing of Spanish immigrants in the American country translated into less immigration and therefore less cultural relevance of Spanish communities. However, despite their low demographic flow, the impact of this group of immigrants was relatively significant in New York, where three-quarters of the Spaniards who entered the country did so through this city (Rueda Hernanz 1993).

Diaspora studies on migratory movements have created contexts over which we can theorize about the transformation process of the first generations of Spanish immigrants in the United States during the last two centuries. The Spanish diaspora is just one example of the many different peoples who arrived from Europe during those centuries and shaped the multiculturalism of the continent. Each diaspora was different, and the Spanish one, small and mostly localized in New York as the point of entry for many of its citizens, had its literary representation also centered, mainly, in that state. In the words of Braidotti (2011),

> In its diasporic version, through the innumerable Little Italy's, Little Greece's, and Spanish Quarters, Europe revealed its true face as a concoction of diverse cultural, linguistic, and ethnic groups with a high level of conflicts. Not all diasporas are equal, though they get homogenized by the gaze of the colonial observer (2011, 32).

To illustrate the literary representation of the Spanish immigrant diaspora in the United States in the second half of the nineteenth century and the first half of the twentieth century, I have selected the most pertinent texts about these Spaniards, most of them physically concentrated in New York

City. There are six relevant texts under study; however, in the following pages, I have also included the works of Konrad Bercovici and Julio Camba as examples of early literary representations of the Spanish communities. They are significant for understanding the construction of the space of Spanish immigrant literature in the United States. In my opinion, all these texts are essential to comprehend the representation of this community, characterized by continuous change through time and space.

Of Romanian origin and an immigrant himself, Konrad Bercovici is the first relevant literary representative of the Spanish community in the United States. In 1924 he published *Around the World in New York*, a travel book about the different communities living on Manhattan Island in New York City: "Slavs from Russia, Celts, Teutons, Gauls, Romans, Iberians; people from the yellow sand deserts of Syria, people from the green and snow-clad mountains of Switzerland, Lowland people, Highland people, the worst and best of every race, of every nation" (1924, 3). This is a book about Bercovici himself, who traveled through the metropolis, moving around from one district to another while studying every foreign quarter between the Hudson and the East River on Manhattan Island. In the book, divided into sixteen chapters, Bercovici travels through the epicenter of the city, explaining his encounters with the most *important* foreign communities that had shaped New York's tradition of cosmopolitanism. Bercovici himself becomes the protagonist of this guide to New York, where touring the city is synonymous with touring the world.

Bercovici goes from the Syrian Quarters to Greece, passing through the well-known neighborhoods of China Town or Little Italy, discovering the African continent, the Gipsy Quarters, or the Balkan countries, leaving his adventures in European countries like Spain, France, Germany, Hungary, and Czechoslovakia, and people from other "scattered nations" (Bercovici 1924), such as Poles, Armenians, and Scots, to the end. One of the chapters is dedicated to the Spanish immigrant community in New York, located around Manhattan's 14th Street, between Chelsea and the West Village, which "encompasses all that lies between Seventh and Eighth Avenues" (1924, 277). The author's first-person descriptions of these communities create the true value of this work. He provided a detailed depiction of early twentieth-century migration in New York City, and especially that of one of the first Spanish communities in the American metropolis.

Julio Camba is considered one of the few Spanish writers who stands out in the history of literature for his work as a journalist. Born in 1884 in the coastal town of Villanueva de Arosa, in the Galician province of Pontevedra, Camba, like many Galicians of his generation, immigrated to Argentina while still a teenager (Redondo Carrero 2017). Once there, and after encountering anarchist circles, he was forcibly repatriated back to Spain, where he remained until 1908. That year he was sent to Istanbul, where he began his work as a foreign correspondent (Camba 2008). In 1917, he published *Un año en el otro mundo*, a compilation of his 1916 articles where he recounts his first stay in New York City. Camba writes chronicles about the reality of the United States, interspersing historical events with accounts of his own experience as a foreign correspondent in the metropolis (Camba 2013). He also describes the customs of the inhabitants of New York City and cites the most *important* news of the American city against the backdrop of the Great War. In his writings, Camba explains that the vision of Spain in the United States comes through the culture and the experiences of the Spanish citizens who migrated to the new American nation. Thus, for example, Camba mentions how Americans perceived Spanish culture through the work of Ignacio Zuloaga or the Hispanic Society, albeit in a very limited way, for they evidence a lack of deep understanding of Spanish history, culture, and society (Camba 2013).

In 1932, Camba focused once more on New York City with the publication of *La ciudad automática* (republished in 2008). In this work, he mentions again the presence of Spaniards in different areas of New York City as well as other communities from different parts of the world. *La ciudad automática* is a sociological approach to the establishment of the Spanish community in the metropolis, ranging from the Sephardic Jews in Seville Street, through the Mediterranean Bowery of the Spanish, Portuguese, and Greeks, to the España Negra[45] between the 110th and 116th Streets. Camba does not forget to include references to Spanish gastronomy in the city either, with *paella valenciana*, *caldo gallego*, and *arroz con pollo* at the forefront. Throughout this work, Camba is frank. In his opinion,

45 Camba refers to Spanish Harlem as Black Spain due to the multicultural variety of the neighborhood, dominated at the time by immigrants of Puerto Rican origin, many of them with African roots.

Americans neither love nor hate Spaniards; according to him, the United States does not understand Spain. For them, he adds, Spanishness is a mixture of stereotypes ranging from the Spanish Inquisition to Château Sevilla,[46] from bullfighting to Christopher Columbus, and sometimes not even that, leaving a sad and painful confession about the scarce relevance of the Spanish community's presence in New York City as a whole. Camba feels that Spanish migration is discreet, little known, and deprived of the importance of other European countries such as Italy, Greece, or Ireland.

For Camba, the Spanish immigrants in the metropolis are characterized by a singularity that adds diversity to the American way of life of the established Anglo-dominant culture. The dominant and the dominated are described as immersed in a culture shock that goes both ways. Camba points out how Spaniards are seen as exotic by American society (Camba 2008, 60) while they endeavor to maintain their identity in their Iberian gastronomy, their music, and their religious traditions. On the other hand, the automatism of the inhabitants of New York as described by the journalist is portrayed by their way of living, working, and even eating, in contrast with the Spanish immigrants' lifestyle. For example, the act of having lunch in American culture is depicted in *La ciudad automática* as no more *important* than drinking coffee or orange juice. Unlike Spaniards, for whom the act of having lunch is almost a gastronomic ritual, for Americans this meal does not go beyond eating something quick and light, such as a sandwich or a cake (Camba 2008, 44). Besides, the author indicates that whereas the average American takes little time to devour his food in order to continue working, the Spanish immigrant is accustomed to sharing the table with other people, whether they are family, friends, or co-workers. Such is the *importance* that Camba gives to food as a cultural element that he even maintains that, unlike his compatriots, Americans do not see the need to cook or produce elaborate dishes, so they enjoy more freedom to do other things, i.e., dedicate even more time to their jobs.

However, Camba also mentions that Spanish immigrants are gradually adapting to the lifestyle of the "automatic city" of New York. In the case of gastronomy, for example, to which the author devotes numerous lines,

46 Camba mentions Château Sevilla as a typical Spanish restaurant in New York City

he indicates that his compatriots also dare to try the typical dishes of the host country, such as the famous Boston beans, "una especie de judías con jamón, constituyen el plato favorito de los españoles en los restaurantes automáticos" (Camba 2008, 58).[47] Throughout his chapters, Camba analyzes topics as diverse as American wines, which he compares with Spanish, Italian, or French wine, or the multicultural relevance of places as *madrileños* as Sevilla Street, where "un recién llegado de Birmingham o de Atlanta es mucho más extranjero que yo en Sevilla Street, donde el concepto de extranjerismo no tiene un caracter politico, sino un caracter municipal" (2008, 69).[48] As in Bercovici's work, Camba also explains how Mediterranean countries have come together to coexist in Manhattan's Bowery, and describes the area between the 110th and 116th Streets, between the Fifth Avenue and the Eighth Avenue, as one of the most relevant areas of the city, filled with Spanish shops and businesses: "Veamos las muestras de las tiendas y los anuncios luminosos: «Doctor Rogué, cirujano dentista,» «Pastelería de Simón,» «Campoamor. Comidas y bebidas,» «Librería Sanjurjo,» «Librería Cervantes,» «Nuestra Señora de Guadalupe,» «La Flor Asturiana,» «El Patio,» «Teatro San José,» «Billares Rodríguez» ..." (2008, 73).[49] And where people from any other Spanish-speaking country, such as Mexico, Argentina, Cuba, or the Dominican Republic, also coexist, creating one of the most *important* Spanish-speaking communities of the metropolis:

> En el teatro de San José no son únicamente el gallego, el catalán o el baturro quienes hacen las delicias del público con sus acentos respectivos. A la par de ellos salen a escena el jíbaro de las Antillas, el pelado mejicano, el atorrante argentino. etc., etc. Se bailan jotas y sones, sardanas y rumbas, pericones y

47 "a kind of beans with ham, the favourite dish of Spaniards in automatic restaurants."

48 "a newcomer from Birmingham or Atlanta is much more of a foreigner than I am in Sevilla Street, where the concept of foreignness has not a political character, but a municipal character."

49 "Let's see the samples of the stores and the illuminated advertisements: «Doctor Rogué, surgeon-dentist», «Simon's Pastry Shop,» «Campoamor. Meals and drinks,» «Sanjurjo's Bookshop,» «Cervantes' Bookshop,» «Our Lady of Guadalupe,» «The Asturian Flower,» «The Patio,» «Theatre San José, » «Billiards Rodríguez»..."

> muñeiras, peteneras y jarabes. Se tocan la guitarra, el cajón, los palillos, el güiro, la pandereta, la marimba. Se canta flamenco y pampero y se alternan alalás con vidalitas o malagueñas con corridos. (Camba 2008, 74)[50]

Camba describes the Spanish Harlem, or El Barrio, the East Harlem neighborhood in Upper Manhattan, as one of the most relevant neighborhoods where immigrants from Spain mix with others from Puerto Rico, Cuba, and the Dominican Republic (Federal Writers Project 1995, 268). According to the author, the different neighborhoods inhabited by immigrants in New York are social places where several Spanish communities develop beside the control exerted by the Anglo dominion, but they are not the only ones. Other immigrants from different countries, races, languages, or religions also have their own space in the city:

> Y es que en una ciudad de formación tan cosmopolita no puede ser extranjero nadie. Si Nueva York tiene una característica es precisamente la de su diversidad de razas idiomas, cocinas y religiones, y cuando yo, por ejemplo, quiero ver los barrios más típicos neoyorquinos, me voy a sus barrios exóticos. Estos barrios, que en otras partes estarían considerados como colonias, son los que dan aquí la nota casticista y tienen hasta un Antonio Casero o Roberto Castrovido: el señor Bercovici, que, como era de esperar, resulta haber nacido nada menos que orillas del Danubio. (Camba 2008, 55)[51]

It is important to note that, at the end of this fragment, Camba himself mentions Konrad Bercovici as the first relevant figure to know and describe these neighborhoods, including the Spaniards themselves. Bercovici, like

---

50 "In the Theatre San José it is not only the Galician, the Catalan or the baturro who delight the audience with their respective accents. Along with them, the Antillean jíbaro, the Mexican pelado, the Argentinean atorrante, etc., etc., come on stage. They dance jotas and sones, sardanas and rumbas, pericones and muñeiras, peteneras and jarabes. They play the guitar, the cajón, the palillos, the güiro, the tambourine, the marimba. Flamenco and pampero are sung, alternating alalás with vidalitas or malagueñas with corridos."

51 "In such a cosmopolitan city, no one can be a foreigner. If New York has a unique characteristic, it is precisely its diversity of races, languages, cuisines, and religions, and when I, for example, want to see the most typical New York neighborhoods, I go to its exotic neighborhoods. These neighborhoods, which in other cities would be considered as colonies, are the ones that provide the *castizo* note here and they even have an Antonio Casero or Roberto Castrovido: Mr. Bercovici, who, as expected, happens to have been born on the banks of the Danube, no less."

Camba, also came from Europe, the continent from which a large part of the immigrant population of the metropolis came at the beginning of the twentieth century (Kraut 1982). Like Bercovici, Camba toured the island of Manhattan and saw the different communities of French, Italians, Armenians, Hungarians, Chinese, and Spaniards living in the metropolis during the decades following the publication of Bercovici's *Around the World in New York* (1924).

However, it is Felipe Alfau's second novel, *Chromos* (1990), written in 1948, that constitutes another fundamental work about Spanish immigration in the United States. In this text, Alfau explores the concept of "Americaniard," a term coined by the author at the beginning of *Chromos* through the character of Don José de los Ríos, a Spanish doctor who immigrated to New York:

> This, a word of his own composition, he had begun originally to employ when referring to the Spaniards in the Americas and at one time might have included Latin Americans, but he had gradually varied the meaning until at present it applied to Spaniards in New York. (1990, 13)

Set in New York in 1940, Alfau himself is the unnamed protagonist and narrator of this story, accompanied by his two other friends, "Americaniards" like the author himself: Doctor Don José de los Ríos and Pedro Guzman O'Moore Algoracid, nicknamed "The Moor." The novel shares many parallels with *Locos* (1936). There are new characters, but also many of those who appeared in Alfau's first novel. Moreover, the stories in *Chromos* also take place in a café, El Telescopio. As a result, it is impossible to understand *Chromos* without reading *Locos* and to understand *Locos* without reading *Chromos*. The characters originally come from the former novel and complete their development in the latter, culminating in a classical immigrant story.

Chromos is a unique immigration story written by a Spanish immigrant who, after settling in New York, novelizes his personal experience with the dominant American culture while examining his own. The Iberian culture of the author is then portrayed through the three main protagonists of the story (the narrator, Don José, and Don Pedro) to explore the space created by Spaniards in the metropolis and how they experience their culture as hybrid subjects in a city with a predominant Anglo-American culture. Alfau stresses the importance of language in entering the new host culture since, once learned, English transforms the Spanish immigrants' perception of their situation as cultural, and they become self-conscious of it:

> The moment one learns English, complications set in. Try as one may, one cannot elude this conclusion, one must inevitably come back to it. This applies to all persons, including those born to the language and, at times, even more so to Latins, including Spaniards. It manifests itself in an awareness of implications and intricacies to which one had never given a thought; it afflicts one with that officiousness of philosophy which, having no business of its own, gets in everybody's way and, in the case of Latins, they lose that racial characteristic of taking things for granted and leaving them to their own devices without inquiring into causes, motives or ends, to meddle indiscreetly into reasons which are none of one's affair and to become not only self-conscious, but conscious of other things which never gave a damn for one's existence. (Alfau 1999, 7)

The whole cultural experience is reinforced by the importance Alfau gives to learning a new language while keeping their native one alive. As a result, knowing both Spanish and English is a feature that connects the protagonists with both their culture of origin and their culture of adoption, creating a bond that, according to the author, changes the way they relate to their surroundings and interact with people in-between cultures.

For decades, the works of Bercovici (1924) and Camba (1932) were the first relevant references to Spanish immigration in the United States and, more specifically, in New York City. These are two introductory books that, although not biographies or novelized narrations based on real situations happening to the Spanish immigration in the American country, constitute a first approach to the phenomenon of literary representation of this migration during the first half of the twentieth century. The fact that *Chromos*, written in the 1940s, was not published until 1990 made the works of another American author of Spanish origin, Prudencio de Pereda, the main reference of Spanish immigration literature in the United States with *Fiesta* and *Windmills in Brooklyn*. However, it was not until 1953 that de Pereda published *Fiesta*, a semi-autobiographical work where he describes his homecoming to Spain after living for decades in the United States. This is the first novel about the Spaniards' immigration experience in New York and their return to their homeland shed.

In the first chapters of the novel, Ros is accompanied by his uncle Bernabé in the village of Mozares, visiting the houses of his neighbors and relatives while he recalls who they are and the circumstances that led them to stay. As the story progresses, and the fiesta approaches, the role that Ros plays in the festivity becomes clear, to the delight of some and the anger of others. The fiesta is none other than a performance at Easter consisting of the dramatization of the passion of Christ in which the protagonist is recommended for the role of the Nazarene. This circumstance brings back old envies and quarrels among the inhabitants of Mozares. The news of the death of Blas Miguenz, one of the candidates for the role of Jesus, brought by a pair of the Civil Guard from the village next to Villarcayo, complicates the choosing of the best candidate:

> "He died in prison?" Ros said.
> Anastasio looked to see who was asking this. "They shot him!" he said harshly. "Le fusilaron." There was a harsh objectiveness about the understood "they." "They shot him in celebration of the Day of the Race." That was the impending 12th of October. Ross had heard that Republican prisoners were still being executed on the eves of holidays. The work was done by Falangist squads. (de Pereda 1954, 114)

As a result of Blas' death, the candidates for the Nazarene are reduced to a few men from Mozares and Ros himself. Their final performance of the Passion of Christ is obscured by the enmities developing among the candidates, which concludes with the tragic end of the play. At the same time, the protagonist struggles to recover part of his Spanish culture using the *fiesta* as an excuse to remember his origins. He tries to reaffirm with his actions his conditions of return. As a hybrid subject, Ross is constantly reminded by the rest that the role he plays in the village is marked by his condition of in-betweener, as the American and the Spanish cultures encompass his own self.

Prudencio de Pereda's second major work is *Windmills in Brooklyn*, published for the first time in 1960 in English, rediscovered when translated into Spanish and republished in 2015 by Editorial Hoja de Lata. *Windmills in Brooklyn* is a flashback from *Fiesta*, a pre-sequel of his first novel. *Windmills in Brooklyn* is set in the New York of the 1920s and narrates the childhood and youth of little Prudencio with his family and their family's friend Agapito. Both *Windmills in Brooklyn* and *Fiesta* are presented by Prudencio de Pereda as semiautobiographical novels: both texts constitute a continuum in the life of the author, combining reality and fiction. *Windmills in Brooklyn* focuses on the childhood and youth of the author, while *Fiesta* continues the story two decades later to narrate his adulthood.

De Pereda was born in Brooklyn on February 18, 1912, to Spanish immigrant parents. He grew up in one of the several communities founded by Spanish immigrants between the late nineteenth and the beginning of the twentieth centuries in New York City. He served in the army in World War II. He also lived in the American Midwest and in Spain, where he visited his parents' families in the small village of Mozares, located in the Castilian province of Burgos. However, de Pereda lived most of his life in and around the Big Apple. He graduated from the City College of New York. De Pereda was a multifaceted author who worked as a scriptwriter, librarian, and interpreter while he developed his passion for writing (de Pereda 1960). After retiring, he lived in the State of New York until he died in 1985. When Prudencio de Pereda writes about his childhood in *Windmills in Brooklyn*, he helps to reconceptualize the idea of immigration in a context that enables the reader to have a privileged point of view of the Spanish newcomers as a minority who had to fight in a predominant Anglo-American world with a different dominant language, religion, and culture. Both novels are unique and not-so-well-known testimonies to the reality of Spanish immigration in New York and its *importance* during the first decades of the 1900s.

Pinnick Kinnick Hill: An American Story/Las colinas sueñan en español (2003), by Gain W. González, is possibly the least-known work on Spanish immigration in the United States, mainly because it is the only one not set in New York City. Unlike the rest of the works that conceal the real scarcity of Spanish migration literature in the United States, González's work remains a revolutionary representation of the Spanish immigrant novel outside the city of New York. The novel has the particularity that it can be read both in English and Spanish, since both versions intermingle page by page, allowing its reading in both languages almost simultaneously. Written in the 1970s, González writes about a reality that was already dying out when he wrote about it: the *important* presence of Asturian immigration in West Virginia (González 2003). This autobiographical novel narrates the life of the author, a first-generation son of a Spanish, mainly Asturian, immigrant community in Harrison County, a mill town in the early twentieth century. Many of the Spaniards who migrated to this area worked in the American zinc factories while struggling to preserve their identity, traditions, and customs. This book, partly a memoir, partly a novel, is a unique depiction of the Spaniards who decided not to settle in cities of the East Coast, such as Tampa or New York, where the Spanish communities were bigger, but instead went deep into the country searching for a better life while creating a story of struggle, resilience, and discovery.

Teresa Morell and her father, Claude Morell, wrote one of the latest relevant experiences of the Spanish immigrant community in New York: *The Lower East Side Kid That Made It Good: The Autobiography of Claude Morell* (2007). The book recounts the life of Claude Morell, who, in 1928, at eleven months old, immigrated to New York with his parents. The family settled in the Lower East Side of Manhattan Island, between the Brooklyn and Manhattan bridges, where he lived for thirty years (Morell 2007). In the text, historical events interlace with Morell's memories of his own existence. The author recalls his life in New York, his adventures as the son of Spanish immigrants in the Big Apple and a member of the community of compatriots to which they belonged. *The Lower East Side Kid That Made It Good* is a reference work for understanding the assimilation process of Spanish immigrants and their descendants in the United States and how a first-generation immigrant like Morell adapted to the metropolis living between two worlds, that of his Spanish culture of origin and that of his American culture of reception. At the same time, Teresa Morell allows the reader to develop their own vision as a second-hand witness of the life of her father and his changes through decades of experiences and historical events. To understand Morell's narrative better, the author uses his experience as a witness and inhabitant of the metropolis in order to reveal a closer view of life in the city. The way that Morell uses language to depict the events and experiences in New York is essential to understanding his perspective as a narrator who is both a witness and a descendant of Spanish émigrés and can understand and describe the invisibility of those immigrants.

Las hijas del Capitán (2018), by María Dueñas, is the most recent work about the Spanish migration to the United States. Set in New York in 1936, the novel focuses on the lives of three young girls from Málaga: Victoria, Mona, and Luz Arenas. Their father, Emilio Arenas, an old sailor, buys a tavern in the city, El Capitan, and dies suddenly in an accident in New York Harbor shortly after bringing his daughters and his wife from Spain. As a result, the three siblings are forced to mature and evolve to adapt to the new American culture. María Dueñas's *Las hijas del Capitán* (2018) presents a broad depiction of these new immigrants that transforms the reader's conception of Spanish immigration in the United States. It is an intense work of archaeology of the period surrounding the Spanish Second Republic and the civil war that followed, bringing "at the state's margins, a memory… emerging of a 'Spanish' Civil War" (Anderson 2006, 202). This is a space where Dueñas tries to recreate the result of her research on the Spanish community in New York based on the work of Professor James D. Fernández. She creates a fictional representation of her discoveries in a similar way that de Pereda transmits his experience and memories as a witness to his readers. It is in this context of experiences and memories where transculturation emerges.

3.3. *Morriña*: The Return to the Imagined Spain

The way authors such as de Pereda, Morell, Alfau, González, and Dueñas make their narrations allows readers to become first-person witnesses to the struggles of these Spaniards, which would not have been possible by using a simple objective narration of the historical events or by the simple numbers and statistics of the myriad of immigrants who arrived in the American country. The main difference between the first five works of authors of Spanish origin who grew up in the United States and Dueñas's work is the tone in which the first ones are written as compared to the last one. Although Dueñas's novel is based on real historical context and inspired by the personal testimonies and by primary and secondary sources of her research in New York, it is still a work of fiction where the main protagonists, the Arenas sisters, emerge from the writer's mind, not from the reality of Spanish immigration in the city. As a result, the reality of those authors of Spanish origin who have lost contact with their imagined Spain has two very distinct characteristics. First, the works of de Pereda, Morell, Alfau, and González are written in English. Their linguistic and cultural hybridization was complete when they wrote them, and they freely preferred to write these works in English even though they could have done so in Spanish. The second characteristic is the written expression of the authors' longing of the main characters to return to Spain, to see the country one more time or for the first time in their lives. The autobiographical narrative allows these writers to revisit their childhood or youth, recalling the testimonies of their lives and those of their compatriots in the United States. Additionally, they also include homesickness for their country of origin. Spain is revisited for some of these authors and never returned to for others.

Prudencio de Pereda shows both cases in his works. The Spaniard who, after immigrating to the United States, wishes to return to Spain but never does. This case is personified by the figure of Don José. From the beginning of the story, the reader is reminded that little Prudencio's grandfather hopes to return to Spain because he only immigrated to the American country reluctantly:

> My grandmother's brother had come to the United States some years before and made an immediate success as *teveriano*. He wrote glowing letters to my grandmother, telling her of the wonderful opportunities and the trade and urging her to make José, my grandfather, see reason and come to America. Does he want to be a waiter all his life? the brother would ask. He'd felt very bad when she'd married a waiter. He was her only brother and they were very close.
> Grandfather was content. He didn't want to leave. (de Pereda 1960, 16)

Finally, however, Don José had agreed to his wife's requests, influenced by the constant letters they received from his wife's brother, and, together with little Prudencio's mother, who was a baby then, decided to go to New York, where Don José would become a *teveriano*:

> The letters got more boastful, and then pleading. Finally my granduncle sent enough money to pay first-class passage for all three, and the pressure was too much for my grandfather. He consented, and he came to the United States with his family—to a tenement district in Hoboken, New Jersey. They moved to Brooklyn shortly after, when my aunt was born, but to a tenement district again, and they had never lived better than that. Grandfather, as my mother would say in ending these stories, was just not a good salesman. (1960, 16)

The reality faced by many Spanish immigrants was not very different from the one depicted in this segment. Many of them crossed the Atlantic under false promises of a better life, but on many occasions the work offered was harsh and poorly paid and did not allow the immigrants to save enough to return to their country of origin, not even to visit it again. Don José wished to return to a Spain that did not exist, that he imagined and idealized, and if it ever was real, the wars, economic crises, and social changes that the country had gone through during the decades he was away would have made it unrecognizable in the eyes of little Prudencio's grandfather.

Eventually, most Spanish immigrants resigned themselves to the fate that had befallen them. De Pereda uses his grandparents to express the acceptance of their fate, of not being able to return to Spain. When at the beginning of the second part of the novel, Don José agrees to take charge of the party of the Spanish Benevolent Society, La Nacional, in Brooklyn, he also accepts that he will have to stay forever in the United States:

> "'I can do it,' Grandfather said. 'I can do it—in some way.' Later, he said to Grandmother, 'Now that I'm sure I will never go back to my own country, I want to do something in this one. Something worthy of me'" (103).

In the case of Prudencio's grandmother, it took her longer to accept her fate, and it is not until the last chapter of the book that she resigns herself to staying in New York:

> In the years after my grandfather's death, Grandmother lost much of her bitterness. She never came to like America or its way of life, but she knew now that she would never go back to Spain, and she was resigned to spending her last years here. (172)

In the end, like most of the immigrants in the United States, a large part of the Spaniards who migrated did not return to Spain. The fact that they had formed a family whose younger generations felt American and did not have the homesickness or the memories of their parents made many choose to stay, accepting the American way of life.

On the other hand, there was the case of the Spanish immigrant who, after years of working and living in the United States of America, managed to return to Spain, even if only for a short visit, like Ros Varona in *Fiesta: A Novel of Modern Spain*. De Pereda himself visited Spain to stay at his parents' village and used his character and alter ego, Erostrato Varona (nicknamed Ros), to explain what his return to Spain was like. Ros returns to Spain in the late 1940s. It is 1948 in Mozares and the protagonist, Prudencio's doppelganger, returns to his family's village fifteen years after his last visit. The novel begins with Ros's arrival at his little *pueblo* at dusk when a little Citroën taxi takes the protagonist to his aunt's big house. It has been fifteen years since his last visit to Spain in 1933, in the thick of the Second Spanish Republic. The Spain that Ros knew no longer exists.

His memories of the Second Spanish Republic have been replaced by a new landscape: a military dictatorship led by General Francisco Franco. Besides, many of the protagonist's relatives are no longer alive, which leaves Ros with his uncle and aunt as his only family members to lead him around the new Spain of the dictatorship. When Ros stepped off the boat in Santander, the memories of the Spanish Civil War are still present. Some of the initial symbols of the victors are still visible but faded:

> The ruins he saw were small and cleanly swept and light in the sun. He saw the photos of Franco, but there was little feeling about them. The pictures were not lighted—either by the interest in them or by a flash in themselves. He saw many flags and uniforms, but the flags were getting dusty, and he had seen many, many uniforms in Spain on that first visit. They had been worn with more spring then.
>
> The whole strange apathy was even more apparent when he stopped at a small shop window in Santander to look at some statuettes of the "Absent One"—the dead Primo de Rivera, Falangist Saint and Martyr. It was in a street that he had walked down to get away from the city, and the statues were cold and white and very dead. (de Pereda 1954, 18)

Coinciding with his arrival, the village is going to celebrate an Easter *fiesta* that only takes place every ten years and that Ros himself is unaware of, not having experienced it since he immigrated to the United States when he was very young. This *fiesta* makes the plot around which Ros's stay in his family's village revolves. He experiences a culture shock as a returned immigrant with a new hybrid personality that changes his life forever.

In the case of Alfau's *Chromos*, there are five references to nostalgia (or lack of it) in the novel. The first one is at the beginning, when Ramos, one of the Spanish immigrants looking for a better future in New York City, finds himself thinking about his country of origin soon after he arrived in the metropolis:

> His thoughts reverted to Spain, but there was no real regret or nostalgia. He had come to the wrong place, or the wrong people, and that was no reason for turning back. He wanted to find a section of the town and of its people more in harmony with himself. He realized that it was more important to find one's class of compatriots than one's country compatriots, but his ignorance of the language deterred him. (Alfau 1999, 79)

Ramos's yearning for Spain is not a question of national identity, but rather a question of class identity. He has only been in the metropolis for a short time, and he still does not miss his country, but rather his social class and the ease of relating to its members without language barriers. His ignorance of the English language prevents him from adapting to the host country, which makes him stay in the Spanish community in the New York neighborhood of Batavia Street next to Roosevelt Street. This nostalgia is indeed present in the character of another Spanish immigrant, García, who indeed misses his country:

> I feared what I might see there, but then I looked at Garcia and I have never seen this melancholic Spaniard look so sad, so crushed by nostalgic despair. I could well imagine what went on in his soul; his desire to recapture and relive the past, an imaginary past that might have been; his frustration and feeling of inadequacy which he shared with so many of his countrymen, his racial sadness and national regret, his love for the unattainable and for his own stories, his poetry and his romanticism, the complications of having to express his race and identity in terms of another. (Alfau 1999, 356)

At times, the longing for one's country of origin was assumed by a number of Spanish immigrants in the United States. Some, like little Prudencio's grandfather, Don José, accepted their fate with resignation. Others, however, like García, the writer friend of the narrator of *Chromos*, were overcome with despair as time passed and saw that they could not return to their country of origin. In these cases, the acceptance of their fate was a drama that not everyone could overcome and carry with enough fortitude to be able to conceal it from others. In the end, few Spaniards were able to see Spain again. Most of them rebuilt their lives in the United States and created a family in the American country, where their children already considered themselves, in most cases, more American than Spanish.

3.4. Spanish Communities and Societies

The fact that Spanish people often traveled together in search of new job opportunities in the United States and that many of them were from the same region, province, and town helped to create communities of Spaniards that served as support for the newcomers. For decades, they were a catalyst to maintain part of their Spanish identity while acquiring features of the new dominant American culture at the same time. While the migratory flow continued in the first decades of the twentieth century, the communities were strong. Their societies organized *fiestas* and events dedicated to maintaining the cultural and religious traditions and festivities of Spanish origin. As a result, societies became an inescapable part of the collective memory of Spaniards in the different Spanish communities. The memory of Spain that these immigrants had maintained their national identity. The new generations assimilated into the American society but at the same time were imbued with the national spirit of a country they had not lived in and only knew from what their parents and grandparents had told them. These societies became escape valves for many Spaniards who found in them a way to maintain part of their Spanish identity and to share their memories of Spain with their peers. The communities and societies created in the United States are unique instruments to inform about how the Spanish immigrants "returned" to their country through the assimilation of the culture of their country of reception.

Since the late nineteenth century and during the following decades, Spanish immigrants have continued to arrive in the United States. However, it was not until the 1950s when Spain began to establish a proper account of this migration. The Instituto Español de Emigración (2018), created in 1956 during General Franco's dictatorship, recorded 14,433 Spaniards in the United States between 1946 and 1980. This figure seems insignificant if we consider that during the second half of the nineteenth century and the first half of the twentieth century, more Spaniards migrated to the United States than during all previous centuries (Fernández and Argeo 2014). As Fernández and Argeo underline about these previous decades,

> By the time of the outbreak of the Spanish Civil War (July, 1936), the presence of Spanish immigrants in the US was peaking, in terms of numbers and cohesiveness. Most, though not all, of the immigrants, supported the elected government of the Spanish Republic; and though their clubs and associations they mobilized to send aid to the Republic, and to lobby the US government to "Lift the Arms Embargo on Loyalist Spain." After July 18, 1936, virtually all the picnics, dances and sports matches of the Spanish colonies and their clubs throughout the US became fundraisers for the Republic... It was during these difficult times of solidarity and strife, that the Spanish immigrants seemed poised to emerge into public visibility. (Fernández and Argeo 2014, 182)

In addition, Spanish migration to the American continent during the Spanish Civil War (1936–1939) and the decades that followed did not come to a halt, due to the serious impoverishment of Spain and of the rest of Europe during and after the Second World War. However, after the

1950s, its number began to decline rapidly. As for the relationship between migration and the Spanish Civil War, Fernández and Argeo explain that…

> For many, the outcome of the Spanish Civil War—a country destroyed, a dictatorship in place—dashed any immediate dreams of returning to Spain. With that door closed tight, assimilation would become the order of the day, particularly for those immigrants who had children. American schools, service in the US armed forces, and post WWII prosperity would finish dissolving the glue that had held together communities of Spanish immigrants all over the United States. Because the main components of that glue were a common dream—of someday returning to Spain—and a common plight—the shared hardships of immigrant life. (Fernández and Argeo 2014, 202)

The socio-economic situation of Spain would improve until 1959 thanks to the economic reforms of the technocrats and the beginning of the country's openness to the Western Bloc with the visit of President Eisenhower to the country (Palacios 2013, 156). This helped Spain to regenerate its market in the Western world after years of isolation, not even being able to benefit from the Marshall Plan.

In Manhattan, touching Midtown, bordering Chelsea to the north and the West Village to the south, is 14th Street, the main thoroughfare of the community of Little Spain. This was to be the Arenas family's real neighborhood in the Big Apple. The enclave was not as compact as that of Cherry Street, probably because, as Dueñas indicates after her own research,

> Esta zona de la Catorce y sus alrededores, pese a contar con un amplio contingente de compatriotas, se alzaba sobre otra idiosincrasia diferente a la de su antiguo barrio, otra manera distinta de ser, más hilvanada en el tejido de la ciudad y menos concentrada en su propia esquina. (Dueñas 2018, 35)[52]

The Arenas would live in a modest flat on the fourth floor of a building on the corner of La Catorce and Seventh Avenue, with two rooms, electricity, running water, and a toilet inside the flat; much more than what they left behind in their native Málaga. A genuinely Spanish neighborhood with its characteristic smells of food, its shouting, and folklore, which had

52 "This area of the Catorce and its surroundings, despite having a large amount of compatriots, arose over a different idiosyncrasy to that of its old neighbourhood, a different personality, more woven into the fabric of the city and less concentrated in its own corner."

in its best days a population of around 30,000 inhabitants, of which only a few vestiges remain today.

The places of the community that María Dueñas presents us with are a synthesis of real places located in the aforementioned street, of others brought from areas of great Spanish influence such as Cherry Street or Brooklyn, and of others of her own creation. Spanish societies in New York City were always connected with each other. From Southeast of Manhattan to the West Village, Queens, or Brooklyn, Spanish immigrants and their societies moved around the metropolis, sharing events, members, and even space. La Nacional-El Centro Español, the Spanish Benevolent Society, is a good example. Located at 207 West 14th Street, between the Seventh and the Eighth Avenues, La Nacional prides itself on being the oldest Spanish society in New York. Its main missions were to welcome and help Spanish immigrants and to serve as a meeting point for compatriots (La Nacional 2015). This is epitomized in the personality of Emilio Arenas, a member of the association. It was there that the news of his death first arrived. He was the one who initially offered to pay for his burial in Calvary Cemetery (Dueñas 2018, 14, 37, 53, 57).

Officially founded in the autumn of 1868 as a social center to help Spanish immigrants, although its origin seems to go back to the first decades of the 1800s (Fernández and Argeo 2014, 58). Fernández and Argeo underline, as a key year, the importance of 1868…

> for the history of Spanish immigration to the United States, as it marks the beginning of what will eventually be known as the "Ten Years War" in Cuba (1868–78); the beginning of the end, that is, of Spanish sovereignty in the American hemisphere. The initiation in 1868 of Cuba's last 30-year-long push for independence from Spain had direct and profound consequences on our story, as it can be linked both to the founding of New York's oldest organization of Spanish immigrants—La Nacional, which was created precisely to assist Spaniards fleeing from revolutionary violence in Cuba- as well to the removal to Key West, Florida, of an important part of the Cuban cigar industry. 1898, the year of the end of the Spanish-Cuban-American war is also of crucial importance to the story of Spanish immigration to the United States; first, because Spain's defeat would send the country into an economic and moral tailspin, a "desastre" which would prompt hundreds of thousands of Spaniards to seek a better life elsewhere. (2014, 221)

The turn of the century was traumatic for Spain and marked the end of a global empire that went back to the fifteenth century. The Disaster of '98, with the loss of Puerto Rico, Cuba, the Philippines, Guam, and the rest of the possessions spread between America and Asia, meant not only the disappearance of Spain as a transoceanic power but also the establishment of the United States as a new emerging world player that would continue gaining power until its consolidation at the end of WWII. For Spain, 1898 was in many ways the end of an era, the end of an Old World empire that had discovered the New World:

> An 1898 also marks a point of no return for U.S. interventionism in the American hemisphere; the subsequent proliferation of political, economic, cultural and transportation links between the Spanish-speaking Americas and the US would significantly affect the immigration patterns of Spaniards, just as it would create employment and business opportunity for them in the US. (2014, 221)

La Nacional headquarters has been for many decades the center of the old Spanish community of Little Spain, a landmark to Spanish immigrants who arrived in New York City from Latin America and Europe looking for a new beginning (2014, 58):

> Chelsea is known as a conservative Irish Catholic community despite the presence of Spanish, French, Scottish, and other national groups. Although typical Manhattan tenements, small business establishments, and apartment houses make up most of the district, here and there an old theater or cafe reminds Chelsea of its past as an amusement center in the 1880's, and a relatively large number of local ancients helps give the neighborhood a "preserved" quality. (Federal Writer's Project 1939, 151)

As a result, La Nacional became one of the most *important* places that offered new immigrants a place for orientation, a warm meal, a first job, or a place to stay. Consequently, La Nacional has become a living testimony to the evolution of Spanish immigration in New York City for more than 150 years. It is an example of why memory must be preserved through centuries in order to not forget, and it serves as a living witness on the changes that the Spanish community has experienced over the years (La Nacional 2015).

La Nacional is one of the oldest buildings in the neighborhood. Its twin buildings, located at 241 and 243 West 14th Street, seem to have changed with time, while 239 seems to be stuck in time. Its red door, preceded by the American and the Spanish flags, welcomes the visitor to its four stories. On the second floor of La Nacional, we can find the headquarters, and next door, in suite number 2, is the office of the Abraham Lincoln Brigade. The rest of the upper floors are bedrooms rented for hospitality service (La Nacional 2015). La Nacional also includes a Spanish restaurant with the same name in the basement of the building that has been renovated and become a landmark in the neighborhood. Many distinguished Spaniards have visited or stayed at La Nacional: from the Spanish painter Joaquín Sorolla, who, according to legend, gave the society a painting that disappeared years later, to Federico García Lorca; from Pablo Picasso and Salvador Dalí to flamenco guitarist Paco de Lucía (La Nacional 2015).

Very close to La Nacional was Casa Moneo at 218 West 14th (Casa Galicia, Memoria 1949, 45). It was open for almost sixty years, from 1929 to 1988, and it soon became a food reference not only for Spaniards and other Spanish-speaking citizens but also for New Yorkers in general. Casa Moneo operated as a grocery store with products from Spain, but one could also find other types of articles such as perfumes, pots and pans, shoes, and so on: "Alguien más pedía una ristra de ajos, dos pastillas de jabón Lagarto; de los ganchos colgaban morcillas, chorizos y sobrasadas, olía a encurtidos y a vinagre" (Dueñas 2018, 29)[53]:

> Se las llevó a la trastienda, una estancia repleta de cajones, sacos y estantes cargados de mercancía. Había comestibles dulces y salados, desde turrones de almendra hasta enormes tarros de cristal lleno de aceitunas aliñadas; había boinas y guitarras, alpargatas, castañuelas, paellas, botas de vino: nadie diría que se encontraban en pleno centro de Manhattan, a un tiro de piedra del río Hudson, a escasas manzanas de Unión Square. (2018, 50)[54]

It was the owner of Casa Moneo who offered the daughters a temporary job for a few hours, and it is Mona, the middle of the three, who accepted it, thanks to which she met people who had a transcendental impact on

53 "Someone else asked for a string of garlic, two bars of Lagarto soap; black pudding, sausages and sobrasadas hung from the hooks, it smelt of pickles and vinegar."

54 "He took them to the back room, a room filled with crates, sacks, and shelves laden with merchandise. There were sweet and savoury groceries, from almond nougat to huge glass jars full of seasoned olives; there were berets and guitars, espadrilles, castanets, paellas, wineskins: no one would think they were in the heart of Manhattan, a stone's throw from the Hudson River, just a few blocks away from Union Square."

her future: "Por fortuna doña Carmen Baraño, la propietaria, no tardó en rescatarlas: otra vasca de Sestao con bata blanca, las uñas pintadas de rojo intensa y los sesenta a la vuelta de la esquina" (Dueñas 2018, 49).[55] The Moneo house, which has one of the few telephones in the neighborhood, was also part of Luz's clandestine life. Another important building on the street, opposite Casa Moneo, was Casa María:

> Casa Maria (Spanish Settlement) 215 West 14th Street, under the patronage of the Augustinian Fathers of the Assumption. The object of this Association is to promote the temporal, social, mental, moral, and religious welfare of young women, particularly for those dependent upon their own exertions for support. Address Mrs. M.A. Lopez, Manager. (Directory Social and Health Agencies of New York City 1914)

The Casa María building is very close to La Nacional, where Sister Lito resides. She is the nun who tries to help in the dispute with the shipping company thanks to her law degree and the great friendship she has with Mrs. Milagros Couceiro, a neighbor of the Arenas family. According to Bercovici,

> The house is on Fourteenth Street between Seventh and Eighth Avenues are built on very narrow strips or front-age land. And each one, even though of the same height as the next one, is built in an individual style. There are houses of red bricks with black-painted windows and doors, and deep set-in sills over the round archway. And between a red and a gray house there are suddenly looms up a yellow-painted stucco building, with narrow oblong windows and red-painted lucarnes between them. There is the Casa María, of rough yellow stucco, with beautifully lined windows and vaulted doors that are barred with wrought-iron Byron. The basement entrance is as mysterious as the descent into one of the underground piazzas around the Alhambra. (1924, 285)

Due to the presence of Spaniards in the neighborhood in 1901, the Church of Our Lady of Guadalupe, also known as Nuestra Señora de Guadalupe, was founded by Augustinians of the Assumption between the Seventh and the Eighth Avenues next to La Nacional at 229–231 West 14th. It became the first Spanish-speaking Catholic parish in New York City, not only for people coming from Spain but also for the people coming from south of

55 "Fortunately, Doña Carmen Baraño, the owner, did not take long to rescue them: another Basque woman from Sestao in a white gown, her nails painted bright red and the sixties just around the corner."

the Rio Grande and with Spanish roots from Cuba, Puerto Rico, Mexico, or the Dominican Republic. One of the most successful Spanish immigrants who arrived in New York from Puerto Rico was Prudencio Unanue (6 April 1886–17 March 1976). Prudencio was born in the small village of Villasana de Mena, in the region of Castile and León, in northern Spain. In 1903, Prudencio immigrated to San Lorenzo, Puerto Rico, where he created a small food distribution business. In 1918, he moved to New York City, where he studied business at the Albany Business School. In 1921, Prudencio married Carolina Casal de Valdés (1890–1984), a Galician immigrant from Pontevedra (Wepman 2008). In 1922, he opened a food store called Unanue and Sons, "as an individual proprietorship, doing business as a food broker" (United States 1961, 578). In 1937, Prudencio "changed the business to a wholesale and jobbing operation" (578–79) and founded Goya Foods, Inc. Nowadays, the food company is one of the most *important* American producers of a brand of foods in the world (Wepman 2008).

The Church of Our Lady of Guadalupe was the first Spanish-speaking Catholic church in the area. It was built in 1902 due to the growth of the Spanish immigrant population since the late 1880s and 1890s (Fernández 2011, 19). According to the 2006 Preservation Plan of the 14th Street and Union Square by the Columbia University Graduate School of Architecture,

> The building occupied by Guadalupe is a mid-nineteenth-century brownstone that has been masterfully converted from a posh row house to a double-height sanctuary, complete with a monumental entrance, side chapel, tiny balcony, and clerestory. This transformation, which makes Guadalupe extremely rare, if not unique, in the city spanned two decades and involved several notable architects one of which was Gustave Steinback. Steinback, known for his work on religious projects, designed No. 229's classically proportioned Spanish Revival façade in 1921. Although the church remained extremely popular, it was consolidated with nearby St. Bernard's parish and closed in 2003. Today, Guadalupe is clear architectural trace of Little Spain. (Columbia University 2006, 9)

Two adjoining buildings were joined in the construction project, with a façade that juts out from that of the flanking buildings. For more than a hundred years it served as a center for prayer and religious celebrations: weddings, baptisms, communions, confirmations, funerals, masses in honor of the patron saint of Spain, etc., until 2003, when it changed its location due to the decrease in the number of its parishioners; it is then when it merged with the parish of San Bernardo, located in the same street, between the Eighth and the Ninth Avenues. Today the old premises are empty and closed to the public, and it is here where María Dueñas places the wedding between Victoria, the first-born of the Arenas family, and the widower Luciano Barona. Built in 1868, St. Bernard's Church was founded by Irish Catholic immigrants and their descendants at 328 West 14th Street, only one block away from the parish of Our Lady of Guadalupe. Our Lady of Guadalupe at St. Bernard Church is the result of a parish merger of the Manhattan parishes of Our Lady of Guadalupe and St. Bernard's Church in 2003.

Another business that was part of the everyday life of this street and which appears in *Las hijas del Capitán* was La Artística, a photography studio run by Paul Pérez. He oversaw capturing the events of the colony, both personal and social, even in its summer resorts. Pérez specialized in weddings and children and all kinds of photographic work. "Paul D. Pérez. El fotógrafo de la colonia. El único que donó todos sus servicios a la causa española. Desea a todos muy felices Pascuas y Próspero Año Nuevo. 239 West 14th Street. N.Y. Tel. Chelsea 3–7569" was how it was advertised (Casa Galicia. Memoria 1944, 15).[56] In the novel, he is responsible for capturing the wedding photo between Victoria and the tobacco dealer Luciano Barona.

Another *important* landmark in the community was La Bilbaína, a renowned restaurant located in front of the Church of Nuestra Señora de Guadalupe (Fernández 2011, 19–20). Its owners, Gaspar Cuadrado and Joaquina Herrera, were originally from the province of Valladolid. Later, their son-in-law, Avelino Castaños Garay, continued the business (Aguirre and San Sebastián 2018, 143). There, the wedding between Victoria and Luciano is celebrated in the novel in a splendid way, with the menu detailed in one of its pages:

> Sentadas ahora en el comedor de La Bilbaína frente a las mesas prolongadas, primero recibieron con ojos llenos de incredulidad las grandes fuentes repletas de entremeses, luego los magníficos troncos de merluza a la vasca en sus cazuelas de barro, después los cortes de vacuno—beef-steaks, los llamaban—; hasta una tarta nupcial de la Valencia Bakery hubo de postre. Y vino, que no faltará el vino. Y

56

sidra El Gaitero y coñac español Lepanto y anís Las Cadenas, procedente toda de la bodega Mediavilla de la Ciento dieciséis. (Dueñas 2018, 292)[57]

Other establishments were located on La Catorce, such as Lavandería Irigaray or Funeraria Hernández, but their location corresponded to other neighborhoods: the Spanish American Laundry, whose owner was Don Enrique Irisarri, located at 38 Cherry Street (Aguirre and San Sebastian 2018, 126). The Funeraria Hernández, run in the novel by the Puerto Rican don Fidel Hernández, appears in an advertisement of the time as A.R. Hernández, funeral director (Casa Galicia Memoria 1944, 26) or, as Funeraria Hernández (Casa Galicia, Memoria 1948, 46), both references with the same address at 219 Atlantic Avenue Brooklyn. Morán boarding house on 16th Street, on whose rooftop Mona, Luz, and Fidel rehearsed, could very well correspond to La Avilesina, 130 East 16th St., which existed at the same time and in the same street, owned by María Álvarez, the Avilesina (Fernández 2011, 24). There are other Spanish-run establishments near La Catorce that retain their genuine location in the novel, such as El Chico at 80 Grove St. at the corner of Sheridan Square, El Patio at 17 Barrow Street, or Jai-Alai at 82 Bank Street (Dueñas 2018, 223–25).

Mountain holiday destinations were very popular with the Spanish colony. Villas, farms, and hotels rented out their rooms to compatriots in the summer season to escape the heat of the big city. Places such as "Villa Alonso," a small farm in Newburg (Fernández 2011, 30), "Villa Rodríguez" in Plattekill, the oldest of them all (2011, 33), or the famous "Hotel Rifton" near the Catskills, run by an Asturian couple, which became a hotel complex with more than a hundred rooms, ballrooms, and a lagoon for water activities (2011, 31–33); they were a continuation of the way of life that could be had in any summer village in the Iberian Peninsula: funfairs, pilgrimages, baths, games, group activities, patron saint celebrations, etc.

57 "Seated now in the dining room of La Bilbaína in front of the long tables, they first received with eyes full of disbelief the large platters full of hors d'oeuvres, then the magnificent logs of Basque-style hake in their clay pots, then the cuts of beef steaks,-as they called them-; there was even a wedding cake from the Valencia Bakery for dessert. And wine, there was no shortage of wine. And El Gaitero cider and Spanish cognac Lepanto and aniseed liquor Las Cadenas, all from the Mediavilla winery in the Ciento Dieciséis."

It is in this area of the Catskills, some 160 km from New York City, where Mona and Luciano spent their honeymoon (Dueñas 2018, 308).

Brooklyn is the new setting where Mona moves to after her wedding to Luciano, specifically to Atlantic Avenue because they have their flat above the tobacco shop where the Alhameño has been working for years. Although a little further away from the Alhameño community and the Salmerón group, with whom Luciano was very close during his first wife's life, and with whom he keeps in touch:

> Éramos un grupo de unas treinta familias y vivíamos en edificios de apartamentos muy cerca los unos de los otros. La sección de Brooklyn donde vivíamos era Park Slope. En la quinta avenida (de Brooklyn) había muchos edificios que tenían seis apartamentos. Me vienen a la memoria los números 147, 151 (el mío), 155, 157 y no olvidemos el 123 donde estaba el Grupo Salmerón. A la vuelta estaba el número 1 de Lincoln Place donde vivían muchas familias alhameñas. (Amate 2011, 76)[58]

The area was bordered by Flatbush Avenue and Lincoln Place in the north, between the 4th Avenue and Prospect Park West, and South Park Slope in the south. To the west was Prospect Park, one of the green lungs of Brooklyn, a regular meeting place for Spanish immigrants in the area, where families of Andalusian, Asturian, Galician, or Basque origin spent their leisure time outdoors on the weekends (2011, 63).

One of the most relevant enclaves of Spanish immigration in New York City was Casa Galicia de Nueva York-Unity Galicia Inc., located today at 3709, 31st Avenue, in Astoria, Queens. Although it was officially founded in 1940, the origins of Casa Galicia go back at least to the 1920s, when the first Galician Center was established at Union Square. However, the Wall Street Crash of 1929 affected the center, and it disappeared due to the economic crisis. Many of its members were integrated into El Centro Español-the Spanish Benevolent Society, located only a few blocks away from Union Square. On July 18, 1936, the Spanish Civil War began, which entailed

58 "We were a group of about thirty families, and we lived very close to each other in apartment buildings. The section of Brooklyn where we lived was Park Slope. In the Fifth Avenue (in Brooklyn) there were a lot of buildings with six flats. I recall 147, 151 (mine), 155, 157 and let's not forget 123, where the Salmerón Group was. Around the corner was number 1 Lincoln Place where many families from Alhama lived."

"una escisión en los proyectos e imaginarios sobre España abrigados por los emigrantes, que ya se venía larvando desde el período de la dictadura de Primo de Rivera. Disputas en centros y asociaciones de emigrantes, divisiones entre una entidad prorrepublicana y otra profranquista, marcaron un antes y después" (Liñares Giraut et al. 2007a, 29)[59]

One of the most famous groups at the time was the Frente Popular Antifascista Gallego. Created in 1937 by Galician immigrants in New York City who decided to support the republican cause (González 2000). At the end of the Spanish Civil War, as Galician immigrants kept coming from Spain, the Galician Antifascist Popular Front left aside its political name, and its members became part of Casa Galicia.

One of the most famous immigrants in exile was the Galician thinker and writer Alfonso Daniel Rodríguez Castelao, who had been sent by the government of the Spanish Republic to look for support in the United States. After the triumph of General Franco's army on April 1st, 1939, Alfonso Castelao decided to exile himself in Argentina in 1940, but before leaving, he gathered with many Spaniards, many of them Galician, to speak to them about the necessity of creating a new Galician Center to preserve their traditions, their culture, and the Galician language (Libro de Memoria 1945).

In 1940, shortly after Alfonso Castelao left, Casa Galicia was founded and became one of the most *important* societies, along with La Nacional, el Centro Asturiano, el Centro Vasco, el Centro Balear, el Club Obrero Español, el Círculo Valenciano, and La Sociedad Naturista Hispana, among others. The founders of Casa Galicia were mostly Galicians. In 1945, after World War II, Alfonso Castelao returned to New York and was named its first honorary member (Libro de Memoria 1945), and since 1951, Casa Galicia has honored his memory annually. According to the first Libro de Memoria of Casa Galicia (1941), on November 2, 1941, after the previous Casa Galicia disappeared in a fire on Columbus Avenue, a floor was temporarily used at 105 West 63rd Street until a new building was bought by

59 "a division in the emigrants' projects and imaginaries of Spain, which had been brewing since the period of Primo de Rivera's dictatorship. Disputes in emigrant centres and associations, divisions between a pro-Republican entity and a pro-Franco entity, marked a before and an after."

Unidad Gallega at 313 West 59th Street for $20,000. In 1948, the Libro de Memoria mentions the possibility of having the building expropriated due to a new project at Madison Square Garden. At the beginning of the 1950s, the City of New York decided to start the project of renewal of the West side of the metropolis between the 50th and the 70th Streets, including the building bought by Casa Galicia at 313 West 59th Street. Therefore, in 1954, Casa Galicia decided to move to 153–159 West 64th Street, and a year later, in 1955, el Grupo de Juventudes de la Casa Galicia was created to encourage the new generation to continue with the work of the previous generations (Libro de Memoria 1955, 3).

In the Libro de Memoria of 1958, the Board of Directors indicates that due to the renewal of the metropolis, Casa Galicia set out to look for a new place for the society while it continued with the different departments that organized all the events of the Unidad Gallega: la Sección de Intereses, de Fiestas, Recreo y Orden, Propaganda, Ayuda Mutua, Cultura, Comité de Damas, Restaurante y Cantina (Libro de Memoria de 1963, 11–12). The Libro de Memoria of 1959 points out that a new building had been bought in Manhattan at 405 West 41st Street, New York 36, N.Y. On July 25th, like every year, Casa Galicia celebrated "el Día de Galicia o Santiago" and invited representatives from Spain and members of other Hispanic societies, like the Centro Vasco, the Sociedad Naturista Hispana, the Ateneo Cubano de Nueva York, La Nacional, the East Side Spanish American Club, the Club Progreso de Boston, the Spanish American Citizens Club of Queens, and the delegate of the Basque Government to the United States (Libro de Memoria 1959).

During the same year, Casa Galicia and La Nacional organized a banquet on October 12, after their gathering with other Hispanic societies, like La Sociedad Hispánica Cívica de Queens Inc., the Cátedra Abraham Lincoln: Escuela de Estudios Metafísicos, or the Sociedad Cívico-Cultural Bello Ideal Puertorriqueño Inc. "ante la estatua de Colón *español*, en el parque central"[60] to celebrate the discovery of America by Spain and the Catholic Monarchs (Libro de Memoria 1958, 14). In 1970, Casa Galicia bought Webster Hall and the Annex at 119–125 East 11th Street, in the East

60 "in front of the statue of Spanish Columbus, in the central park."

Village (Libro de Memoria 1969-70, 5). After almost twenty-five years in their new location, Unity Galicia decided to take advantage of the increase in the value of land in the East Village, and the members of Casa Galicia saw an opportunity to improve the revenue of the society and decided to move to a new location at 37-09 31st Avenue, in Astoria, Queens, in 1994. Webster Hall is still owned by Unity Galicia, and it is currently rented and used as a concert venue and night club (Libro de Memoria 1993–1996, 2).

Worth mentioning as an *important* society in New York City was the Centro Vasco-Americano Sociedad de Beneficencia y Recreo, also known as the Centro Vasco-Americano Benevolent Society Inc., founded in 1913 by Spanish immigrants from the Basque region in Northern Spain. The Centro Vasco-Americano was originally located in the first Spanish settlement of New York, in Manhattan. In the beginning, the Centro Vasco-Americano was at 41 Cherry Street and then moved to 48 Cherry Street (Totoricagüena 2003, 99–100), a few blocks away from the Spanish Benevolent Society. One of his most illustrious founders was Valentín Aguirre, a Basque immigrant from Monte Sollube, in Biscay, who helped the new Spanish immigrants to find jobs, in New York City or would send them to another American state where he had contacts and knew they would find a good job (2003, 15). Aguirre had arrived during the migration wave from Spain and the Spanish territories of the Caribbean (Cuba, Dominican Republic, and Puerto Rico) and South America. According to Rueda Hernanz (1993, 161), Aguirre was the owner of one of the 32 Spanish export and import companies from New York, which also included tobacco trade companies such as Selgas & Cia.

At the end of the nineteenth century, the number of Spaniards had increased in the United States after the Cuban War of Independence (1895–1898) and the Spanish-American War (1898). Aguirre originally established a boarding house at Cherry Street, Casa Vizcaína, where he lived with his wife Benita Orbe, near the Manhattan Piers of the Brooklyn Bridge, where many Spaniards lived after arriving from Ellis Island, creating the first Spanish neighborhood of the City. Cherry Street is in Lower Manhattan, between the Two Bridges neighborhood and the Lower East Side. In the early 1900s, Aguirre moved his business several times until he decided to establish it at 82 Bank Street, close to the Spanish Benevolent Society on 14th Street. When Aguirre moved to Little Spain, he founded Santa Lucía

Hotel, and in 1922 the Restaurante Jai Alai, literally *Happy Party* (the Basque name for the Basque game *cestapunta* or *basket tip*), where his wife Benita Orbe became a famous cook. As La Nacional, Aguirre helped new Spanish immigrants to find jobs, and in 1920 he decided to create his own travel agency, advertised as a place "Al Servicio de la Colonia," or "At the Service of the Community" (Totoricagüena 2003, 74).

In Aguirre's Travel Agency, he helped many Spanish immigrants find their first job, a place to live and even to move to the west of the United States to places like Montana, Utah, Wyoming, Washington, Oregon, California, Nevada, or Idaho, the latter state was very popular among Spanish Basque immigrants, who moved to the city of Boise where mining, ranching, and sheepherding were already a popular employment destination from the 1890s, especially after the establishment of La Sociedad de Socorros Mutuos, or Mutual Aid Society, created by the Basques in the city of Boise to coordinate and bring family, friends, and neighbors from Spain, many of them from Biscay (Totoricagüena 2003, 55; 75).

According to Álvarez Gila, when Spanish immigrants arrived in the United States, some stereotypes were rampant, and some people believed that there was a certain predisposition of some Spanish regional groups for the activities they came to develop in the host society. It was widely believed that, for example, "los anados eran robustos y aptos para los trabajos de gran esfuerzo; [y] los vascos porfiados óptimos para el trato del anado..., y en los Estados Unidos, como pastores de ovejas" (Liñares Giraut et al. 2007a, 42–43).[61] However, it seems that the origin of this idea of Basques and sheepherding has its origin in 1849, when, during the California Gold Rush, the brothers Pedro and Bernardo Altube, Antonio Jáuregui, or Miguel Leonis succeeded in the cattle industry by providing food for the new settlers and wool to the textile industry on the East Coast (2007, 45).

As an example of the *importance* of the Spanish manpower at the beginning of the twentieth century, in 1919, The Literary Digest highlights the *importance* of the Spanish laboring class in the United States during World

61 "The Galicians were robust and apt for strenuous work; [and] the stubborn Basques excellent for handling cattle..., and in the United States as sheepherders."

War I (1914–1918) as Spanish immigrants represented a large percentage of the unskilled workers in many industries in the country:

> The larger percentage of Spanish immigrants in this country are of the unskilled laboring class. Before the war the tide of immigration was heavily on the increase. Shipping conditions during the war naturally caused a slackening in the numbers of Spaniards bound to our shores. Yet during the war, we are told by a reputable authority, from 30 to 40 per cent, of the unskilled workers in munition-plants, shipyards, mines, and other industries were Spaniards from Spain. (The Literary Digest 1919, 40)

As many other Spaniards, the Basques who stayed in New York City attended the Spanish-speaking Catholic Sunday mass at Nuestra Señora de Guadalupe on 14th Street, where for many years there was a Basque priest (2003, 85; 100). However, it was not until the 1930s when the Spanish immigrants who lived in New York City received full spiritual care from the Catholic Church. As Núñez Seixas highlights,

> la Iglesia católica española descuidó por completo la atención espiritual a los emigrantes españoles entre 1880 y 1930, siendo muy escaso el número de clérigos destinados a zonas de amplia presencia de emigrantes españoles... De ahí que la jerarquía católica española sí tomase cartas en el asunto a partir de 1946, cuando se restableció la ley de emigración de 1924. Para evitar que los emigrantes se descristianizasen en su periplo por extraños lares, las Comisiones Católicas de emigración asumieron tareas de control y supervisión, y los curas españoles... se convirtieron en un vehículo de identificación permanente entre una España católica identificada con el régimen franquista y la nostalgia de los emigrantes. (2007, 20)[62]

According to Rueda, between 1933 and 1935, in New York City there were seven "Centros Benéfico-Asistenciales, Iglesias o Capillas atentidos por clero español" (1993, 243):

---

62 "the Spanish Catholic Church completely neglected the spiritual care of Spanish emigrants between 1880 and 1930, with very few clergymen being assigned to areas with a large presence of Spanish emigrants... Hence, the Spanish Catholic hierarchy's reaction after 1946, when the 1924 emigration law was re-established. To prevent emigrants from becoming de-Christianised on their journeys to foreign lands, the Catholic Emigration Commissions took on tasks of control and supervision, and Spanish priests... became a permanent vehicle of identification between a Catholic Spain in tune with the Franco regime and the nostalgia of the emigrants."

- Iglesia de Nuestra Señora de Guadalupe (229 West 14th Street) (1933–35).
- Iglesia de la Medalla Milagrosa (114th Street and 77 Saint Nicolas Avenue) (1933–35).
- Iglesia de la Esperanza (156th Street and Broadway) (1933–35).
- Iglesia de la Santa Agonía (98th Street) (1935).
- Day Nursery of San José de la Montaña (432 West 20th Street) (1933–35).
- Convento de las Madres Reparadoras (14 East 29th Street) (1933–35).
- Casa de María (221 West 14th Street) (1933–34) (1993, 245).

In 1946, the City of New York began its plans for urban renewal and purchased "la mayor parte de la calle Catherine, Cherry y Water" (Totoricagüena 2003, 116).[63] Due to this renovation, the Centro Vasco-Americano had to move to a different location but kept participating with other Spanish societies in different activities such as the Columbus Day parade (2003, 119). The Board of Directors decided to move temporarily to a nearby building at 95 Madison Street and later moved to two different locations on East Broadway between Pike and St. James Place. The area was an Italian quarter before it became today's Chinatown (117). In 1952, the Basque-American Center had to move back to 63 East Broadway, a few blocks away from 95 Madison Street (118). However, in 1955, the Basque-American Centre had to move back to 71–73 East Broadway.

In 1969, the Basque American Centre obtained a five-year lease and moved to 63 East Broadway, close to its previous location (126). However, space problems remained a problem, and the Basque American Centre sometimes used "la Casa Galicia en el Webster Hall, o en el Prospect Hall en Brooklyn" (, 127).[64] In 1973, a friend of a Basque Center member told him that an old two-story Greek Orthodox church in Brooklyn was for sale in a Polish neighborhood. The members of the Basque American Center met once more and finally agreed to "terminar sus veinticinco años de alquiler de espacio"[65] and move permanently to 307 Eckford Street in Brooklyn, where the new members of the Basque American Center still meet today.

The examples of these Spanish societies in New York and their survival through time show how the transculturation of these immigrants was a long process where family, culture, and community affected the way

---

63 "most of Catherine street, Cherry and Wate."
64 "Casa Galicia at Webster Hall, or at Prospect Hall in Brooklyn."
65 "end its twenty-five years of lease."

this transition took place. Although the acculturation process of these Spaniards was constant since their arrival in the United States, the fact that new compatriots continued to regularly arrive in New York until the late 1930s resulted in a slower assimilation thanks to the influence of the newcomers. However, the culture of those people who lived outside the influence of the Spanish communities and societies, as was the case of Spanish intellectuals, began to blur under the influence of the American society where they lived, thus accelerating the deculturation process. As the flow of immigrants diminished, the boundaries separating the dominant and the dominated cultures began to dissolve as well, and Spaniards, along with their second- and third-generation descendants, started to lose their roots as they negotiated their Spanish-American identity, closing the circle of cultural transition with the arrival of the last phase: neoculturation. As a result, most Spanish communities and their societies began to disappear when the feeling of belonging to the United States became stronger than the memory of a Spain that many did not know, no longer existed, or was not remembered anymore.

Chapter 4: The Representation of Linguistic Hybridization

> "Please!" I said, and kept pressing on her shoulder as she tried to sit up. "Please, my soul!" The "*mi alma,*" a term of endearment that I had once heard Agapito use to a Spanish waitress, slipped out without my thinking, and it seemed to touch her because she stopped frowning suddenly, shook her head and laughed, and grabbed both my hands and pulled me down to her.
>
> —*Prudencio de Pereda, Windmills in Brooklyn*

One of the most important aspects of the "Third Space" in these works is language: how their authors use language, if they write their works in Spanish, English, or in both languages, how their characters use words of both languages, and code-switch, which is essential to communicate and to understand their hybridity. The use of either of these two as a "Third Space" language will be dealt with through the analysis of the different narratives, as they offer a variety of uses that are worth mentioning. This "Third Space" language uses words or sentences, even in both languages, on purpose as part of the hybridity of their characters and is able to offer a more realistic representation of the "Third Space" as employed by the authors and the characters themselves.

Throughout the works selected, one of the most relevant elements to analyze as regards the representation of transculturation and biculturalism in the literature of the Spanish immigrants in the United States in the first half of the twentieth century is language. When speaking about identity, but especially about the construction of the American identity, Sollors differentiates between "contractual and hereditary, self-made and ancestral,... between *consent* and *decent*" (Sollors 1986, 5–6). If *descent* relations are relations of "substance," "descent language emphasizes our positions as heirs, our hereditary qualities, liabilities, and entitlements; consent language stresses out abilities as mature free agents and 'architects of our fates' to choose our *spouses*, our destinies, and our political systems" (1986, 6). This linguistic hybridization is an essential aspect not only to examine the cultural transformation of the characters but also of the authors.

The representation of migration in literature helps to create a cultural and historical background that benefits the collective memory of immigrants both during and after the merging process of the dominated and the dominant cultures. In his article, "Acculturation and Identity: The Role of Individualization Theory" (2006), Professor of Sociology James E. Côté points out that to understand the acculturation of immigrants in the context of identity theory, language is one of the tangible resources that immigrants acquire to "help the person to strategize how to, in the first place, negotiate structural passages and penetrate associated barriers, and in the second place, find acceptance and membership in new groups, along with the rewards of membership in these groups" (2006, 34). In other words, it is one of the essential skills in the acculturation process that immigrants use to adapt to the dominant culture. All the authors of the literary works analyzed are fluent in English and Spanish. This fact makes their interpretation of the linguistic reality of the characters they represent a little more truthful. If, in addition, all of them have resorted to their own biographical elements or of those who lived through the process of cultural hybridization as Spanish immigrants to recreate their use of the language, their books allow us to delve into the importance of language in the construction of this new hybrid person.

4.1. Prudencio de Pereda's Portrayal of Spanish Immigration

4.1.1. The *Teveriano*

> For a long time Agapito wrote home as if he were actually in Havana, knowing that his father would construe the United States stamp on the letters as just another indication of *Yanqui* power, but he did tell the truth about his being a cigar salesman—an honest one, of course—and about the wonderful friends he had made.
>
> —*Prudencio de Pereda, Windmills in Brooklyn*

Although the use of Spanish in *Windmills in Brooklyn* is scarce, there is one Spanish word that recurs throughout the novel regardless of the moment of the narration. That term is *teveriano*. The analysis of this word and its meaning is essential to understand the importance of the use of language in New York as a "Third Space" and the different interpretations that the hybrid concept of *teveriano* has in the novel. This is a term that condenses the importance of "Third Space" language in New York City, where English and Spanish coexist to describe the work that Spanish immigrants performed in the metropolis. Throughout the story, the first-person narrator describes this Spanish-American transcultural job and its different interpretations of it, a profession created by the confluence of Cuban, Spanish, and American cultures, resulting in the unique figure of the *teveriano*. At the beginning of the first chapter, Prudencio introduces the topic of tobacco to the reader:

> I thought when I was young that you worked according to your nationality. We were Spanish, and my father, grandfather and uncles were all in the cigar business. There was a definite rule about this, I believed—a law. I thought so particularly during those times that I listened to my father and the other men of our family talk business, and heard them complain bitterly about the cigar business and about what a dishonorable trade it was and how they were cursed the moment they took it up. (de Pereda 1960, 3)

The hybridism of the "cubaneidad" of the tobacco business studied by Ortiz in *Contrapunteo cubano del tabaco y del azúcar* in Cuba as something specific to the country's hybridism, is transferred by immigrants of Spanish origin when they emigrate to the United States of America, especially to places like Tampa in Florida and New York. Prudencio explains that the monopoly of the cigar business in the city does not belong to immigrants of Cuban origin with Spanish roots, but to Spaniards who, although some may have connections with the island, for the most part, have never been to Cuba but have internalized the cigar business as something intrinsically connected to their Spanish culture. It is this Cuban hybridism of tobacco within the Spanish and American cultures that makes the case of the *teverianos* unique. However, according to Prudencio, there is an aura of shame surrounding the cigar business that he does not understand. For little Prudencio, his father's shop is an idyllic place, a colorful store with cigarette boxes, hookahs, and lighters that provide the shop with a magical atmosphere for a boy like him. Moreover, the clientele is wealthy and well-dressed, with an air of superiority that amazes the narrator:

> This used to surprise me—especially in regard to my father—because on the rare visits to his store it had seemed like a wonderful place. It had a broad, rich-looking, nickel-plated counter, neatly stacked with bright colored boxes of cigars, and with shining hookahs and lighters standing along its top. The floor was white tile, and the inside wall of the store was a great mirror. The customers I'd seen had been well-dressed men with booming voices, rich gold chains around their full stomachs, and canes and gloves in their hands. There had been an air of wealth and strength in that store as I remember it. (de Pereda 1960, 3)

Prudencio is nonetheless struck by his father's behavior when he refers to the cigar business and how he disowns it, indicating that he would never allow any of his sons to go into the family business: "If I permit any of my sons to go into this business!" (1960, 4). Little Prudencio claims to admire his father for his ideas; however, as a child, he believed that the cigar business was a job he and his brothers were destined for, even though they also considered themselves Americans. According to González López-Briones, "The family ties are so strong for the author, that as his grandparents are not integrated into the American life, he feels a foreigner. This is one of the main features of the novel" (1997, 122). When de Pereda inhabits the novel as little Prudencio, he transmits this feeling of in-betweenness. He connects his status as a Spaniard and as an American with the work of Spaniards as *teverianos* in the United States, a hybrid profession because of the amalgam of cultures that have encountered each other. In this case, the Spanish with the Cuban and the dominant Anglo-Saxon American.

But then, what is a *teveriano* according to little Prudencio, the narrator? Is it simply selling cigars of dubious origin and quality? As the reader can see, the definition of *teveriano* depends on each character's point of view. For most of the Spaniards in the colony, like Prudencio's father and Don José, being a *teveriano* is a curse. For Agapito, it is one of the most fascinating jobs and a fine way of earning a living and becoming a rich man in order to return to Spain and live as a wealthy man. And to little Prudencio, it seems that it is a mixture, like his hybrid persona, of both things. At the beginning of the story, the reader must wait for a few pages for the protagonist to introduce the figure of his grandfather, Don José, and discover that, indeed, little Prudencio's family lives off the cigar business, but that there is a very specific job, the *teveriano*, that seems to be even more unfortunate than the others. Little Prudencio's father and uncles seem to work at their cigar shop, and it is left to Don José to face the daily arduous task of being a *teveriano* in the streets of New York City.

Little Prudencio, however, does not care what his family thinks. He is in an acculturation phase at this stage of the novel, and the Spanish culture is still the main part of his identity: "I had heard all this at home—listening eagerly because the *teveriano* was certainly the most interesting of all the cigar men—but I'd never been able to connect the fabulous stories of *teverianos* with my mild, sad grandfather" (6). For little Prudencio, the concept of *teveriano* is positive, defining it as an ideal possibility that Spanish immigrants have of obtaining a job in the metropolis, and this is personified by the figure of Agapito. Agapito López represents everything little Prudencio imagines the perfect *teveriano* to be. He is young, intelligent, and elegant. Agapito is the most successful of the *teverianos* in the Spanish community and is, therefore, admired by the protagonist and, at the same time, envied by the rest of the Spanish *teverianos*: "I did envy Agapito's good fortune, but it was hard for me to feel bitter against Agapito personally as many Spaniards did" (50). Prudencio is aware of this imbalance between what he thinks and what others think, and yet he remains faithful to his idyllic definition of the term and of the character, not without contradictions. As the story unfolds, it is up to the reader to create their own definition of what a *teveriano* is, so its meaning may be as varied as their interpretations. *It is important to note* that the word *teveriano* is a Spanish term that cannot be translated as such, and the narrator chooses not to do so. As a result, if being a Spanish immigrant in the United States, and more specifically in New York City, is to be an "Americaniard," being an Americaniard who engages in the cigar business selling door-to-door is to be a *teveriano*.

4.1.2. From Andalusia to Brooklyn

De Pereda, son of Spanish immigrants, spoke both English and Spanish fluently. He was bilingual and, as a result, was able to write in the two languages interchangeably. He served, for example, in the U.S. Army from 1941 to 1944 as a Spanish language censor of letters for the U.S. Bureau of Censorship. He was also a translator and translated Alberto Gerchunoff's *Jewish Gauchos of the Pampas* from the Spanish in 1953. De Pereda experienced biculturalism both as an immigrant descendant and as an author in New York City, inhabiting his works as a character himself. Most of his manuscript collection is in English, as well as his three only novels: *All the Girls We Loved* (1948), *Fiesta* (1954), and *Windmills in Brooklyn* (1960).[66] As mentioned before, the three main characters in his last work, *Windmills*

66 Prudencio De Pereda Papers: 1935–1973. Manuscript Collection. MS-01107. Harry Ransom Center: University of Texas at Austin.

in Brooklyn, represent a different way of integrating the English language, as they are all culturally Spanish individuals. The protagonist's grandfather, Don José, is an old Spanish immigrant who was forced by his wife's family to migrate to the United States and become a *teveriano*. Don José does not speak much English and finds it difficult to integrate into New York society. The fact that he does not speak much of the language hinders him in his work, and he does not manage to become a successful *teveriano* like Agapito. On the other hand, in matters of linguistic hybridization, Agapito represents the successful assimilation of a Spanish immigrant into American society.

Although it is mentioned that he has a strong Spanish accent in English, he can speak it fluently and even takes advantage of the fact that everyone knows he is an immigrant to play dumb and fool those who want to take advantage of him because of his status as a newcomer. Finally, there is the case of little Prudencio himself. As a son of Spanish immigrants living in a community surrounded by his nationals in New York City, he is, like the author himself, bilingual. Agapito's company makes little Prudencio participate in a series of quixotic adventures, already hinted by the title of the book, where the young boy, sometimes in the company of his grandfather, experiences mechanics more typical of the stories of *El Lazarillo de Tormes* or *Don Quijote de la Mancha* than of the American metropolis. The character of little Prudencio chooses a controlled assimilation where his Spanish identity is mainly preserved by the Spanish language that he still uses to communicate with his family, especially with his grandparents, as well as to maintain a kind of umbilical cord with his culture of origin where respect for the elderly, a peculiar attitude towards death (also present in Morell's work), and the typical stereotypes of the United States about Spain are intertwined to build this novel.

Windmills in Brooklyn is written in English with some Spanish words to highlight when the Spanish characters speak in their mother tongue, which is most of the time, and also to emphasize their identity as Spanish immigrants. However, when the characters speak in English, the narrator makes sure that the reader notices it: "I heard the big man say something to Grandfather that Grandfather didn't answer. 'No speak English, eh?' the big man said, and laughed" (de Pereda 1960, 14). On this occasion, the worker at the bar uses the lack of English to construct the "other" out of the figure of Don José, who does not speak the language. It is used by the worker to identify Don José as an immigrant at the same time that he tries to take advantage of Agapito, as he thinks that he is Cuban and, therefore, inferior to him and easy to take advantage of. This "otherness" creates a border inside the "Third Space" of New York City where those who speak English think that they are in control of the space since they control the language of the culture of dominance in the metropolis. This barrier is overcome by Agapito, who learns the language and uses his picaresque skills to move from English to Spanish, from the dominant culture to the dominated culture of "the other," depending on the situation and the economic profit that he can make. De Pereda demonstrates that whoever wants to succeed in the United States must move in-between, using English when necessary, depending on the context and the moment.

The knowledge of a language is a good example of how this transition between cultures evolves in the Spanish immigrants and their descendants. In Smokowski, Rose, and Bacallao's "Acculturation and Latino Family Processes: How Cultural Involvement, Biculturalism, and Acculturation Gaps Influence Family Dynamics" (2008), the authors explain that "children of immigrants tend to acquire English as their primary language… more rapidly than their parents" (2008, 296). They also point out that young immigrant descendants usually become, as in the case of little Prudencio and his grandfather, translators of their family elders (296). However, this does not mean that new generations are not willing to preserve their culture of origin, but rather how they have opted to assimilate to thrive and become more mature at a young age (296). According to Rueda,

> asistimos, en muchos casos, a la protección consciente de sus valores propios, por considerar que merece la pena conservarlos: la lengua española (aunque se propugna un bilingüismo siempre enriquecedor), la estructura fundamental de la familia, la religión, los usos y costumbres (1993, 181).[67]

Prudencio's father, like his grandfather, belongs to the first generation of immigrants. However, unlike his grandfather, little Prudencio notes

67 "We are witnessing, in many cases, the conscious protection of their own values, because they are considered worth preserving: the Spanish language (although bilingualism, which is always enriching, is advocated), the fundamental structure of the family, religion, customs and traditions."

that his father speaks very good Spanish: "He once said, in his correct, intense Spanish" (1960, 4). Besides admiring his father for his ideas, as a young boy, little Prudencio notices that language plays an important role in his life. As most second-generation Spanish immigrants, he speaks both English and Spanish perfectly. Thus, language becomes the peak of biculturalism for him. As a Spanish immigrant descendant, little Prudencio, who is fluent in both Spanish, his family's tongue, and English, the most widely spoken language in the United States, will always live in two realities. This will create an ambivalent relationship between his culture of origin and the sociocultural state of mind created by the country of reception, a cultural hybridism that is understood both by first- and second-generation immigrants and used by them to assimilate at ease: "Going to Grandmother's had some responsibility, for... I know I would often have to act as a translator" (1960, 5). This indicates that little Prudencio's mastery of English and Spanish is equal, and, therefore, there is a clear case of bilingualism that will accompany the protagonist throughout his process of transculturation: first, Prudencio in New York, and then Ros in Mozares.

In *Windmill in Brooklyn*, most of the time there are no Spanish words, and the reader must interpret the situation to decide if they are using one language or another. For example, when Agapito leaves little Prudencio and his grandfather alone at the bar to get more boxes of cigars, Don José addresses his grandson in Spanish, even though the whole dialogue is written in English in the text:

> I could smell the whiskey on his breath as he bent down. 'Get thee out of here,' he said. 'Act as if thou art going calmly.' My grandfather always used the familiar 'thee' with us, and his voice was calm and easy now, but I could see that he was sweating badly" (1960, 14--15).

It is said at the beginning of the book that Don José only speaks a few words in English; by deduction, the reader knows that Don José is speaking in Spanish and the "thee" to which little Agapito refers is the informal "tú" to address people in a familiar way in the Spanish language.

The use of the Spanish words in *Windmills in Brooklyn* is scarce and not accidental. De Pereda uses them when he wants to underline something special about the text, but the use of words is almost anecdotal, with sentences such as "Agapito Lopez was born in a little *pueblo* in Galicia" or " 'Until Saturday night, *hijo*,' he said." The truth is that de Pereda's characters, like the author himself, inhabit the "Third Space" of New York City, and they move smoothly in a narration almost fully written in English where little Spanish is present.

4.1.3. The Tragedy at Mozares

Fiesta is also written in English; however, it has more Spanish words than *Windmills in Brooklyn*, even some short sentences, although the narrator always offers a translation: " 'No sabia, Tía.' He had known she was sick; he had not realized it was real" (de Pereda 1953, 14). Set in Spain, the reader knows that the characters are actually speaking Spanish. As in the case of *Windmills in Brooklyn*, most of the time the characters do not even use Spanish words at all, but because of the context, the reader understands that they are always speaking in Spanish: "Her voice sounded just like Aunt Felipa's as he remembered it, but heard over a clear, long-distance phone or through a tunnel" (15). Sometimes, it is the omniscient narrator who translates the words, " 'Well. Very well! Guapa. Muy guapa!' Beautiful, he thought. Very beautiful" (32), and sometimes they are just left untranslated: "No, *hombre*, you don't" (33). However, *it is important to highlight* that the use of Spanish words in *Fiesta*, unlike *Windmills in Brooklyn*, is constant, and the reader is aware of it.

Americaniards' use of English instead of the Spanish languages in *Windmills in Brooklyn* indicates that Spanish immigrants are adapting to the "Third Space" of New York City by assimilating the *importance* of the language of dominance as part of their assimilation to the Anglo-American culture. This is manifested in the workplace: Agapito has been quick to learn English since his arrival in the United States; he understands that if he wants to be a successful *teveriano* and better than the rest of the Spaniards around him, he must speak English. This is reflected soon in Agapito's success in his job: "Only Agapito did well. He did as fabulously as ever, and it seemed more than ironic to my family that he should continue to send his money home instead of trying to get into the 'big' money" (de Pereda 1960, 49).

Although Agapito formally acculturates to the American culture and begins this process by learning English, he always maintains his Spanish identity, and when he reaches his neoculturation stage, he keeps considering himself Spanish, although he has changed, and his job is in New York:

> Agapito was a Spaniard and he lived in Spain. America was the place he worked in; being a *teveriano* was just a job that he did well. He had no illusions about America, and so he hadn't been disappointed or fooled as we all had (49).

Agapito's hybridity is the proof of the successful cultural transformation of a Spanish immigrant represented in de Pereda's work. The other clear example is that of Prudencio/Ros, although in this case the process is slower and will take de Pereda's alter ego several decades to achieve hybridity. The hybrid language used by Don José, Prudencio, and Agapito in *Windmills in Brooklyn* is not present in *Fiesta* as the "Third Space" is located in Mozares, where there is no need for Ros to use English. As a result, the hybridity is only in the writing of the story, as the whole novel is in English, but the reader knows that the events narrated actually happened in Spanish.

4.2. Claude Morell's *The Lower East Side Kid That Made It Good*

> My father was quite proficient with Sicilian because it was very similar to our *Valenciano*
>
> — *Claude Morell, The Lower East Side Kid That Made It Good*

This opening quotation alludes to Morell's family's bilingualism from Spain. One interesting aspect of the biculturation of Morell's novel is the numerous references to the use of language that can be found. According to him, the Valencian language is internalized in his family as something normal. Unlike the rest of the works analyzed, on this occasion, the narrator, and sole protagonist of the story, starts from a Spanish bilingualism where the Spanish and the Valencian languages are spoken at home thanks to the fact that Morell's family is of Valencian origin, like many of the Spaniards who immigrated to New York City during the first decades of the twentieth century:

> I was born in Spain on November, 12th 1928 in a little village named ORBA on the Mediterranean coast. The province is called ALICANTE. It is one of the three provinces which comprise the region of VALENCIA. I did not stay in Orba very long. The following year on October, 5th 1929, eleven months after my birth, I arrived in the United States to begin on the luckiest journey of my life. (Morell 2008, 1)

The author recalls that his father made wine for about twenty-five years, between 1936 and 1960. He started three years after the end of prohibition and became quite successful. One of the reasons for this success could be found in his ability to learn languages. Morell's father was a polyglot who spoke Sicilian, Valencian, English and Spanish, which made him an excellent businessman, not only in dealing with those who spoke English, the language of the dominant American culture in the metropolis, but also among other Spaniards who had businesses related to catering, and even Italians, especially those of Sicilian origin.

In relation to the Italians, Morell, as González does in discussing the German accent of Mr. Ahrens in *Pinnick Kinnick Hill*, transcribes the words of *La Bossa*, Claude's father's boss at work, before moving from 54 Market Street to 100th Street: "Before we departed *La Bossa* told him with that lovable Italian accent, 'Joe, YU GONNA HAV A LOTTA TRUBLE IN DATTA PLACE', and she was right!" (37). The fact that the narrator transcribes the Italian accent with which *La Bossa* advises his father not to move corresponds with Braidotti's statement when she speaks of the polyglot nomadic subject as "a linguistic nomad," "a specialist of the treacherous nature of language, of any language" (Braidotti 2011, 29). Morell transcribes the interaction in English using the Italian accent of his neighbor to convey the crossing of cultures confirmed by the linguistic hybridization of the inhabitants of New York that lived during his youth in the metropolis in an immigrant neighborhood where Spaniards and Italians communicated with each other in English, as the dominant language, instead of doing it in their own languages, despite the similarities between Spanish and Italian. In this way, both Claude and his father could cross linguistic borders, the dividing lines of the borderlands, to assimilate into the multilingual American migrant culture. The fact that the family lived in Little Italy with immigrants, mostly Catholics, from Italy, Spain, Ireland, and Poland, made the integration of the family even more successful, to the point of participating in other immigrants' festivals, such as the San Gennaro Festival celebrated by Italians in September:

> It was called the San Gennaro Festival. Various activities took place on several days, but what I enjoyed the most was walking from Bayard Street to Houston Street, with lots of people around me and looking at the variety of stands on my left and right. They consisted of many games of accuracy with balls and shot/guns, card games, and lotteries, etc. If you were successful you were rewarded with money, a toy or a doll. The most appetizing stand had to be the one with Italian sausages, smothered with peppers and onions, or meatballs immersed in a thick tomato sauce. My choice was inserted into Italian bread, and while I was

> waiting impatiently for my change of money, half the bread and its ingredients had disappeared into my mouth! (Morell 2008, 10)

The multiculturalism of the immigrant community in Little Italy was led by a group of "others," individuals that, like the Spaniards, came from the south of Europe but in greater numbers, the Italians. As part of the control exerted by the Anglo-American culture in New York City, there were also neighborhoods controlled by the dominated cultures, subjugated by the mainstream culture, but which could dominate other cultures in turn. These situations only occurred in areas where large numbers of immigrants from a particular place were concentrated, creating bubbles of power. Thus, although the Anglo-American culture dominated the metropolis, these dominated cultures built their own power structures, creating small imagined communities in their own image, as were the cases of Little Italy, Chinatown, or Little Spain.

When Claude Morrell was four years old, he went to the apartment of Mr. and Mrs. Nardone, who were the tenants, and saw that the door was open. Claude entered the house and saw Mrs. Nardone's father in a corner of the living room, in an open coffin: "I was puzzled and frightened, so I left the apartment and quickly descended the stairs" (Morell 2008, 13). He went down to talk to his parents because he was scared and did not know what he had seen: "When I arrived at my apartment on the ground floor, I immediately described to my parents, in Spanish, what was happening on the fifth floor" (13). The fact that he spoke to his parents in Spanish is relevant because it shows that they had spoken to him in this language since he was born. The narrator rarely mentions the language he speaks in each situation, but it can be deduced from this and other similar situations that he always spoke to his parents in Spanish or Valencian. His parents also spoke to him in these languages, and their interaction at home must have always been like this:

> Thoughtfully, and with care, my mother explained that he had died and was going to heaven in the sky. I understood the word *CIELO* (heaven in Spanish), but I had never heard the word *MUERTO* (dead in Spanish), nor what it meant! (13).

Another relevant example of the use of language appears in one of the adventures that Claude's father and his uncle experienced in New York City during their first visit. They wanted to find a job as soon as possible, so they approached a group of men working with picks and shovels on a long ditch in the street. It was the very first week of their arrival, and they did not speak any English, so they had to use sign language to indicate to the foreman that they wanted to work:

> He smiled and coarsely made them understand where to purchase a peak and a shovel at a nearby corner. In a few minutes they were back with the newly purchased tools. The workers in the ditch looked up and instantly began to laugh. To them, this was hilarious. Here they were, with newly acquired tools, purchased with the limited money they possessed, and to be ridiculed and humiliated! Was it a terrible joke or a misunderstanding? Maybe he assumed that they wanted to buy a pig and a shovel for personal reasons! This was a sad day for two ambitious young men. (22)

Morell does not clarify whether what happened to his father and his father's uncle was a misunderstanding or a joke of the foreman and his men, but everything seemed to indicate that it was more the latter than the former, since the Spaniards did not get the job; they spent the little money they had on a pick and a shovel, and, in the end, the narrator indicates that it was a sad day for both. Moreover, Morell continues his description of "lost in translation" situations in which misunderstandings, teasing, and difficulties due to not speaking English were not uncommon: "Because of language difficulties, many immigrants that arrived in the United States were subjected to numerous unfortunate incidents; some were embarrassing, others were sad, and some were funny" (22). In the theory of the Third Space, language is essential to understand the real borders that divide the dominant culture and the dominated one. In *The Lower East Side Kid That Made It Good*, Morell stresses the *importance* of language to communicate with the new dominant language of the new American community still in construction. Spaniards, like many other immigrants who arrived in the United States, find it difficult to learn a new language and are often victims of the language barrier. Morell is aware of that division, as his hybrid persona allows him to understand both sides of this cultural clash. Morell, as narrator, transfers to paper the testimony of his father and his father's uncle during their first trips to the metropolis. This first part of the author's biography is based on the memory and recollections of his elders, who tell him about the greatest difficulties they encountered, including learning English.

In relation to the author's own use of Spanish in his adolescence through the 1940s, the narrator gives some tips about the possibility of still using it outside the family circle with his teenage friends of Spanish origin:

> The total group consisted of many people, exceeding more than 25 persons. Most of us were first generation children of immigrants from Spain. I will give a partial list of names: Manny Zapata, Henry Portela, Sonny Gonzalez, Pepe Paz, Manny Suarez, Oscar Bilbao, David Suarez, Joe Estrada and many more. Some of the girls were: Marie Gonzalez, Emily Portela, and the three sisters, consisting if Carmen, Rose and Dolores Suarez. (Morell 2008, 90–91)

The fact that most of these teenagers were of Spanish origin and all of them had a Hispanic last name could indicate that Spanish was still spoken among them and that Morell kept a good Spanish-speaking level through the 1940s. However, that must not have been enough for his parents, who decided to send him to the Spanish Benevolent Society-La Nacional on 14th Street to learn Spanish grammar. As Morell points out,

> My folks not only wanted me to be proficient in the English language, but they were also convinced that I should have the capacity not only to speak, but to read and write the Spanish language. I totally agreed on this matter. (121)

Young Claude had the possibility to continue his cultural transition as a hybrid person through language thanks to his parents' use of Valencian and Spanish at home, his contact with other Spanish-speaking children, and a Spanish professor, Don Vidal y Plana, "who had taught for many years at the university in Madrid, Spain" (121). Don Vidal taught him Spanish at La Nacional with twenty other students, "the majority of [whom] where not Spaniards" (Morell 2008, 122). According to Morell, "The grammar was invaluable and has been an asset throughout my life, not only in Spanish but in the use of the English language" (122), which only reinforces Braidotti's postulates on the figure of the polyglot nomadic subject and their ability to create the cultural and linguistic identity necessary to navigate the time and location of New York City, where a "Third Space" is created by the Spanish immigrants.

4.3. Gavin W. González's *Pinnick Kinnick Hill, An American Story*

> And when Juan brought out some English stories and began to read, the family would sit entranced, listening to his modulated voice translate the English script into the Castilian tongue.
>
> —*Gavin W. González, Pinnick Kinnick Hill*

Las colinas sueñan en español and *Kinnick Hill, An American Story* represent the two versions of a narrative that cannot be understood if read only in English or in Spanish. The manuscript, originally written in the former language, includes numerous words and phrases in the latter one, indicating the writer's intention to incorporate code-switching, so amply used by Spanish immigrants in the zinc community. This code-switching also appears when the protagonist is still in Spain:

> "Que hay, Juanito? Como se siente?"[68]
> "It's just a small punture. It'll be all right in a day or so." (González 2003, 21)

The fact that González includes these leaps from English to Spanish and from Spanish to English, even when the action takes place in Asturias, is not only curious but also demonstrates how González himself, as narrator and secondary protagonist of the novel, inhabits the "Third Space" both in Harrison County and in the Spanish region. Throughout the novel in English, it is normal to find some clarifications from the narrator about the meaning of the Spanish words or phrases scattered in the novel. This shows that the author's main intention is to address his work to an English-speaking audience, but not always, which suggests that some knowledge of Spanish and Spanish culture is expected on the part of the reader:

> Emilio planned to open a grocery, where he would sell imported products from Spain. They would include garbanzos, azafrán, alpargatas as well as chorizo, longaniza, callos, morcilla and regular staples of canned goods, sugar, and other common items. There was such a store in St. Louis being run by a former resident of Naveces. (2003, 35)

This language alteration is not apparent in the Spanish-translated version of the work, which detracts from the author's original intention to be read in English but offers the monolingual Spanish reader the opportunity to read the work.

González's manuscript presents the bilingual reader with the possibility of alternating the process of reading from one language to the other, and the translation, although correct, makes the nuances of the original version, which contains a greater linguistic richness condensed in the use of Spanish as a secondary accompaniment to the narration of the events that take

68 "What's up, Juanito? How are you feeling?"

place. However, this use of code-switching gets lost in the Spanish version. Thus, for example, during the 1909 strike of the Spanish workers in the factory, when the plant's superintendent, the German-born Otto Ahrens, arrives at night at Juan's house, the narrator is talking about his father's chores: "Father was kept busy going out to the farms to buy the beef cattle that he would dress out in the field, and in raising a family" (49). The original dialogue in English is as follows: "Father greeted the man by saying, 'Bienvenido, Señor Ahrens. Esta es su casa.' 'Buenas noches, John.[69] I have come up the mountain to ask of you a favour' " (53). In the Spanish version, the protagonist's switch from Spanish to English is not noticeable, as he translates the entire sentence into Spanish and its corresponding punctuation: "Mi padre saludó al hombre diciendo: 'Bienvenido, Señor Ahrens. Esta es su casa.' 'Buenas noches, John. He subido a la montaña para pedirte un favor' " (52).[70] Similarly, as the conversation continues, the narrator refers to Mr. Ahrens' thick German accent, even indicating by writing how it sounds to him:

> "I vill come to the point," Ahrens said in his accented English. "I vood like to find out vat it is your countrymen vant from me. Dey all valk out and I don't understand all dey vant."
> My father replied, "What they want, I already know. They cannot afford to be spending the greater part of their checks on shoes and work clothing. It's that simple."
> "Vy they don't tell me? Ve can settle this matter vithout work stoppage. Vill you try to help me get the men back to vork?"
> "I will be glad to do my best. Let me get you some beer." (González 2003, 53)

However, when we compare the original version of this dialogue with the translated version, the German accent disappears. The translator does not bother to replicate the possible phonetic transcription of Mr. Anrens's English into the Spanish language. As a result, the dialogue is poorer and unfunny:

> "Iré directamente al grano –dijo Ahrens con su peculiar y marcado acento en inglés—. Quisiera que usted se enterara de lo que quieren sus paisanos de mí. Están todos en huelga y no entiendo lo que quieren."

---

69 'Welcome, Mr. Ahrens. This is your home.' 'Good evening, John.'
70 My father greeted the man saying, 'Welcome, Mr. Ahrens. This is your home.' 'Good evening, John. I've come up the mountain to ask a favor of you.'

> Mi padre replicó: "Lo que quieren, ya lo sé. No se pueden permitir gastarse la mayor parte de su salario en zapatos y ropas de trabajo. Así de simple."
> "¿Por qué no me lo dicen? Se puede arreglar este asunto sin necesidad de parar el trabajo. ¿Me ayudará usted a hacer que los hombres vuelvan a emprender el trabajo?"
> "Me agradará hacer lo que pueda. Déjeme que le traiga algo de cerveza." (González 2003, 52)

This failed translation of Mr. Ahrens's accent and use of code-switching will be repeated every time the plant's superintendent intervenes, but it is not the only case. On the other hand, the fact that Mr. Ahrens must talk to Juan Villanueva because his workers do not speak English and Mr. Ahrens speaks little Spanish shows that the process of acculturation of the workers in the zinc factory is delayed due to the isolated situation in the furnace. This loss in translation choices is just an example of the *importance* of the original version of the text, which is necessary to understand González's work in all its splendor and whose translation, although useful for non-English speakers, is not sufficient to cover the linguistic aspects represented in a novel about Spanish immigrants in West Virginia. The shortcomings of the Spanish version of the narrative allow the reader to understand the importance of the original manuscript, which projects in its pages a more truthful and useful version for those who wish to know the effect of transculturation on Spanish immigrants in the United States and its literary representation.

4.4. María Dueñas's Calle 14

> Saludó entre los aplausos, soltó unas frases en inglés que ellas no entendieron pero que debían de ser bastante graciosas porque todo el mundo las acogió con una monumental carcajada.
>
> — *María Dueñas, Las hijas del Capitán*

Las hijas del Capitán is the only work analyzed here that was written almost entirely in Spanish. Except for a few isolated phrases in the novel, "we have the best prices in town" (Dueñas 2018, 36), "You know what I mean, right?" (186), and so on, the rest is narrated from the point of view of a third-person omniscient narrator who knows everything about the characters and what is going to happen and who uses the Spanish language to tell the story. One of the defining elements of the "Third Space" is language. The fact that the author has decided to write the experience of immigration to the United States in Spanish from the point of view of the Arenas sisters offers a different point of view from the other works analyzed here. Dueñas created a representation of migration literature in this novel but with little representation of the English language and, therefore, of code-switching, although throughout the novel, references are made to this switch from Spanish to English by several of the characters who interact with the Arenas sister:

> Si los meneos del bus le ponían a Mona difícil seguir el hilo narrativo, tampoco la ayudaba el acento de este hijo de puertorriqueños nacido ya en Manhattan que a veces decía cosas con un acento y unas palabras que ella no entendía, y otras veces dudaba y se atascaba y se iba al inglés y después tenía que retroceder para volver a intentarlo. (Dueñas 2018, 210)[71]

On this occasion, for example, Mona's contact with Fidel Hernández, the Puerto Rican who worked in the family business at the funeral parlor and organized the burial of Emilio Arenas and imitated Carlos Gardel singing in El Chico, takes place with a dialogue in Spanish. The young man, son of the owner of Funerarias Hernández and fervent admirer of Carlos Gardel, shares Luz's artistic aspirations but also supports Mona in her project to transform Las Hijas del Capitán into a nightclub, becoming an active participant in the reform. He is the unconditional friend and the secret admirer of the youngest of the sisters. To help them as much as possible, he sacrifices hours of work, endures parental scolding, and pulls strings. He shows how close the coexistence between Spaniards and the other part of Hispanic immigration is. However, although both speak Spanish, Mona herself refers to the fact that on occasions the boy would switch to English, and this is something that is not reflected in the text as in other works, as was the case in the original English version of González's *Pinnick Kinnick Hill, An American Story*, where these code-switching dialogues are shown.

On the other hand, the fact that Dueñas's work is the only fictional one, although its historical background is real, limits the representation of the

71 "If the shakiness of the bus made it difficult for Mona to follow the narrative thread, she was not helped either by the accent of this Manhattan-born son of Puerto Ricans who sometimes said things with an accent and words she didn't understand, and sometimes hesitated and got stuck and switched to English and then had to try again."

use of language by the characters in the story, which makes the narrative simpler. As a result, *Las hijas del Capitán* lacks the characteristic hybridism that the writings of de Pereda, González, Morell, and Alfau use to inhabit the "Third Space," both as writers and protagonists of their own stories, using language as a subjective element of their own where the voice of the authors and the voices of their characters intermingle inside the narration. Dueñas's vision is, therefore, a construct influenced by her status as a writer of the twenty-first century who draws on the memory of the past of these Spanish immigrants to create a reality according to the standards of the present day, although it does not necessarily correspond to an accurate representation but rather to an adapted construction of the process of transculturation experienced by the Americaniards who lived in New York City during the 1930s.

The use of the Spanish language is also connected to identity. The fact that for most of the book, the reader is reminded that Victoria, Luz, and Mona do not speak much English until the epilogue indicates that their identity is tied to the language of their culture of origin. At the beginning of the novel, while they try to reject English, they also attempt to avoid transculturation by limiting their interactions outside the neighborhood and Spanish-speaking communities of the metropolis:

> "Mona seguía metida entre las mantas, con la espalda apoyada contra la pared que hacía las veces de cabecero, el pelo desgreñado como una leona morena y el uniforme de camarera hecho un guiñapo. Sus hermanas llevaban un largo rato hablando como cauces desbocados, arrebatándose una a otra la palabra sin miramientos para ponerla al tanto de lo que ocurrió primero con Sendra y después en Casa María." (Dueñas 2018, 130)[72]

As the story unfolds, however, the sisters become more and more immersed in the city: first by interacting with other Spanish-speaking New Yorkers and then by themselves, embracing their cultural transition and gradually beginning to use some English words. Initially with simple ones, "Ella

72 Mona was still tucked between the blankets, her back against the wall that served as a headboard, her hair disheveled like a brown lioness and her waitress uniform in tatters. Her sisters had been talking for a long time like wildcats, snatching at each other's words without a second thought to fill her in on what had happened first with Sendra and then at Casa Maria.

querría haber sabido replicar en inglés, pero le faltaban las palabras, así que farfulló espontánea entre dientes:—¡Sorry a tu padre, a ver si tienes cuidado, idiota!" (162),[73] and little by little with a few more short sentences: "—Voy yo a pedirlo—anunció Luz queriendo ganar tiempo. Sin esperar respuesta, se acercó al portero con su inglés de los montes—. One taxi, please!"[74] (Dueñas 2018, 427). Throughout the novel, however, Dueñas emphasizes the lack of need, real or not, for Spanish immigrants to use English to move around New York City in the 1930s. The fact that Dueñas's work is not based on the author's life as an immigrant or descendant of immigrants and is only inspired by the historical and cultural context of Spanish migration in the United States implies that linguistic hybridization is hardly represented in the novel. In addition, the fact that *Las hijas del capitan* is the only work originally written in Spanish means that this work of literature has less importance in matters of hybridization and language analysis, which determines its limited impact in this regard.

4.5. Felipe Alfau's *Chromos*: The Spanish New York City Novel

> The moment one learns English, complications set in. Try as one may, one cannot elude this conclusion, one must inevitably come back to it. This applies to all persons, including those born to the language and, at times, even more so to Latins, including Spaniards.
>
> — *Felipe Alfau, Chromos*

The opening of the novel, which is one of the best-known and most repeated quotations of Alfau's masterpiece, is a full-fledged declaration of intentions. The narrator points out that his friend Don Pedro has no problem in stating that while a person who only speaks Spanish is more direct, English speakers do have serious difficulties in their everyday lives because they question their existence and make problems out of the simplest

73 She wished she could have replied in English, but she lacked the words, so she mumbled spontaneously through her teeth: -Sorry to your father, be careful, you idiot!

74 "—I'm going to ask for it—said Luz, trying to gain time. Without waiting for an answer, she approached the doorman with her hillbilly English—. One taxi, please!"

things. On the other hand, Spanish speakers, among whom the author differentiates between Latinos and Spaniards, are described by Don Pedro as less complicated people. Speaking Spanish makes them straightforward and simple, whereas if a Spanish speaker, like a Spaniard, begins to speak English, Don Pedro points out that this "is indeed a most incongruous phenomenon. On the acquisition of this other language, far from increasing his understanding of life, if this were possible, only renders in hopelessly muddled and obscure" (Alfau 1999, 26). The dominant Anglo-American culture is, therefore, directly connected to the English language, while the culture of those who speak Spanish, especially immigrants from across the Atlantic, are more temperate people who tend to make life less complicated and, as a result, enjoy it more. However, when the two worlds collide, it is the Spanish immigrant who suffers the most, as s/he must deal with his/her linguistic hybridization amid his/her cultural transformation.

Felipe Alfau was born in Barcelona in 1902. The son of an upper-middle-class family from Northern Spain, they soon settled in Guernica. At the outbreak of the First World War, the family decided to travel to New York, where they began their journey as members of the Spanish community in the metropolis (Martín Gaite 1993). Alfau wrote four books in his lifetime, all of them in English. *Old Tales from Spain* (1928), a collection of children's short stories in Spain; *Locos: A Comedy of Gestures* (1936), written in 1928, published in 1936; *Chromos*, a continuation of *Locos*, finished in 1948 and published in 1990; and Alfau's final work, *La poesía cursi*, a compilation of poetry written by the author since the beginning of the twentieth century and published in 1992. *Locos* constitutes the first of the author's two novels, a metafictional work about a series of short stories that intersect in the Café de los Locos in early twenty-first-century Toledo. Divided into eight stories, Alfau's *Locos* uses stereotypes to describe both his characters and the comical situations where the action takes place. In *Locos*, the line between the narrator and characters is blurred, and the division between reality and fiction becomes the most innovative aspect of this work, a book where the characters take control of the narrative by choosing their own path.

In the case of Alfau and his work *Chromos*, as indicated before, the entire novel is written in English, as is also the case with Morell's *The Lower East Side Kid that Made it Good*. Alfau's novel lacks the code-switching found in the texts of de Pereda and González, with no exchange from English to Spanish. However, the prose of the book is not standard American English. According to Alfau himself, *Chromos*'s writing style is "half English and half my own creation, the result of an immigrant experience" (Stavans 1993, 151). This Spanish or Iberian English is the result of Alfau's experience as a young immigrant, as he was already a teenager when he moved to the United States of America.

Alfau, the character and narrator, considers that his English skills are not very good, "Well, I don't know about that. My English is not so good" (1999, 56); this leads him to think that he is not ready to write the book in the first place and, much less so, in English. The character even thinks about writing the novel in Spanish abroad, where he considers that the reception could be more favorable:

> I am not thinking of publishing it in Spanish here. I have in mind one or two publishing houses in Latin America, or perhaps even Spain, although I would rather—but what I was really thinking is that you might help me with the English translation. I will show you some other parts I have already written out, even if they still need a little polishing. (1999, 56)

However, the reality is that Alfau did write *Chromos* in English. As a result, the Third Space language that he used combines English writing with his knowledge of the Spanish language, creating a well-written Anglo-dominant language that uses elements of the Spanish-dominated one. This language can be better understood if there is previous knowledge of both English and Spanish on the part of the reader. This means that the phenomenon of the linguistic hybridization of the novel can only be fully appreciated by those who speak both languages and, as a result, by those who have also experienced the phenomenon of such linguistic hybridization.

The quixotic influence exerted by de Pereda's *Windmills in Brooklyn* on Alfau's works can be seen through his characters. In the case of the novel analyzed, *Chromos*, the Cervantine touch is provided by their three main characters: Doctor Don José de los Ríos, Don Pedro Guzman O'Moore Algoracid, nicknamed "The Moor," and the author himself, an unnamed narrator whom Don Pedro de Guzman commissions to write a book, the very same delivered to the readers, about the "Americaniards" (Alfau 1999, vi):

> I am not thinking of publishing it in Spanish here. I have in mind one or two publishing houses in Latin America, or perhaps even Spain, although I would rather—but what I was really thinking is that you might help me with the English translation. I will show you some other parts I have already written out, even if they still need a little polishing (56).

Alfau coins the new term through the character of Doctor Don José de los Ríos, who defines "Americaniards" as those immigrants of Spanish origin who settled in the United States and whose hybridism gave them a new identity between the Spanish culture of origin and the American Anglo-Saxon dominant culture of reception. One of the clearest examples of de Pereda's quixotic influence on Alfau's works is the author's description of Don Pedro at the beginning of the novel:

> He was changeable and he was complicated and, in his manner of speaking, it would have been interesting to trace the wanderings of this complex variable over the subconscious plane and evaluate the integral of his real conclusions. To me, he was an absurd combination of a slightly daffy Irish- Moorish Don Quixote with sinister overtones of Beelzebub and the only Irishman I ever heard speak English with an Andalusian brogue. (Alfau 1999, 10)

The parallels between de Pereda and Alfau are numerous. While it is true that de Pereda was born in New York to Spanish parents and Alfau emigrated from Spain with his parents at a very young age, both lived in the city during the last golden years of Spanish immigration and watched its final decades of the rise in the first half of the twentieth century and its ultimate decline through the second half of it. As de Pereda, Alfau returned to visit Spain during his adulthood. He did it in 1959 when the dictatorship of General Franco was fully established in the country, and Spanish immigrants were opting for immigration to other parts of Europe, such as France, Switzerland, Belgium, the United Kingdom, or Germany (Muñoz Sánchez 2012). Similarly to their characters, both authors are nomadic subjects, "Americaniards" who decided to return to a country that only existed in their minds, a fictional nation that was replicated as mere imagined communities by Spanish immigrants in New York City. In their novels, Alfau and de Pereda reproduced their experience as hybrid selves during the first decades of the twentieth century in the American metropolis. Their characters, like themselves, move in-between worlds, the Spanish and the American Anglo-American culture, building their own as they go through the different stages of transculturation, just like many other Spaniards had done before.

Chromos was completed in 1948 and is set during the 1940s when Alfau was writing the book. In this narration, Spanish immigrants who occupy the Third Space do so because they live in a country that is not their own. The change of location of their native land of origin and the new country of reception changes their identity, as there is a clash between cultures that transforms them into hybrid individuals by also changing their language, which also becomes hybrid. According to Said,

> There are highly significant deformations within the new communities that now exist alongside and partially inside the recently coherent outlines of the world English group, a group that includes the heterogenous voices, various languages, and hybrid forms that give the Commonwealth its distinctive and still problematic identity. (1990, 6)

Outside the Commonwealth but inside the English-speaking world, there is another country: the United States of America. In this country, Spanish immigrants can also experience "deformations" that change the individual into a new hybrid person, but it seems to have a negative meaning for Said, who uses this term instead of "transformations," a much more positive term as to the cultural transformation of the new communities. In the period when Alfau wrote *Chromos*, this "transformation," or "deformation" as Said points out, went on happening for decades, although the sap of the new generations has become less and less relevant as their numbers continued to decline due to the new immigration laws that affected the number of Spaniards who could arrive in the country and the issue of citizenship. As a result, Alfau's work focuses not so much on the lives of those newly arrived Spanish immigrants who have to make a living and search for a place to work and live in, but also on the experience of three individuals fully settled in New York society who move in-between cultures.

On the other hand, the character of the Spanish immigrant and writer García, a friend of the narrator's and obsessed with the style of *Chromos*, represents Alfau's intention to minimize the *importance* of his style by creating a character who shares the narrator's interest in the novel while, at the same time, allowing the writer to inhabit the Third Space as an author/narrator writing and describing a novel and reviewing it as the reader reads it:

> He was looking at me again in that way that suggested that I would wind up doing a lot of translating and perhaps a little collaborating too, although Garcia was quite impervious to suggestions, and I did not relish the thought. Translating being my business and means of livelihood, I am naturally disinclined to take on extra work, particularly of doubtful remuneration. Besides Garcia knows as much English as I do and is a professional writer which I am not. Maybe he likes to read to me and tell me stories. (1999, 77)

Alfau even allows himself at this point to joke and ridicule his own ability as a writer by giving García a predominant role in the construction of the narrator's work, thus creating a constant presence inside and outside the Third Space that Alfau seems to enjoy, while the reader becomes a participant in the construction of two different and, at the same time, equal works. Alfau's narrative is self-conscious. He chooses to immerse himself with the reader to understand the complications of speaking two languages while living in-between cultures, sometimes even three. Many of the Spaniards who arrived in the United States during the first half of the twentieth century spoke not only Spanish but also the language of the region or province from which they came, as was the case of Galicians like Agapito, Valencians like Claude Morell, or Basques like García.

In this regard, the narrator alludes to the trilingualism of his friend, for which he uses the flashback of the vacation time that García enjoyed in a small village of Vizcaitia[75] as a kid, where some local neighbors, Lanky Chapelo and El Gorriti, used both Spanish and the Basque language, or "vascuence," to communicate with each other. El Gorriti was the owner of the village's tavern of the same name. He also owned the *frontón* where the villagers used to play what the narrator describes as handball, probably referring to the Basque game or "pelota vasca," and kids used to go see them play:

> Besides there were always a few ball players drinking in the tavern of the Gorriti who also owned the frontón and it was good to listen to their talk about the game as the kids admired the players very much. (Alfau 1999, 58)

Lanky Chapelo was not a very good one except when he had a good day. When Little García and his friend entered the tavern, they noticed that both friends were having a conversation:

---

75 Vizcaya

> He was talking to el Gorriti in Spanish and el Gorriti answered little and in Vascuence. They all could speak Vascuence and el Gorriti could also speak Spanish, but they always spoke Spanish and el Gorriti was the only one around who spoke Vascuence most of the time (61).

Alfau points out that some of these immigrants from Biscay were fluent in both languages and could indulge in constant code-switching if both the speaker and their companions spoke both languages. When the Basque immigrants arrived in the United States, they learned English but kept speaking Spanish to other Spaniards and "vascuence" to those Basques who also spoke their regional language.

Chapter 5: Cultural Hybridization and the Creation of the Americaniard

> There was another man behind the counter, standing further back. He had his jacket off and his sleeves rolled up, but he didn't have an apron on. He was a big man with a red face, and he was smoking a big cigar. He had a gold chain across his vest and two big rings on his right hand, and he looked like one of my father's rich customers. When I stared at him, he winked at me and laughed. He'd been watching Agapito and my grandfather, who were leaning on the counter with their feet on the brass rail. Agapito had been talking in Spanish and laughing as he and my grandfather drank their whiskey.
>
> The big man walked up to them slowly and patted the cigar boxes. Agapito turned his head suddenly, in surprise, and then smiled at the big man and bowed to him.
>
> —*Prudencio de Pereda, Windmills in Brooklyn*

My analysis of the representation of American literature on Spanish immigration in the United States is focused on the spaces chosen by the respective authors in the texts selected: New York City in the State of New York, Harrison County in the State of West Virginia, in the United States, and Mozares, in the province of Burgos, Spain. Cultural transformation marked by the combination of the Spanish culture of origin and the Anglo-American culture of reception in the United States of the time gave rise to the creation of a new individual defined by Alfau as the Americaniard, a new American individual of Spanish origin who lives in the States intermingling in both cultures. The process of transformation from the acculturation stage to the neoculturation stage means that the Spanish migrants can be aligned as "the Other" by the ideologists of the dominant culture while the newcomers accept the new culture and lose part of their culture of origin and finally create a new cultural context where both cultures are combined to give shape to a new hybrid subject.

It could be argued that, on this occasion, the "Other" can be the Spanish immigrant, or the Americaniard, as the main characters of the selected works are sometimes born in the United States, although they may consider themselves as both Spanish and American. They are portrayed by the authors as individual subjects, under the influence of the dominant Anglo-American culture, who undergo a cultural transformation based on factors such as the age of the immigrant's arrival or the Spanish community they were born into. As a result, the cultural transformation of these characters is different depending on the generation to which they belong (first generation, 1.5 generation, 1.75 generation, second generation, etc.) and the influence of the Spanish culture of origin and the Anglo culture of dominance in their individual lives. "Third Space" writers present their subjective sides of the truth and of the past of Spanish immigration in the United States by creating a narration where the Americaniards may be "othered" in the country as they evolve according to their experiences and the interactions existing between their culture of origin and the culture of reception. The hybrid character created may be excluded or not.

5.1. De Pereda's Memoirs: *Windmills in Brooklyn* and *Fiesta*

As previously mentioned, in de Pereda's *Windmills in Brooklyn*, the narrator's name is never mentioned. Being an autobiographical novel and a Bildungsroman, readers witness the evolution of the protagonist/author from childhood to youth and in *Fiesta* to adulthood. For Ros as de Pereda's alter ego, I have chosen the author's own name, Prudencio, to differentiate him from de Pereda the writer. De Pereda does his best to avoid mentioning the narrator's name, although the construction of the space and time in which the protagonist's life takes place makes it easy to find out who he really is and to notice that the writer is in reality basing the character on himself. Throughout the two parts of the novel, the narrator changes his identity to a hybrid cultural identity. The boundaries of his Spanish culture of origin and his Anglo-American culture of reception are negotiated to create a new individual in-between cultures, in-between identities. In the six texts selected, the boundaries between the main characters are constantly redefined as they are culturally transformed.

As a result, while at the beginning of the novel little Prudencio identified himself mainly as a Spaniard, "We were Spanish" (de Pereda 1960, 3), he wrote, having been raised in a family of Andalusian origin where both parents and grandparents were part of a community of Spanish immigrants, partially rejecting his American identity, his evolution becomes more complicated as he left his immediate environment and ventured into the metropolis: "We took a trolley—an open summer trolley—and stayed on till the end of the line, and I saw that we'd come to the dock section" (8). This first adventure with his grandfather Don José and Agapito, the first of many to come, transforms little Prudencio's view of the *teveriano*'s world. The first element that proves this change is happening is language, as he uses Spanish only at home with his family and his friend Agapito, while English is used to move freely in the metropolis, without even leaving any trace of his Spanish origin. The development of his life shows how an Americaniard like little Prudencio connected to the typical values that were assumed of a Spanish immigrant family of Andalusian origin abroad: respect for elders, the *importance* of the family, and religiosity, evident in the first two vital stages of his life.

Religion is always present in de Pereda's characters. In the case of Prudencio, it is the Catholic religion. His help in the church at mass determines the character's childhood and youth, especially in his relationship with death. That connection between religion and death is present both in *Windmills in Brooklyn* and in *Fiesta*, as little Prudencio seems to prophesize the future of the adult Ros Varona when he mentions his fear of death:

> Death had always been and important part of life in the Spanish colony. I had felt it as a child, without knowing why. When I began to study Spain and read Spanish authors, I saw that death had always been an obsession with the Spanish people. To the Spaniard, "death, too, is a fiesta," says V.S. Pritchett, and the important thing here is the special meaning that the word "fiesta" has for the Spaniard, and for Pritchett. (1960, 91)

However, this is not only a reference to the protagonist and the rest of the Spaniards' view of death in *Windmills in Brooklyn*. De Pereda, through his young narrator's self, connects the novel with *Fiesta*, chronologically posterior in his Bildungsroman but written six years before. De Pereda lives in Little Prudencio, as he already knows that a *fiesta* is going to end in death. The narrator seems to allude to the tragic outcome of the *fiesta* in Mozares and its inhabitants in which he participated.

Death is also present in little Prudencio's life through the figure of Agapito. Agapito is not from Andalusia, like the narrator's family, but from Galicia, and when the Spanish Civil War starts in 1936, Agapito decides to take his family to New York City. However, when they migrate from Spain,

Agapito's younger son dies of an attack of appendicitis in Nova Scotia, and his second youngest son, fourteen at the time, dies of pneumonia soon after (90). Despite these events, the narrator says that he was always afraid of death anyway, but, nevertheless, he always enjoyed attending the Spanish wakes with respect:

> There were two main groups at these wakes: the people in the front room who sat with the family of the dead around the coffin, and the group in the back rooms that could talk more freely. It was understood that everyone should spend some time with both groups but, toward the late hours of the night, the men usually drifted to the back room and the grieving women stayed in the front. I used to like to sit in the back room because you heard more stories there, about *teverianos* and about Spain. (92)

Little Prudencio's fear of death seems more a matter of respect than psychological, since in both parts of the novel, mention of the death of loved ones is constant in the narrator's mouth. The concepts of death and family constitute the main pillars of the culture of the Spanish immigrants in New York. Thus, for example, before the end of the first part of the novel, the narrator informs that Agapito is going to die, although he will continue to be present throughout the author's youth in the second part of the book:

> Agapito died just before V-J day.[76] I heard later that he had died quietly at home after a short illness, with the sounds of his grandchildren's voices in the next room. The oldest grandson, of course, was named Agapito. Agapito's wife had died a year before, and he was buried with her and his two sons in their family plot in a new cemetery in Queens. He had never gotten back to Spain to live. (95)

Like most immigrants of his generation, Agapito never returned to Spain. As soon as he managed to raise enough money, he took his family to the United States and, at the end of his life, fulfilled his late wife's wish, i.e., to donate her dream house in Galicia to a local order of nuns: "Agapito complied with her wish. He paid for the final furnishings and turned the house over to the nuns" (de Pereda 1960, 95). At the end of the novel, in chapter 6, the narrator mentions that first his grandfather Don José and his grandmother died a few years later (de Pereda 1960, 172), thus closing the story of his youth, marked by the deaths of the two people who best

---

76 V-J day: Victory over Japan Day, 2 September 1945.

represented the Spanish identity and the figure of the two people that the protagonist loved the most.

At the beginning of de Pereda's *Windmills in Brooklyn*, there is a dialogue that introduces the character of Don José, little Prudencio's grandfather,[77] a *teveriano* or street vendor of cigars, one of the most popular and despised jobs that Spanish immigrants began doing when they first arrived in New York City from Spain or from the former Spanish territories of the Caribbean, mainly Cuba, where Spaniards had learned the value and the trade of *habanos*:

> She often criticized Grandfather for his lack of business sense and his otherworldliness, and once when she was doing this to a friend, the woman objected and defended my grandfather. "Don José is a man of great integrity," she said. "That is worth more, much more, than your business sense. He has ideals, like the great man of the world. He is like Quixote, like a true Don Quixote. "Yes," Grandmother said, in her cold, beating way. "A true Don Quixote. Unfortunately for all of us, though, there are no windmills in Brooklyn." "But one can suppose!" the friend said. "One can suppose!" (de Pereda 1960, 1)

Windmills in Brooklyn, like *Fiesta*, is an autobiographical narration where de Pereda recounts the evolution of the character of Prudencio through his childhood, youth, and adulthood. *Windmills in Brooklyn* begins in the 1920s: these are the years after WWI, and the author provides a local color to the experiences of the protagonist in the small Spanish colony of Brooklyn, first as a little boy and then as a young man. There, Prudencio learns the great lessons of life thanks to his grandfather and his friend Agapito, who teach him about the importance of the community and how the business of the *teverianos* works, selling cigars door to door all over the city, while both characters represent two very different sides of the same coin. The process of assimilation of the character of little Prudencio is to be analyzed as part of the second generation of Spanish immigrants who were born and raised in the Spanish community abroad. However, his experiences as a child and a teenager correspond more to those of a first-generation immigrant who keeps his native language and whose process

77 As explained earlier, to avoid any confusion to the reader, I will refer to de Pereda as the author and to Prudencio as the protagonist of the story.

of assimilation is influenced by his attachment to his culture of origin and country.

The flow of Spaniards leaving their country for the United States during the second half of the nineteenth century and the first half of the twentieth century was constant. However, the effect of the American culture on the new settlers was different depending on the age of the newly arrived: those who came to the foreign country when they were merely infants or those born in the New World. In "Amériquestrans culturelles—Transcultural Americas" (2010), Jean-François Coté refers to transculturation as

> the notion of dominance, with culturally non-dominant groups engaging in the process of appropriating and transforming some of the cultural practices and representations of the culturally dominant group, a process that may also occur to some extent in the other direction. (2010, 16)

That is especially true in the case of the Spanish immigrants who arrived in New York City in the first decades of the twentieth century, as the first generations managed to preserve their language and traditions and created a space of inclusion for these Spaniards arriving from the other side of the Atlantic. According to Pérez Firmat,

> an immigrant group... passes through three stages in its adaptation to a new homeland. Initially the immigrant tries to deny the fact of displacement. I will call this first state "substitutive," for it consists of an effort to create substitutes or copies of the home culture. This is translation in the topographical sense only, an undertaking that engenders all of those faint doubles of foreign places that speckle the American urban landscape. (1996, 7)

Little Spain was one of the five communities in New York City with a high population of Spanish immigrants and descendants. The five Spanish communities were:

- In Cherry and Roosevelt Street (Lower East Side Manhattan).
- In the 14th Street, between the Seventh and the Eighth Avenues and the neighbourhoods of Chelsea and the West Village (Little Spain, West Side Manhattan).
- In East Harlem, Upper Manhattan (Spanish Harlem or El Barrio).
- In Willow Place, Columbia Place and Henry Street (Brooklyn).
- In Astoria (Queens).

Pérez Firmat clarifies that enclaves like Little Spain did not get their "Little" name because of their size in square miles or population, but because of their "diminished status as a deficient or incomplete copy of the original." (1996, 7). Thus, Little Spain and the rest of the Spanish communities in the United States were created as a consequence of a process of imaginary construction, as Anderson indicated, of the different regional representations of the Spain to which they belonged. However, as they were groups of local or provincial Spaniards, they were subject, as Pérez Firmat explains, to the imperfections and limitations of not being able to replicate in its totality the cultural variety of their country of origin.

The second stage in the adaptation to a new country is "destitution," when "gradually the awareness of displacement crushes the fantasy of rootedness" (7), thereby losing the place of origin as the reference of the construction of the individual as a human being. Thus, first-generation immigrants lose a "place to stand on" and, as a result, "rather than nostalgic, they now feel estranged and disconnected" (7). It is a mental and cultural transition that makes Spanish immigrants aware of their Americanness, despite the fact that they keep considering themselves as Spaniards in a land that is becoming their home, a place where homesickness seems to slip away as the second generation constructs their hybridism between their culture of origin and that of reception. As de Pereda illustrates:

> By the time they had made their fortunes, their children, who had all been born here, were happy Americans, their own parents in Spain had died and their brothers and sisters had stopped writing from there. They still considered themselves Spaniards—they spoke little English and never thought of themselves as Americans—but they were bound now by an American life and they felt reluctant to follow a dream alone. (1960, 46)

According to Pérez Firmat, the final stage usually happens after a long period of time:

> As the years go by the foreign country loses its foreignness and "nowhere" breaks down into "now" and "here," into a concrete time and place... Destitution gives way to institution, to the establishment of a new relation between person and place. (1996, 11)

It is a moment of complete break with the past. The loss of their past self makes first-generation immigrants take this stepping stone as an opportunity to lay new foundations (11). In the case of Prudencio's grandparents and parents, the 1880s, when they probably arrived in New York City, was a time of nostalgia and substitution; by the 1890s, when it had become evident that they were not going to return to Spain and were there to stay, their prevailing attitude was destitution; and in the 1900s with the conformation of a younger generation of Spanish Americans, "destitution gave way to institution" as a "feeling of nostalgia and disorientation are probably tempered by a sense of emplacement" (1996, 11).

Decades went by, and the flow of Spanish immigrants diminished, and the influence of American culture increased.

> although the concept of transculturation views cultures as adaptative and dynamic, it also emphasizes the idea that the cultures in contact with one another are distinct and structurally embedded in a historically established power relation where one tends to dominate the others (e.g., a modern metropolitan culture on local traditional or ethnic cultures). (Benessaieh 2010, 16)

Therefore, the effect of the American culture on the first generation of Spanish immigrants would be different from the one this culture has on the second generation, usually born in one of the numerous Spanish communities spread throughout the country. The following generations of the new Spanish-Americans were more integrated into the so-called American way of life and, in many cases, almost fully assimilated into the new culture of reception.

Literature about the transculturation process of twentieth-century Spanish migrants in New York City can also offer a testimony about the events and memories that these Spaniards experienced in the metropolis. As Ricoeur explains, "testimony takes us 'with one bound to the formal conditions of the 'things of the past' (praeterita), the conditions of possibility of the actual process of the historiographical operation' " (2006, 161). When people talk about history, they refer to the study of past events, while memory is the subjective remembrance of those events. When talking about the past, *it is important not to* confuse memory with history; however, both concepts are intermingled and necessary to create a complete landscape of previous events. For example, Dueñas's *Las hijas del Capitán* is a work of fiction based on a real historical background about the Spanish immigrants in New York City in the 1930s. However, the rest of the works chosen are based on the real experiences of their writers. Thus, the way that Dueñas's characters perceive and interact with the metropolis is her own interpretation, based on different primary sources, such as personal narratives, photographs, and official data, but also secondary sources. However, the way de Pereda describes his family life during the 1920s is not different from the testimonies of those Spaniards who had to immigrate to the United States to escape hunger, war, or repression.

In considering how *Fiesta* and *Windmills in Brooklyn* were created, the time frame of the author's biography is essential to understand the relevance of his work. De Pereda published his first novel in 1954. Like the protagonist of his novel, he had previously returned to Spain, but in the case of de Pereda, it was during the Spanish Civil War, when he met Ernest Hemingway, with whom, for some time, de Pereda worked. *Windmills in Brooklyn* was published in 1960, more than forty years after the events narrated. This is not to say that his and Alfau's *Chromos* were not written earlier, but the dates of their publications indicate that considerable time passed between the events narrated and their respective releases. Regarding the historical background and the recollections of de Pereda and how he remembers the past, *it is essential to consider* when he wrote his novels and what the time lapse was between the events that inspired these pages and when they were put in black and white. Both stories were written years after the events that inspired them. De Pereda was born in New York in 1912, but *Windmills in Brooklyn* was not published until 1960 and *Fiesta* until 1953. The first one was printed when de Pereda was forty-eight years old, but the narration of these events on his childhood memories was more than three decades old. In this work, de Pereda uses New York City as a Third Space. Part One of *Windmills in Brooklyn* is set in 1920 and Part Two is set around 1928. In both cases, New York's Roaring Twenties determine the historical background of this migration story. Furthermore, when de Pereda published *Fiesta*, based on his stay in Spain years before, he was already forty-one years old, but the visit he novelized was described as if it was still recent. De Pereda uses his parents' village of Mozares as a Third Space, and the whole story is set in 1948, in the thick of Francoist Spain and after World War II, that is, fifteen years after his last visit to Spain in 1933.

In de Pereda's *Windmills in Brooklyn* and *Fiesta*, Prudencio "the writer" and Prudencio "the character" take turns to portray the three stages of transculturation. De Pereda, the author, inhabits the "Third Space" as the protagonist of his own stories while he is in constant dialogue with himself to occupy the space and time of the two characters Prudencio and Ros. The process of transculturation experienced by de Pereda's alter ego (divided into these two personas) is captured in the two novels. The first one, *Windmills in Brooklyn*, includes little Prudencio (acculturation) and young Prudencio (deculturation), while the second novel, *Fiesta*, includes the third stage of transculturation (neoculturation) with the character of Erostrato (Ros) Varona as an adult Prudencio in his last phase of hybridity, where the author's flashbacks of his stay in Spain become the final attempt to inhabit the "Third Space" of his Spanish-American culture.

During Part One of *Windmills in Brooklyn*, there is a cultural shift in little Prudencio: acculturation. The American culture begins to take precedence over the Spanish one. First, in the form of the constant criticism of the *teveriano* profession made by most of those around little Prudencio: " 'Agapito is the best *teveriano* there ever was,' Grandmother said. 'I hate *teverianos*, but I don't hate Agapito' " (de Pereda 1960, 23). Little Prudencio likes *teverianos*, especially Agapito, because he and his work as a *teveriano* represent everything that little Prudencio relates to Spain, which, of course, is positive. The second shift from little Prudencio's Spanish culture to the American one is through language. Through the permanent use of the English language outside his home, the Spanish one becomes something secret, an internal method used by Spanish people to communicate among themselves as the rest of the population did not understand their native language. Little Prudencio begins to perceive Spanish as a tool for secrecy and lies, personified especially in the figure of Agapito and his tricks as a *teveriano*: "We both took a long sip of the ginger ale—it was flat—and the Agapito put his glass on the counter and reached the cigar boxes down to me. "Go over to the door," he said, in Spanish" (80–81).

However, young Prudencio also experiences biculturalism in the second half of the novel, as the process of deculturation had mainly happened between Part One and Part Two of *Windmills in Brooklyn*, after which there is a time gap. During Part Two: The Good Pair, young Prudencio is presented as a deculturized young man. He has lost all contact with his grandfather Don José, who represents the old cultural values that the Spanish immigrants brought from Spain. This process of deculturation is materialized by the protagonist himself at the beginning of Chapter 5 when he indicates that he never thought of resuming contact with his grandfather and, therefore, with his grandfather, but he did:

> He had stopped selling cigars a long time ago, and so he did not need a guide or translator, but we never even went out for walks together now. Grandfather stayed mostly at home, and I saw him only when I went to visit. That was an often, because I was in third year of high school at the time, with a difficult program, and had to study very hard. I began to think of myself as grown up and as an American. (101)

Young Prudencio's link to Spain has almost disappeared. The protagonist himself affirms that he has already begun to see himself as an American citizen, and since he does not have to guide and translate for his grandfather Don José, he does not need to use the Spanish language either. However, it is in this second part of the book that biculturalism appears, when the elements of the dominant American Anglo-Saxon culture are already well established but some of the elements of the dominated Spanish culture are still preserved. Young Prudencio regains the use of the Spanish language with his grandfather by helping him organize the *fiesta* for the Spanish Benevolent Society as chairman of the Entertainment Committee of La España in Brooklyn: " 'I'll help you,' I said. I felt a sudden rush of the old feeling I'd had for Grandfather when I saw how alone and brave he seemed. 'I'll help you in this thing if you want me to' " (103).The final stage of the process of transculturation, i.e., neoculturation, is also combined with biculturalism in *Fiesta*. As the alter ego of adult Prudencio, Ros Varona, returns to his parents' village of Mozares, he ends up giving shape to his new cultural self and recovering part of his forgotten past by intermingling his well-established American culture with his recovered native Spanish one.

This change of culture is reflected, as in the previous novel, in the protagonist's use of language. Throughout the story, Ros is in his family's village. The book is written in English, but it is taken for granted that all his interactions with the inhabitants are in Spanish. This is suggested by the constant use of Spanish words inserted in dialogues written in English and by their subsequent "translations" for the non-Spanish-speaking reader:

> The man stopped talking to Eusebio right away and went. He said "Adiós!" to the group. Then Heraclito and Leandro started to move away, Leandro first. "Hasta luego!" he said in the same quiet, controlled, voice. "Until later." Heraclito waved his arm. (1953, 84)

However, at times, it is Ros himself who sometimes slips out English words or phrases, demonstrating that his hybrid identity is latent in the

Anglo-American culture that is now dominant in his self: "He might be 'separated,' but he was not used to death. 'I'm not accustomed to death,' he said in English" (1953, 118). This code-switching is mentioned only a few times in the novel; however, the translation of words and phrases from Spanish to English is a constant practice in it, indicating the *importance* granted by the author to the reader's understanding as well as Ros, the language, and, therefore, the biculturalism in which he finds himself.

In these two novels, the author is also the main character. de Pereda is the author's surrogate; however, in *Windmills in Brooklyn*, he uses a first-person point of view, whereas in *Fiesta* there is a third-person omniscient narrator. De Pereda inhabits the Third Space both in New York and in Mozares. For the writing of the two biographical novels, de Pereda has experienced these places firstly as a witness, secondly as a character in his own works, and thirdly as an omniscient narrator who captures and relates as much as he can while he writes and moves between the American and the Spanish cultures. De Pereda as an author has experienced transculturation and biculturalism before his alter egos. He is perfectly aware of the cultural shift and hybridism that little Prudencio, young Prudencio, and Ros Varona experience in the novels.

De Pereda was born in New York City, but his character presents himself as an "Other" in both stories, an in-between world person depending on the space. In New York, both little and young Prudencios are part of a Spanish community in the metropolis; they do not belong to the Anglo-American society *per se*, but they are in a process of cultural transition. Prudencio is not an immigrant but an American citizen who fights his personal war between two worlds. The Spanish immigrant as "the Other" in American society is easier to explain in the case of Prudencio's parents and grandparents, who were born in Spain and arrived in the country when they were older.

The case of Ros in *Fiesta* is the opposite. After fifteen years away from Spain, he has lost contact with his Spanish family. The time Ros has spent in the United States has gradually reduced the number of people that he knows in his parents' hometown. His return to Mozares is characterized by the lack of familiarity with the place: "There was only a strange woman waiting there…, he had been so shocked to find no one there, no one he knew" (1954, 9). Ros is the "Other" in Spain, the American, or as the people in the village call him, *el Inglés*: "It must be the trip, Inglés. The long trip" (1953, 10). The people of the village he knew are either dead or very old and sick: "Aunt Felipa, his father's sister, and Uncle Benito were very sick, the woman was saying" (1954, 10). Ros's sense of otherness is acute, as those who might have recognized him as one of their own in Mozares are no longer present. Ros is thus a stranger in his own homeland, an Americaniard who has lost the close ties that used to bind him to it in the past.

Windmills in Brooklyn is divided into two parts. "Part One: Agapito" relates to the process of acculturation of the protagonist, little Prudencio, and it focuses on his childhood and on his relationship with his grandfather Don José and with their common friend Agapito. In the first half of the novel, little Prudencio presents himself as an American born of immigrant Spanish parents and grandparents living in New York City, where he undergoes acculturation, thus becoming an "Americaniard." His Spanish and American identities are balanced thanks to the fact that he lives in Brooklyn with his family, close to one of the Spanish communities of the city, while attending an American school. Although there is a conscious defense on the part of the author of these characters' Spanish identity under the hegemony of American culture, each of them reacts differently to acculturation. Some of these characters remain more rooted in Spanish culture with their religion and traditions, while others embrace American culture, abandoning most or all of the distinctive elements of their culture of origin.

Little Prudencio discovers Spanish culture through his family and those around him, but especially through his grandfather Don José and his friend Agapito, two nomadic subjects who have traveled from Europe to America, in Don José's case via Africa, through a never-ending journey until he finally succeeds in settling in New York City. Don José tries to resist the weight of the hegemony of the American culture in the metropolis through his own work as a *teveriano*. He tries to avoid acculturation, while Agapito embraces being a *teveriano* with success. Don José's lack of affection for American culture is perceived by the absence of nerve in his job. He lacks the competitiveness of Agapito in his work as a cigar seller. Don José is utterly uninterested in learning the English language: "My grandmother spoke only about ten words of English, and my grandfather just a few more" (de Pereda 1960, 5). Agapito's case is just the opposite. His work as a *teveriano* is an opportunity for him to move between cultures by changing his identity to the most appropriate in his work as a salesman. Agapito is not the same person when he is with little Prudencio's family, where he is attentive and chivalrous, as when he is working as a *teveriano*, where he is misleading and phony.

Only little Prudencio and Don José witness this identity switch. Agapito makes an effort to learn English and does not hesitate to improve his personal appearance to distinguish himself from the rest of the Spanish *teverianos*. Unlike Don José, Agapito is aware of the American way of doing business and the mentality required for street vending in New York City and takes advantage of it in each of his sales. As a child, little Prudencio was aware of the contrast between his grandfather and his friend and did not hesitate to comment on the different situations where this cultural clash between the Spanish native culture and the American culture of domination took place. At the same time, little Prudencio is a second-generation immigrant who was born and raised in the Spanish community. He speaks Spanish and English perfectly but uses the former when he is with his family and friends and the latter when other people are present.

To understand the complexity of the interactions between little Prudencio and the world around him, *it is important to examine* those scenes where the process of assimilation and acquisition of the dominant culture is present and how this is incorporated into the native culture. Little Prudencio's assimilation was during his childhood more a process of integration, or biculturalism, as he managed to keep his culture of origin intact while adopting many elements of the Anglo-American culture, especially the English language. This is reflected in little Prudencio's idea of having a good job as part of the American work culture and in the fact that he did not receive any official education from any Spanish institution in New York City, like La Nacional, but from one of Brooklyn's schools: "Mother said she wanted to be near a nice school for us boys" (de Pereda 1960, 6), he writes. Prudencio acculturates to the American culture in a natural manner, as part of his everyday life.

According to the description provided in the novel, the job of a *teveriano* was a tough one. Little Prudencio's grandfather represents the figure of the quixotic character, an idealistic and unrealistic Spanish immigrant who, a victim of circumstances and due to the economic situation of Spain, was forced to emigrate to the United States in search of a better life, proving to the reader that the first cultural clash experienced by the first generation of Spanish-American citizens who had been born in Spain went through the process of transculturation in a more violent way. Values such as honor, truth, and chivalry provided Don José with success as a salesman. This first generation felt torn away from Spain, as in most cases they never returned to their country of origin, while nostalgia made them hold on to the idea of a nation that existed in their memory, an idyllic construction of their homeland, where they would never return. As Pérez Firmat asserts, "the exile knows his place, and that place is the imagination" (1996, 10). However, he also observes that "imaginings cannot sustain one indefinitely. Sooner or later reality crashes though, and the exile loses the place that never was. His or her reaction to the collapse of substitution is vertigo, disorientation" (10). Little Prudencio's grandfather represents the hard truth of the *teverianos*, first-generation Spanish immigrants who believed at the beginning they could eventually return to Spain: "All *teverianos* talked about going back to Spain—if only to die there, as some of the older ones said—but they rarely did" (de Pereda 1960, 46). Despite wishful thinking, the older they got, the more they realized that they were never going back, and all that remained was the feeling of bitterness and nostalgia for a country that did no longer exist but in their minds.

As for Agapito, he represents the personification of the character of the picaresque novel, a Lazarillo who, thanks to his youth, social skills, and clever lying, manages to succeed where little Prudencio's grandfather is unable to due to his idealistic moral integrity. At times, this will help Agapito to succeed as a salesman, while at other times he will get into trouble from which it will not be difficult for him to escape. Prudencio, first as a child, then as a young man, learns to love his grandfather and Agapito differently while commenting on how migration and transculturation have affected them in different ways. Don Jose's dignity, pride, and honor represent the ideals of what he thinks every Spaniard should have, the figure of honor of Don Quixote that little Prudencio's grandmother bitterly criticizes: "A true Don Quixote. Unfortunately for all of us, though, there are no windmills in Brooklyn" (de Pereda 1960), an expression that gives the novel its title.

From Agapito, little Prudencio learns that life is not as easy as it seems and that shortcuts may help or hinder depending on the personal skills and a combination of talent, hard work, and luck. However, in both cases, loyalty and compassion are presented as two values shared by both characters and seem to be commonplace among Spanish immigrants. *Windmills in Brooklyn* is a novelized truth, a realistic fiction that depicts in a local-color mode the life of those Spaniards and their descendants who assimilated with greater or lesser success in a country and a society that was not originally their own. Prudencio's memories and recollections in the company of his grandfather and Agapito represent a more innocent reality, but with less fiction than could be imagined.

At the beginning of the book, Prudencio explains through his grandmother, who knows her husband's values of honor and loyalty, the reason for the title *Windmills in Brooklyn*. The grandfather is like Don Quixote; however, "there are no windmills in Brooklyn," or perhaps there are, but in this case, the giants are not windmills but skyscrapers full of an American culture and way of doing business that the grandfather does not quite understand. New York is a city that shows the reader how *important* it is for young Prudencio not only to be a *teveriano* like Don José "Quixote," but also an Agapito "de Tormes." This behavior attracts little Prudencio's attention, especially in relation to his grandfather Don José and Agapito.

Little Prudencio has three brothers, and all four of them are already experiencing transculturation. Although generationally the four brothers belong to the second generation of immigrants, by growing up in a Spanish environment, they manage to keep many elements that could be considered as being part of the 1.5 generation. The brothers do not see themselves only as Spaniards but also as Americans. They belong to an in-between generation in which transculturation is transforming them, taking the best of both worlds. Their roots are Spanish, their family is Spanish, and they patronize a purely Spanish neighborhood, yet their thinking is becoming more American because they are being educated in an environment dominated by the American culture, represented by such elements as the city itself, the school, and the clientele of the *teverianos*. This is indeed the first sign of acculturation, as indicated by little Prudencio about his older brother Joe, who is just ten years old but considers himself a "wise American.":

> Indeed, even at this time my older brother, who was only 10 but figure himself a wise American, had already begun to do some special errands for my father. He not only would deliver boxes of cigars to the hotels in the neighborhood of my father's store in the borough Hall section of Brooklyn but would even take the elevated and go over the River and into the city to make deliveries. (de Pereda 1960, 4)

At the beginning of the novel, Prudencio is a child, yet he thinks that his life, and that of his fellow Spaniards, is already determined by his origin. However, he also believes that they can have a different future: his older brother Joe wants to be an aviator, Prudencio himself wants to be a bullfighter, his brother Justo wants "a big shoeshine parlor," and his twin Bifanio wants to be a sweeper (4). Little Prudencio is 8 years old, it is 1920, the beginning of the Roaring Twenties, and, although he was born in Brooklyn, he considers himself more Spanish than American: "We were Spanish" (3), he declares. At the same time, he is self-aware of his opportunities as a Spanish immigrant in New York City. When his older brother Joe begins to "deliver boxes of cigars to the hotels" (4), our protagonist is concerned about his sibling's future: "Aren't you going to be an aviator anymore?" (4), as he is worried that being Spanish in the metropolis is connected to the cultural phenomenon of *teverianos* and their stigma:

> He was doomed—just as my father and uncles had been doomed. He would never be an aviator—nor would I ever be a bullfighter; and poor Justo would never have his big shoeshine parlor or have his twin Bifanio as a sweeper. Bifanio hadn't made up his mind yet as to what he wanted to be, but the twins always did things together. (4)

The fact that Prudencio and his brothers consider themselves Americans and, at the same time, Spaniards condemned to be *teverianos* gives an idea of the process of acculturation in which they find themselves. Joe, Prudencio's big brother, begins to run errands for the family, going alone from one side to the other of the city, taking the trolley or even the subway: "Then, he would take the el or even the subway to deliver the cigars" (4–5). At this point, little Prudencio expresses his desire not to be a *teveriano* but indicates his fascination with the experience that working for this Spanish business brings: "I didn't want to get into the cigar business and was afraid of the city, but I would have risked anything to be allowed to ride on an elevated train. And I liked to go to my father's store anyway" (5). His father's store was in the center of the Spanish colony, "in the Boro Hall section of Brooklyn" (4), where Spaniards lived, where he could "get candy at the Spanish grocer's" (5). When Prudencio refers to the Boro Hall section, he means Downtown Brooklyn, being the Brooklyn Borough Hall at 209 Joralemon Street (Nevius and Nevius 2009, 76), an area included by Rueda Hernanz in his map of Spanish neighborhoods in New York City (1993, 88). However, Spanish culture and the culture of the *teverianos* in New York are still very much present in little Prudencio's life, more than at any other time in his life. As the protagonist explains, his first experience of the family business was totally casual and without the help of his brother Joe, and it produced fear and shame in the protagonist, instead of the pride he thought doing a job typical of the Spanish community in the United States would bring him.

After having four boys, his "mother was making still another try to have a girl, a little sister" (5), and Prudencio and his twin brothers are sent away. Prudencio stays at Grandmother's, Justo and Bifanio at their aunt's, but Joe stays at his parents because he "could do errands, make phone calls and generally help around the house" (5). The reader knows that Prudencio's family did not live in the Spanish colony because Joe had to take the trolley to go to his father's store. At this point, the reader can notice this effect of transculturation, more specifically biculturation, as the Spanish-American culture can be defined in the same way as Pérez Firmat speaks about the Cuban American culture, characterized "more by contiguity than by conflict," with "lives lived in collusion rather than collision" (1996, 6). Cuban Spaniards and Spaniards from the Iberian Peninsula blend in a single culture when they talk about their work around Havana cigars. As a result, the Cuban cigar culture brought from the island is transferred to those Spanish immigrants from the other side of the Atlantic, as this is where their new Spanish-American culture meet.

This biculturalism can be seen reflected, for example, in how little Prudencio's grandparents argue over whether Don José should respect the Fourth of July holiday or go to work as a *teveriano*: "On the third day of my stay there—it was the Fourth of July—Grand Father had announced early that he wouldn't 'go out' today. 'Going out' meant going to work" (de Pereda 1960, 6). Don José does not like his job as a *teveriano* and decides to use the excuse of the festivity to do no work. However, Agapito's grandmother, who knows the real reason why he does not want to go out, decides to intervene and forces him to continue selling cigars during the holiday. Throughout the novel, the author indicates how the main characters alternate between English and Spanish when they communicate with each other depending on the situation. In a characteristic situation of diglossia, when they are with other Spanish speakers and in private, the main characters speak in Spanish, whereas when they are in public and in the presence of non-Spanish speakers, they choose to speak in English.

Another case of biculturation that Pérez Firmat considers as contiguity versus possible culture shock is the fact that the family, both Agapito's grandparents and parents, have decided to adapt to American life by living outside the Spanish colony. Prudencio's grandparents move out of the Spanish community of Brooklyn to be closer to their grandchildren:

> Grandfather and Grandmother didn't live in the Spanish colony now. They had moved to only a few blocks from us when we moved to a nicer section of Brooklyn. Mother said she wanted to be near a nice school for us boys, and she wanted a street without business. (5–6)

This proves that the central family structure as discussed by Rueda Hernanaz and Núñez Seixas was fundamental to maintaining the transition of the Spanish community in New York into biculturalism, rather than simply acculturation, where the descendants of first-generation immigrants acquire a new culture while they begin to lose their culture of origin (deculturation) and little by little assimilate into the American culture of reception. This was the case in Prudencio's and his siblings' childhoods but changed as they became teenagers and integrated into the host society, where the deculturation stage reached its full realization.

As a result of this biculturalism, Prudencio and his brother enjoyed the best of both worlds: they were educated by their Spanish parents and grandparents and were in constant connection with the Spanish colony, but at the same time they lived in a residential area in the thick of the American world where, as Prudencio points out, there was "a nice school for us boys… We owned our own house and were on a very nice street. Grandmother's place was on the ground floor of an apartment building, but the street they lived on was very pretty too" (6). The fact that little Prudencio's parents and grandparents left the Spanish colony to live in a residential area of Brooklyn, away from the main business streets and close to a school, is another example of biculturation. In this case, it is not only experienced by the protagonist and his siblings but also by his parents and grandparents, who decide to integrate into the dominant culture by leaving one of the communities where the Spanish immigrant population was concentrated, thus assimilating even more into the American dominant culture of New York City.

However, there are other elements that indicate the generational and acculturation difference between little Prudencio, his friend Agapito, his parents, and his grandparents. One of the clearest examples of how transculturation affected the newcomers was work. The American and Spanish business cultures and work ethics were very different in the nineteenth and twentieth centuries, as the American "live to work" and "can-do" mentality was culturally dissimilar from that of the Spanish immigrants (Kooyers 2015, 8). According to Anderson,

> the failure of the Spanish-American experience to generate a permanent Spanish American white nationalism reflects both the general level of development of capitalism and technology in the late eighteenth century and the local backwardness of Spanish capitalism and technology in relation to the administrative stretch of empire. (2006, 63)

Anderson seems to point out that in the Protestant Anglo-American world, their work ethic, based on the work culture that they extracted from the Old Testament through the Reformation, made the colonists of the Thirteen Colonies successful. However, the lack of success in establishing a capitalist and technologically more developed society would be, according to Anderson, the reason why Catholic Spain was less successful in sustaining its empire. This also explains why, according to Anderson, "the Protestant, English-speaking creoles to the north were much more favourably situated for realizing the idea of 'America' and indeed eventually succeeded in appropriating the everyday title of 'Americans'" (63).

At the beginning of the novel, Prudencio highlights the relevance of having a job in the United States and the different cultural approaches between his grandfather and Agapito. Both men are first-generation immigrants in New York, but they belong to another generation and arrival periods of establishment in the city. Prudencio's grandparents lived first in the Spanish colony for a long time with little Prudencio's parents, who were also Spanish immigrants, while Agapito was practically new to the country, and he is still very young in the first half of the novel. At the beginning of the story, little Prudencio describes Agapito in a very positive light: "Agapito had neat, white teeth and a small black mustache. He had dark Spanish skin, and I thought he was very handsome" (de Pereda 1960, 8). Besides, when compared with Don José, Agapito is described as a successful person, dressed in the stereotypical attire one could imagine for a salesman of the Roaring Twenties:

> Just as Granfather was not, Agapito was the perfect example of the *teveriano*. He was still a very young man and had only been in America a short time, but he was easily the most famous, as well as the most criticized, all the salesmen. He was dressed that day as I imagined a *teveriano* would dress: a fine white linen suit, brown patent-leather shoes with button tops, a bright polka-dot bow tie and a Panama straw hat with a multicolored band. When he came smiling into the front room, I thought he looked like the perfect man of the world, and he seemed to fill the room with brightness. (7)

This description of Agapito as an efficient salesman clashes with the one of Prudencio's grandfather. The latter was "dressed in his best black suit, with a black derby hat, and his face looked very worried. His drooping black mustache made his face look very sad" (8). Through these descriptions, little Prudencio acknowledges, once again, the contrast between the acculturation of Agapito as an American salesman and the resistance to the dominant culture of the traditional Don José. The negotiation of the transition and acquisition of the American culture in both cases is completely disparate. Agapito embraces acculturation, the new American way of life, transitioning from his original Spanish culture to his new American life, while Don José is attached to his Spanish roots not only by his dream of going back to Spain but also by his attachment to his family and his job and his Spanish customers. Prudencio describes him as a "mild, sad grandfather" who "was always very poor" (6), but at the same time he is proud of his roots, and later, once retired, he uses his free time to help the Spanish Benevolent Society in Brooklyn to organize a big *fiesta*:

> I began to think of myself as grown up and as an American, and to feel that Granfather was old and definitely retired, when suddenly he became the chairman of the Entertainment Committee of La España, the Spanish benevolent society in Brooklyn. Every Spaniard we knew belonged to La España, and the chairman of the Entertainment Committee was the most important man in the society. (101)

This attachment to one's roots can also be found in Prudencio's grandmother, for she criticizes anything that has to do with the American world they live in: "She had a great dislike for everything American. She had been a great lady in Spain" (6). Little Prudencio's grandmother consciously rejects any kind of acculturation as she avoids it by not learning the language, by her lack of relationship with non-Spanish people outside her closest circle of family and friends, and even by not celebrating the typical festivities of the dominant culture. This palpable phobia of anything that has to do with American culture has its counterpoint in Prudencio's father's rejection of the traditional Spanish "dominated" job of *teveriano* in New York City. He is even opposed to his sons ending up in the cigar business or in anything to do with the gray environment associated with it: "I knew Miguelín from seeing him at home and at the Spanish dances. He was a little gray man, and his store was dusty and old" (8–9). Miguelín is described as a dark person with a black future as a *teveriano* that little Prudencio should avoid.

The description of Prudencio's grandfather is not much better either. Don José is the opposite of the dynamic Agapito: Agapito is described as a young, self-confident person who radiates light through his behavior and elegant dress code, willing to embrace the dominant American culture. On the other hand, Don José is an old, insecure, dark man like Miguelín and full of sadness. As a first-generation immigrant, Prudencio's father knows the difficulties that Spaniards endured in the metropolis and their struggle in order to be embraced in this new American society. Don José and Agapito are used by de Pereda to portray the two sides of what could become of little Prudencio and his brothers if they follow the path of their grown-ups, an example of what his father rejects of their Spanish origins, while little Prudencio and his brothers experience a process of acculturation to become Americans.

Agapito is always depicted as a successful American salesman. He is also respectful and generous and seems to have plenty of money, which he uses to help Don José and to make more money: "Agapito gave him fourteen dollars… Grandfather wanted to pay, but Agapito stopped him and made him put his money away. Agapito seemed to have charge of everything—he'd paid our fares on the trolley too" (9). However, in Prudencio's first adventure in the company of Agapito and their grandfather, Agapito shows a special skill that proves that the cultural transition of the first generation of Spanish immigrants will never be complete, as he seems to reconnect with his Spanish origins through the picaresque of his actions at a saloon, where he tricks the owner of the place and sells him ten boxes of cigars that he pretends are Havanas.

In this scene, the reader can appreciate the hybridism of Spanish immigrants with Cuban culture through cigars. Thanks to their cultural transition in Cuba, Spaniards are now connected to the *habano*, or Havana cigar. The transculturation between the hybrid Spanish-Cuban culture and that of reception in the United States is represented in the role of tobacco, and especially Havanas, in *Windmills in Brooklyn*. Cuban tobacco culture becomes part of Spanish culture in the United States. The former is assimilated and becomes part of the latter. As a result, the dominant American culture in the metropolis identifies the cigar business with both the peninsular Spaniards and Cuban Spaniards coming from the Caribbean island, mixing both cultures and making them indistinguishable in the eyes of the New York culture. Spaniards become the only nation to dedicate themselves to the work of being *teverianos* due to the influence of Cuban immigrants of Spanish origin in the metropolis.

Ortiz points out that "el tabaco nace para caballero… hasta alcanzar la aristocrática individualidad de la vitola, la marca y el anillo" (1999, 32).[78] At the beginning of the adventure, the owner of the saloon is portrayed exactly in the same parameters as used by Ortiz:

> There was another man behind the counter, standing further back. He had his jacket off and his sleeves rolled up, but he didn't have an apron on. He was a big man with a red face, and he was smoking a big cigar. He had a gold chain across his vest and two big rings on his right hand, and he looked like one of my father's rich customers." (de Pereda 1960, 10)

In little Prudencio's first experience in the world of *teverianos*, Agapito exemplifies Ortiz's representation of the tobacco customer, and especially of Havana cigars, as a sign of prestige and social status, which Agapito uses to deceive the man behind the counter in the saloon. Agapito is aware of the prestige of Havana cigars in the United States: on the one hand, they are symbols of social status, as they are imported products and more expensive than conventional cigars; on the other hand, Agapito knows that Cuban cigars are considered to be among the best in the world, so he not only

78 "tobacco is born for the gentleman… up to the aristocratic individuality of the label, the brand, and the ring."

passes the cigars off as Cuban cigars; he also passes himself off as a Cuban national to complete the deception:

> "Havanas?" the big man said. He had a strong, deep voice.
> Agapito nodded quickly. "Yes! I am from Havana. I am from Havana."
> "I mean the cigars," the big man said, laughing. He had brown teeth but a nice face.
> "Oh! Also, also!" Agapito said. He laughed and kept nodding his head. "From Havana, also. For my friend. I bring them." He pointed outside. "The ship! You understand? From Havana to Spain. I bring them to friend here. I stop off." (de Pereda 1960, 10–11)

This example of Agapito's cultural appropriation indicates how close in cultural terms Cuban and Spanish culture are in the eyes of the dominant Americans, to such an extent that Agapito feels confident enough to pose and pass as a Cuban returning to Spain to see his friend with a few boxes of Havana cigars. He understands the importance of the culture of origin in the dominant American culture when it comes to selling his cigars. It is easier for him to sell cigars as a *teveriano* if he hides his Spanish origin and his profession, so stigmatized by the Spaniards in the business.

Agapito knows that the best way to succeed in the American culture is to blend in a much less honorable and quixotic behavior than the Spaniards represented by Don José, so he uses the English language to communicate more easily with his buyers: "He spoke in short spurts, but he pronounced very clearly" (11). Under this paradigm, Agapito changes his behavior according to the circumstances that may facilitate a sale on each occasion. His acculturation process is conscious and determined by economic and social reasons, for he wants to succeed in the United States in order to be able to bring his wife from Galicia. By contrast, Don José consciously rejects everything that has to do with the dominant culture: its way of carrying out business, its language, its festivities, etc. All this turns the clash between the Spanish culture of Don José and the American culture into an aggressive one. Unlike Don José, Agapito has no problem celebrating the 4th of July if it means he can sell his cigars:

> He stopped smiling and became very serious as he pulled one of the boxes out of the bundle, opened it with his little gold knife and picked out two cigars carefully. He handed them over to the big man and nodded vigorously when the man seemed to hesitate. "For Fourth of July!" Agapito said. He smiled again.

"Happy Fourth of July!" He nodded and pressed the cigars into the man's hand. (de Pereda 1960, 11)

Throughout this interaction, little Prudencio witnesses how Agapitos's behavior changes both his Spanish culture of origin when he interacts with little Prudencio's grandparents at home and his interactions with the culture of reception when he goes on his own or with Don José to sell cigars around New York City. The use of language is fundamental to understanding how little Prudencio perceives his own acculturation process. When adults do not want to be understood, they resort to Spanish: "Agapito held a finger up and turned to my grandfather. 'This one seems to have money,' he said in Spanish. 'This one can pay' " (12). When the time comes, little Prudencio even feels contempt for what Agapito represents for the culture of the people of *teverianos*: "I hated his accent now. His lying" (12). In the end, little Prudencio even pays attention to Agapito's accent, as he is aware of his friend's capacity for manipulation, even while putting them at risk.

Little Prudencio seems to connect this constant code-switching between Agapito and Don José to the contrast between the public and the private, business and family, dominant culture and dominated culture, but also to the times when they want to say something and keep it private from the rest: "Agapito was talking in Spanish then. He must have been talking to my grandfather" (12–13). He is aware of the connection between language and acculturation. He points out the lack of knowledge of his grandfather (13) as well as his lack of interest in using the little English that he seemed to know: "I heard the big man say something to Grandfather that Grandfather didn't answer" (14). Little Prudencio does not say that Don José did not understand the man, but it is the man who assumes that he does not speak the language: " 'No speak English, eh?' the big man said, and laughed" (14). The fact that the man asks Don José if he speaks English is a clear sign of two things: first, that English is the dominant culture's language used in public; and second, that at that time, and due to the large number of immigrants coming to the United States through New York City, it was normal to encounter many people who did not speak English. This scene also shows the change in Agapitos's picaresque behavior, as he interacts with the American business culture through his sales, in contrast with the behavior of Don José as keeper of his Spanish quixotic and honorable values. Little Prudencio's grandfather is constantly described as a "stubborn" and respectable person but without any thought of realism and practicality regarding business.

His grandson takes advantage of the time they spend waiting for Agapito at the bar of the saloon to explain how his grandparents came to New York. Don José used to be a waiter in Spain and in Tangiers, Morocco. While he lived with his Grandmother in Tangiers, little Prudencio's mother was born. At the same time, a brother of Grandmother had immigrated to the United States and had already begun working as a *teveriano* with great success. After much insistence, Don José agreed to immigrate to the United States with his family. They settled first in Hoboken, New Jersey, and then definitively in "a tenement district" in Brooklyn, where little Prudencio's aunt was born (16). However, "Grandfather, as my mother would say in ending these stories, was just not a good salesman" (16). The family's financial situation suffered, and Grandmother blamed this situation on Don José by comparing him to Agapito. This quixotic sense of honor and duty is persistent in Don José: "He glared down at me with a stubborn look. 'No. In no such manner. When we go, we go through the front door. We are men' " (17). Little Prudencio's determination to portray his grandfather as an honorable man versus Agapito as a successful and tricky *teveriano* is an expression of his own process of acculturation, as he becomes aware of the transculturation experienced by Agapito but not by Don José in New York City.

Windmills in Brooklyn's "Part Two: The Good Pair" is a flash forward to Prudencio's teenage years when he is in the third year of high school and recovers his contact with his grandfather after he stopped working as a *teveriano* selling cigars. Eight years have passed since the beginning of the story, and life has changed for its protagonists. In *Cuban counterpoint, tobacco and sugar* (2000), Ortiz defines deculturation as "the loss or uprooting of a previous culture" (2001, 102). This is clear at the beginning of the second half of the book, as Prudencio, now a teenager, has lost contact with his grandfather: "There was a time when I thought Grandfather and I would never be together again. He would never need me again, I thought" (de Pereda 1960, 101). His Spanish connection with Don José and Agapito has blurred. Prudencio has lost part of his Spanish culture due to his acculturation to the American culture since he was a child. The fact that Don José isolated himself after retiring prevented him from going through any significant deculturation, but this was not the case for his grandson.

American education has played an *important* role in the process of Prudencio's deculturation, as he continues indicating that visits were not frequent: "That wasn't often, because I was in third year of high school at the time, with a difficult program, and had to study very hard" (101). At the same time, Prudencio now considers himself more an American than a Spaniard: "I began to think of myself as grown up and as an American, and to feel that Grandfather was old and definitely retired" (101), he says. Don José embodies the Spanish culture of origin, almost forgotten by Prudencio the teenager. However, when Prudencio's grandfather becomes the chairman of the Entertainment Committee of La España, the Spanish Benevolent Society in Brooklyn, his grandson stops abandoning his Spanish culture. Young Prudencio decides to help him organize the *fiesta* of La España: "Grandmother looked at him and then he stared at me. 'Well, you two are together again,' she said in her cold voice" (103). The protagonist reconnects with Don José, one of the two personifications of the Spanish culture. The other one, Agapito, is also present in this second half of the story, but it is obvious that after he acculturates to the American culture as a successful *teveriano*, he has also lost part of his Spanish identity. He is no longer appealing to young Prudencio as he was to little Prudencio because they have both lost part of their Spanish essence.

In this second half of *Windmills of Brooklyn*, Prudencio rediscovers his Spanish identity when he reestablishes contact with his community. Prudencio's Spanish identity had weakened by the acculturation of the American culture. During the first half of the novel, Prudencio identified himself as both Spanish and American. When he decides to return with his grandfather, he rediscovers part of his Spanish identity: "I had written some hints about it to my best friend who was in the country, but he wasn't a Spaniard," as Prudencio was, "and had nothing to do with the Spanish colony," as he still did (114). Young Prudencio points out that his friend does not belong to the Spanish community as a way of differentiating him from the rest and from himself when speaking to him and having a point of view from outside his culture about his personal relationship with the widow Martínez.

Don José leads his grandson in his rediscovery of several Spanish elements. The most *important* one in the second half of the novel is the Spanish *fiesta* dedicated to Manolín, who, according to young Prudencio, is "the greatest Spanish dancer in the world" (120). When Don José and Prudencio set out to organize the *fiesta* of La España, they both seem to rejuvenate and return to the past. Prudencio recovers his almost lost Spanish roots, and his grandfather has one last chance to redeem himself as a quixotic character to defeat the Brooklyn windmills against which his honor and patriotic loyalty have taken him to a life apart from American culture:

> Grandfather had on a white shirt and black tie and had shaved very carefully, and I thought he looked younger than I could ever remember him. He was seventy-two now, but he certainly didn't look it this morning, and he sat very straight and proud as he talked to me. I could see that he was wearing the pants of his best suit, too. I felt more reassured as I watched Grandfather. He seemed just as strong as last night. (120)

It seems as if Don José wanted to defend his Spanish identity against the hegemony of American culture for the last time. In this second part of the novel, young Prudencio recovers some of the memories of his past and makes his grandfather feel useful again. At times, it is even the grandson who is forced to draw on Don José's memories to keep his spirits up: "I tried to keep him talking about his life in Spain and Morocco so that he wouldn't think about the manager and the interview" (125). Both characters help each other to maintain their Spanish identity. Young Prudencio rediscovers his Spanish identity thanks to the contact with his grandfather as a catalyst that keeps the cultural flame alive.

Furthermore, young Prudencio has rediscovered his Spanish identity in a period when deculturation had already been established as part of his identity and continues after the death of Don José. From this moment on, young Prudencio firmly holds on to his process of deculturation. After the death of his grandfather, it is Grandmother who represents the last bastion against American culture:

> In the years after my grandfather's death, Grandmother lost much of her bitterness. She never came to like America or its way of life, but she knew now that she would never go back to Spain, and she was resigned to spending her last years here (172).

This acceptance of her fate as a member of American society, accompanied by young Prudencio's explanations on how his uncle had become a public accountant, gives the reader a glimpse of the process of deculturation that even those who rejected the American culture may still experience in a subtler way:

> Grandmother had security and comfort during this time because my uncle Joe, her son, had a very good job, and there is a kind of ironic justice in this. Joe was a certified public accountant, and it was Grandmother who had insisted that he go to high school and be kept out of the cigar business. She had sacrificed and planned to send Joe through high school and then to Business School at night. Lots of people in the colony—and even some of the family—objected to this. They felt it was out of character, not Spanish. They said, if Joe was to be educated why not make him a doctor or a lawyer—give him a respectable profession. Grandmother said no; that this was a business country and a money country. "It will always be like that," she said. "I want Joselito to have steady work. That's why I want him to be in a business that has to do with money." (172)

At the end of the novel, the reader discovers that Grandmother has also experienced transculturation, in a different way than her grandson, accepting American culture as a means of improving her son Joe's life. In an indirect way, she chose what she believed was best for her family's future over her own culture and beliefs, thus completing her process of cultural transformation, which, although she never accepted it, did affect her, as it had also affected all Spanish immigrants who had arrived on the shores of the United States:

> It was a daydream that he had summoned many times since that first visit to Spain in 1933. Through the depression in New York, through his marriage, through the war, Spain had always seemed like some kind of last hope. It was the one part of his life he had never fully realized; it was the one thing that he could always go back to. (de Pereda 1953, 8)

This opening quotation from *Fiesta* mentions the last hope of many Spanish immigrants after years of living and working in the United States. This excerpt refers to the journey when Ros Varona,[79] a Spanish immigrant who had established himself in the United States, returns to Spain on September

79 In Prudencio de Pereda's short story "The Way Death Comes" (1939), the last name Varona is also used.

23, 1948, to visit his family, fifteen years after his last trip to his country and to his village, Mozares, in the province of Burgos. He is now a war veteran, in possession of a gun after his discharge from the army, who decides to return to Spain after a painful divorce. It is a rainy September at dusk, and only the family's nurse, Candelas, is waiting for him. Candelas represents the Spanish identity from Cuba portrayed in *Windmills in Brooklyn*, as the reader discovers that she had lived in the Caribbean country and smokes cigars. Ros's Aunt Felipa, his father's sister, and Uncle Benito are very sick. Bernabé, his uncle on his father's side from Campo, was waiting for him, but he went to his village to help fix dinner. His wife, Nicolasa, was also sick. The next day, with her uncle Benito, Ros visits the village a few days before October 14, the date when a great *fiesta* that gives its name to the novel will be celebrated in Mozares.

In the village, many of the characters that Ros recognizes from his past want to play the role of Jesus Christ in the *fiesta*. After several meetings, there are five neighbors and candidates selected to play Jesus: Blas, Heráclito, Leandro, Tomás, and Luciano. As the novel progresses, the candidates for Christ become fewer and fewer. Blas, imprisoned for his Republican past, is allegedly shot on October 12, the national holiday: "They shot him in celebration of the Day of the Race" (de Pereda 1953, 114), although he has actually escaped from prison. Heráclito, tormented by his infertility, confronts Ros and beats him until Ros's wife, Rora, defends him. Heráclito escapes but returns to ask for forgiveness and confesses that Tomás has ultimately been chosen for the role. Leandro, the Falangist who used to terrorize his fellow citizens, is killed by Ros when he is beating Tomás for having been chosen for the role of Jesus. In the end, Luciano and Heráclito are chosen to scourge Tomás as Christ. Ros tries to prevent it and even carries the cross to help him (318), but finally, Tomás is crucified and dies on the cross.

Candelas calls Ros *Inglés*, evidencing the process of transition of his cultural identity. He is no longer considered to be a native of the village for many of Mozares' inhabitants, but a visitor from the New World instead. Bearing in mind Ortiz's definition of "neoculturation" as "the consequent creation of new cultural phenomena" (2001, 103), Ros combines his Spanish culture with the American one to create a new identity. In his return to Mozares, Ros's family and neighbors are witnesses to this new hybrid individual. The *fiesta* works as a catalyst to show how he has changed and how the old cultural practices clash with part of the long-forgotten culture of the protagonist. However, Ros still feels insecure as he is regaining his Spanish culture and moving between two worlds. This in-betweenness grants him a unique perspective of the Spanish and American ways of life. Ros, as many other Americans, had been in the army in World War I, and then he met Rica, who had no connection with Spain, and made him forget about Spain and his Spanish family and friends there. When Ros arrived in Mozares, only Candelas greeted him. His family members who still lived there were old and sick. Ros had also lost contact with his friends when he stopped writing them letters.

When Ros opened his bags, there was a "thick folder of sketches at the bottom of the valise... The work was the illustrations for a child's version of *Don Quixote*" (12). De Pereda uses Don Quixote to highlight the Spanish culture that was always present in Ros's life. The author also mentions the noble *hidalgo* in *Windmills in Brooklyn*, where Don José is presented as the very personification of the quixotic figure. At the same time, Ros is convinced that due to his quixotic self, he had to fight for the Spanish Republic during the Spanish Civil War in order to revive his Spanish connection from the bottom of that suitcase that he had taken from Spain back to America. On October 14, the village of Mozares celebrates the Festivity of San Isidro, two days after the Day of the Race, as they called Columbus Day in Spain.

Aunt Felipa stands for the love that relatives felt for the Spanish immigrants who had to leave their country. This love is especially embodied in the character of Ros. At the beginning of the story, the reader discovers that she is dying, just like Ros's connection to Spain due to deculturation. However, old Aunt Felipa still remembers Ros and loves him, as Spanish people never seemed to stop loving their missing immigrants, "deeply, truly, soulfully" (1954, 17). The text under study here offers a good example of the effect of transculturation when Spanish immigrants like Ros, who are already settled in the United States, decide to return to their country of origin. These immigrants are no longer considered "real" Spaniards by their compatriots. They are deculturized by many of their family members and neighbors that, like in the case of Ros, who is called the "inglés," no longer consider them as one of their own. In *Fiesta*, visiting Spanish migrants abroad, like the protagonist of the novel, are considered to be less Spanish than the inhabitants of the village because they have been away.

Ros's impression of Spain is that nothing has changed: "He had not been jolted to attention by anything new" (18). The Spanish Civil War had long finished, and the traces of the war were already fading: "The ruins he saw were small and cleanly swept and light in the sun… The flags were getting dusty" (18). Ros is worried about the detachment that there seems to be between his behavior, who says he has not returned for love, and the love that his Spanish family shows to him: "His aunt's love had embarrassed him. It was too strong" (17). His father's brother, Uncle Bernabé, also expresses his love for Ross the very first morning of his arrival. Bernabé goes early in the morning from the neighboring pueblo of Campo to visit his nephew: "In his uncle, love was a natural expression" (20). Ros had lost contact with his Spanish family when he stopped writing them; however, his ties with his family seem to be renewed as "the fact that Ros had not written had not hurt him" (20), referring to Ros's Uncle Bernabé, and neither did it upset any of his family members, who accepted him again into their home.

Aunt Felipa and Uncle Bernabé want Ros to forget about his failed marriage and his divorce: "We'll make you forget it. You have people who love you here" (21). His Uncle Benito, Aunt Felipa's husband, takes him around the village to meet his surviving relatives and neighbors from his childhood. As a result of his return, the now American "inglés" Ros is confronted with some elements of Spanish fascism that had not been present in the identity of the village and its inhabitants before:

> Another odd detail of the funeral was that Leandro came in full uniform. He looked very neat and handsome, and it seemed to Ross that the uniform was an officer's uniform. It was far too lavish and well cut to be that of a private in any army. Besides, Ros could see no sergeant's stripes. It was Leandro's Falangist uniform, Heraclito told Ros. (126)

Ros, a man discharged from the army, tries to identify Leandro's military rank when he sees the uniform. However, it is Heraclitus who indicates to Ros that the uniform is not that of a military man, but that of the Spanish Falange to which the deceased man belonged, which is why he is buried in very similar clothes to those used in the army.

With Ros's return to his former home in Mozares, the promise he made to return home is fulfilled, the self-made promise of returning one day to Spain after decades abroad. However, the Spanish Civil War and Spain's subsequent dictatorship of General Francisco Franco brought a major change in the village where everyone knows each other and the political and religious ideas of its neighbors are known to all: " 'In this life' meant the life of the pueblos, the life of Spain, *his* life. 'You have everything different in your life, Inglés. Everything is different!' " (126). With the new regime, life in the towns has also changed, causing old quarrels between neighbors to increase due to political ideologies in which Ros finds himself immersed because of his hybrid identity as an American and a Spaniard.

The hope of returning to Spain expressed at the beginning of de Pereda's *Fiesta* by its protagonist Erostrato "Ros" Varona is also reflected in the figures of other characters and works, as in Remedios in Dueñas's *Las hijas del Capitán* (2018) and Don José, de Pereda's grandfather, and in many *teverianos* in *Windmills in Brooklyn* (1960). On this occasion, it is Ros, the adult continuity of little and young Prudencio, who struggles between the American and Spanish cultures:

> If they went on a visit to Spain, they came back very quickly and never went again. Two of the older *teverianos*, of Don Mariano's generation, actually went back to Spain to die—they were both very ill and their families knew they would never come back—but the rest of the *teverianos* are burid in Brooklyn or in the new cemeteries in Queens. (de Pereda 1960, 47)

Ros is an Americaniard, a Spanish immigrant who has spent most of his life in New York City and now returns to his home country in pain after his divorce from the woman he loved, Rica. After many years, he has experienced deculturation and has lost contact with his origins, with his Spanish identity: "The interest he had in Spain now was nothing like so eager as when he had truly wanted to go in those earlier times" (12). The *fiesta* that takes place in Mozares leads Ros to undergo a neoculturation phase, a phase in which the protagonist of this story creates a new identity by mixing his dominant American culture and his native Spanish culture, reinforced by his return to Spain, thus creating a new cultural context.

Mozares is a space that becomes a catalyst for establishing Ros's hybrid identity as an Americaniard. His once partially forgotten Spanish culture and identity are reunited with his adopted American culture as he re-experiences his long-forgotten origins: "As he opened the window on the pueblo and saw that this was really Spain, he remembered the time he had started here. He remembered that that was long ago" (13). The morning after arriving in the village, Ros begins to reincorporate his Spanish identity: "The pueblo had a more familiar look now than when he had first come this evening" (18). However, it is not until Ros is taken around the village that the reader can appreciate de Pereda's creation of the new individual as the final stage of the little and the young Prudencios in *Windmills in Brooklyn*.

During the first tour around the village, Bernabé and Ros encounter Luciano Eneguas, Manuel Enaguas's son, who had taken over his sausage factory, house, and lands from his father. He is the first person to ask about Ros's role in the village's Saint's Day, the celebration of San Isidoro. On this occasion, Ros expresses his early insecurity toward Spanish culture and language: "Ros wondered if he had understood correctly. He had not had trouble with his Spanish yet, but he knew he would slip every once in a while" (25). He is not sure he understands what Luciano has told him about participating in a play: " 'What paper? What do you mean, 'paper'?' 'Paper' in Spanish meant 'role' or 'part' " (25). By pointing at this translation misunderstanding, the narrator underlines Ros's insecurities about his own comprehension abilities in his own mother tongue. However, this does not stop him from successfully incorporating Spanish culture as his own again. The day of San Isisdoro, a Passion play will be performed, and people in Mozares expect Ros to participate in it. Luciano is interested in playing the role of Jesus, "The Christ!" (26). However, Uncle Bernabé explains to Ros that it is not up to Luciano to decide. He adds that the old members of the community will determine that, leaving a door open for the following events to come.

After their encounter with Luciano, Uncle Bernabé and Ros meet Anastasio. He is the oldest man in Mozares, lives alone, and is one of the men who will decide who will play Jesus in the Passion Play. Anastasio welcomes Ros as one more of the villagers who has been away but is still part of the community: "I remember you, Erostrato, son of Erostrato, this fiesta of ours will interest you. Interest you." (27) Anastasio does not refer to him as "el Inglés"; he remembers his name and his father's and invites him to join the *fiesta*. However, Ros's successful recovery of his Spanish identity makes him unruffled by this nickname:

> "If Erostrato can't be here, he should have a son here" (28). Uncle Bernabé explains to Ros that this fiesta is only for people from Mozares. By saying this, Ros is once again included in the community. He is considered a member of the village and as such has the honor of taking part in the festival. Ros's Spanish identity is thus foregrounded. He continues having his American culture, but his visit to the village means the rebirth of his Spanish culture. Ros successfully undergoes neoculturation intermingling both cultures. When Ros and his uncle Bernabé go to visit the latter's daughter Rora and her husband Heraclito, Bernabé reminds Ros of his condition as an outsider by using again the term "inglés." (29–30)

The omniscient narrator explains how other people in the village of Ros's generation had the opportunity to travel and have a hybrid identity, yet they did not. A couple of examples are Luciano and Ros's cousin, Rora. They could have left the village as Ros did. Luciano did not leave because he did not want to:

> He had not wanted to live in Madrid, and he did not want to go to America—meaning Latin America—to make money. He was one of the few who could have gone, too, because his family had had the money to spare for the passage (23).

As can be seen, the narrator indicates that there were very few in Mozares who could afford to leave and Luciano was one of them, but he did not. On the other hand, there are those who wanted to leave and could not. This is the case of Ros's cousin, Rora, who told her cousin on her previous visit about her true intentions regarding her future: " 'I want to get away from this life,' she had said… 'I don't want to marry him. I don't want to stay here' " (30). In the end, however, neither of them had left the village, and their identity had hardly changed. Both were now adults, but the growth of their cultural identity is limited to the village of Mozares and its surroundings with little interaction from outside.

Heraclito is the reminder of Ros's American identity. He constantly calls him "inglés" and expresses his opinion about Ros being in the village during the *fiesta* and the Passion play. Ros is in-between worlds, but for Heraclito, he is an outsider: "The fiesta isn't for you. You know that, *Inglés*" (31). Ros is being "othered" by Heraclito. For him, Ros is not a returned compatriot but an "English man with Spanish roots," an Americaniard who does not belong in the village. The Passion play is only for people from Mozares, not even for their neighbors of Campo. Mozares works for Ros's recovery of his Spanishness, of his Spanish identity long forgotten, and creates an equilibrium between his Spanish and his American culture. For Anastasio, one of the oldest men in the village, Ros is not the "Other"; he is one of them who has been abroad, in the American space, but still one of them. For other villagers like Luciano and Heráclito, Ros does not belong in their "space." Throughout the novel, Heraclito always stresses the word "*Inglés*" when referring to Ros, as a reminder of his distinction: " 'What do you think of her, Inglés?' Heraclito grinned broadly" (32). They have socially constructed an imaginary border separating Ros from Spain and from Mozares. Ros is the "Other" now and cannot belong to both worlds and has a binary position as a hybrid person.

Uncle Bernabé, however, agrees with old Anastasio and thinks that Ros is one of them. Ros reminds him of his American side, "I come from the city" (1953, 35), but Uncle Bernabé insists on Ros's Spanish identity: "You're a Varona, and you're here now, with us. Where you belong" (35). The fact that Ros is in Mozares emphasizes his hybridity and at the same time reinforces his participation in the Spanish culture of origin in the eyes of the older locals, while a part of the inhabitants of his age already consider him an outsider, an "Other." Throughout the novel, this ambivalence becomes more and more evident, until the day of the festival and the Passion play. For those who consider him as one of Mozares, his return is a reunion with the prodigal son who takes part in their most intimate and sacred celebration, only worthy of those who belong to the community. For those who consider Ros an "Other," his presence is an affront to their own identity, which is threatened by his binary position, a hybridity that contains an American and a Spanish culture within.

5.5. Pinnick Kinnick Hill's Story

González is the first-person narrator of his novelized biography of a first-generation American-born son of two Spanish immigrants from Asturias who left everything behind to establish themselves on the hills of West Virginia in Harrison County, in the Pinnick Kinnick Hill of the book title. González creates a fictional family, the Villanuevas, where Juan Villanueva becomes the center of the story, the father of the narrator/alter ego of González himself. The most recent studies of the history of foreigners in Appalachia date back to 1880, when German and Swiss immigrants arrived in the area. Years later, between 1880 and 1920, Eastern and Southern Europeans entered the United States *en masse*. Among these Europeans were a number of Spanish immigrants. González's manuscript, written in the seventies of the twentieth century and hidden for years in a suitcase, constitutes a unique testimony to the literary representation of Pinnick Kinnick Hill as a "Third Space," a unique story of Spanish immigrants in the zinc mines of Harrison County in West Virginia at the beginning of the twentieth century (González 2003, viii).

The importance of Pinnick Kinnick Hill dates back to 1859, when it was first a coal mine and, during the American Civil War, a fort for the northern troops from where the town of Clarksburg could be seen. In 1864, with the American Civil War almost over, the lack of manpower due to the conflict encouraged the arrival of European immigrants thanks to recruitment campaigns that, especially in the 1870s, began to attract foreigners from the old continent with the help of steamship agents. The industrial growth of the United States at the turn of the century further accelerated the transformation of West Virginia, which saw its coal production increase. The refusal of the state's residents to leave their farms and work in the industry favored the massive arrival of foreigners, turning West Virginia and Harrison County into two of the main coal-producing territories between 1897 and 1910 (González 2003, x, xii).

The increase in jobs and businesses led to the growth of the county's population between 1900 and 1920. Many of these were European immigrants from Southern and Eastern Europe, including Portuguese, Spanish, French, Italians, Polish, and Russians. Among these immigrants were families such as Juan Villanueva's, who came to Clarksburg and the surrounding area in the early decades of the twentieth century. During these years, the Spanish population became so large that a Spanish vice consulate was opened in the city in the 1920s (González 2003, xii). The presence of Spaniards in West Virginia produced a pull effect among friends and relatives, which brought more immigrants from the Iberian Peninsula to the American territory. If between 1882 and 1936 it is estimated that more than four million Spaniards arrived in the American hemispheres. The period between 1904 and 1913, saw the greatest influx, especially in countries such as Argentina and Cuba, but also in Mexico, Brazil, and the United States. In the case of the Asturians represented in González's work, the reasons for their immigration were mainly economic, due to the agricultural privatization of the region, affected by growing industrialization, and the increase of taxes and rents (González 2003, xiv). On the other hand, compulsory military service in Spain, with its system of "quintos" that obliged the replacement of one man in five to remain attached to the army, caused those who could not afford a replacement to consider emigrating. This, coupled with ongoing conflicts in Spain such as the Spanish-American War and the Rif War led to even greater emigration. In the case of Asturias, Rueda Hernanz indicates that around 45% of the region's population avoided conscription at this time (cited in González 2003, xiv).

In the case of Juan Villanueva's family, their experience is much more positive and not typical of Spanish immigration. He volunteered to replace another man and do the military service in his place. In this way, he earned money to pay for tickets to the United States with his whole family, first class and from Liverpool, saving the trip from Spain to England thanks to an invitation. Most of the emigration to Harrison County consisted of men first, as did most immigrants from Southern and Eastern Europe. Once settled, the male immigrants often brought their families from their home countries (González 2003, xvi). In 1903, the Grasselli Chemical Company planned to build a factory in Clarksburg. Zinc production began in 1904, and in 1910, Grasselli began the construction of a second factory in Harrison County. By 1913, the second-largest smelter in the United States was in the city of Clarksburg. Other companies, such as the Columbia Zinc Works, opened in 1907, and a third zinc company followed suit in Lumberport, north of Clarksburg (xviii).

The Asturians, with their experience in factories in Avilés, Arnao, Mieres, and Naveces, had no problems finding work in the area between 1900 and 1920 (xviii). This was not the case for Juan Villanueva's family, as they came from a family of fishermen and stockbreeders. However, when they arrived in Harrison County, they had no problem dedicating themselves to zinc. The Pinnick Kinnick Hill zinc factory became the center of the settlement for the Spanish community. During the Great War, the Asturian workers at the Grasselli factory saw their working hours increased and their wages reduced (xx-xxii). However, it was not until the end of the war that they went on strike to avoid accusations of being unpatriotic. In 1919,

Grasselli workers went on strike on several occasions until they won the improvements that they demanded in their jobs (xxii).

Most of the Spanish immigrants, mostly Asturians, who came to Pinnick Kinnick Hill between 1900 and 1920 knew nothing about the place. They came to this area because of the call effect of family and friends working in West Virginia. When Juan Villanueva arrived in Clarksburg, he was surprised that people greeted him with an Asturian accent. González points out that even the Coca Cola ads were in Spanish. The nationality of the immigrants with whom the Spaniards had the most contact was Italian. Italians learned Spanish, so coexistence in the neighborhood was good. In addition, Spanish immigrants with economic problems were entitled to a "suscripción," or an amount of money that the Spanish community obtained through collections in the Clarksburg area (xxiv).

When González wrote his novel in the 1970s, it was the end of an era. From the 1930s onward, there was a decline in Spanish immigration. The zinc industry began to decay in the 1940s and 1950s, and the former workers began to buy the houses where they lived. As work disappeared, the workers became older and retired. The children of the first generation of Spanish immigrants left the area, and ties with Spain began to weaken as the new generations assimilated. While it is true that the first Asturian arrivals maintained a hybrid identity thanks to the community created around the zinc, the disappearance of new migratory flows from Spain, the aging of the first immigrants, and the massive flight of the new generations from the area meant that their *importance* gradually diminished. In the 1970s, the Asturian community was still in contact with families and friends in Spain, Cuba, and other parts of the United States (González 2003, xxvi).

When Juan and his family moved into Nicanor's furnished flat in Saint Louis, he went to the employment office to look for work and was assigned to the city factory in the pottery workshop. However, as soon as he started, he was called back to the office and assigned to the furnace. When Juan asked why the change, he discovered that the Tizadores, "the firemen in charge of each furnace" (33), had found out that he was Spanish and told their bosses. This is the first time that Juan becomes aware of his condition of "Other": "When Juan told him he would not work there, the man told him he couldn't work in any other department" (35). At first, Juan did not understand what was happening. He had just started his new job and spoke good English from his experience as a sailor between Gijón and Liverpool. He does not know it yet, but his identity as a Spaniard, his "otherness," due to his belonging to a nationality considered unworthy by the dominant culture, marked his life in the United States from the beginning. The explanation given to Juan does not satisfy him, and he decides to change locations and leave Clarkston in West Virginia to follow his brother David:

> "You will be hiring a man to replace me in the pottery," Juan said.
> "Yes," the man said, "but he won't be Spanish. Had I known you were Spanish, I wouldn't have hired you."
> "Why didn't you know I was Spanish?"
> "Because your name didn't sound Spanish. I thought Villanueva was a French name. We do have a lot of French men in this part of the city. Besides, you speak English well. None of the Spaniards I know speak English. How do you happen to be so fluent in the king's English? You sure fooled me."
> "You still haven't explained to me why a Spanish person cannot work anywhere but the furnaces."
> "For the simple reason that we tried Americans, Italians, Irishmen, Frenchmen, and Lord only knows what other nationalities, and the only men so far who adapted well to the furnace work are Spanish men." (35)

Upon arriving in Clarkston, Juan's family settled in the town of Coe's Run, about three miles to the east and one of the most important concentrations of Spaniards in the area. After Juan's experience in St. Louis and seeing that the situation in the zinc factory in the area was the same, he decided to move into his brother's house in a room built especially for them. His experience as an "Other" and the role assigned to him in American society also extended to West Virginia. Juan was determined to avoid it and dedicated himself to selling beer through a franchise of the Hoster brewery in Columbus, Ohio:

> He wanted the franchise to become a beer distributor. A few days later, a representative of the company arrived in the village. After talking with Juan, he telegraphed headquarters apprising it of Juan's suitability. The next day, the representative told Juan he'd been accepted. (39)

This decision determined Juan's evolution as an individual, creating a sense of independence in him through his new job. He did not have to be subordinated to others, like the "Tizadores."

According to the narrator, Coe's Run, also known by the Spaniards as Crossetti, grew a lot between 1904 and his birthday in 1909. The fact that González mentions his birth in the Spanish community is no coincidence. The author and narrator inhabit Harrison County as a "Third Space." The novelized biography becomes a way for the author to explain his experience as a Spanish child of migration in the Asturian colony, a relevant part of the story of the Villanueva's family. González is witness to the evolution of the transculturation of the Asturian immigrants in the area in the early twentieth century. The fiction of the Villanueva family is only a screen onto which González projects the life of those around him. However, these descriptions benefit from the writer's discretion. The author changes some of the names of places and people, while at other times he uses real ones to describe the experience of a family that could have easily been his own: "On the other side of the water, Valentin Aguirre would receive them in New York City, where they would be fed and housed until their final destination was determined" (29).

In his description of the Spaniards as "Others" who are not allowed to climb the social ladder to become a fully-fledged part of American society, González also considers the other nationalities that were allowed greater integration, although, apparently, there may not have been differences among them. Most were from Southern and Eastern Europe, did not speak English and had come to the United States, in search of a better future. González is aware of this marginalization of the dominant American culture against the Spanish culture, but not of the other nationalities:

> In the beginning of the settlement, there were about thirty-five families, now Coe's Run had a population of nearly 1,200 people, two-thirds of them from Spain, but also including Italians, Poles, Slavs, Hungarians, Germans, Irish and Native Americans. Most of the non-Spanish immigrants worked in departments other than the furnaces: The ore-storage, the pottery, the machine shop, the yards and the laboratory. (41)

The Spanish community would have to wait for another generation before their children, with a clear hybrid Spanish and American identity, could enjoy the same benefits as the rest as first-class citizens: "The Allied Carbon Company built a new plant adjacent to the smelter, but didn't hire Spanish immigrants. Later the company hired the offspring of the original Spanish settlers" (45). As a result, the most dangerous and hardest jobs in the factory were done by the Spaniards, and it was rare for people of other nationalities to work there too. This situation sometimes caused labor shortages and a worsening of the already poor working conditions of the labor force: "The furnace work was done exclusively by Spanish men. Only during the Great Depression did a few men of other nationalities dare brave the hazards" (45). It took a generation for Spaniards to be accepted as equals in American industry, which shows the fear that the American culture had of the Spanish culture, creating a situation of first- and second-class immigrants in West Virginia that lasted for decades.

With the settlement of the Spaniards in the Crossetti community, the process of acculturation to the American culture began. This process was more successful in the case of the Villanueva brothers thanks to the fact that they stayed away from the factories, and especially the furnace, which oppresses many of their compatriots. They avoided normalized cultural transformation thanks to the constant contact with American culture. These three brothers are the perfect examples of nomadic subjects. From Spain to England and then to the United States, the Villanueva brothers moved across America looking for a place to work and live according to their expectations. After their mandatory arrival in New York City and their encounter with Valentín Aguirre, the brothers took separate ways. Their case is not the only one where the process of cultural assimilation in a new country comes from the establishment of a new business, but it is one of the most representative ones. According to the narrator, there were many businesses established by Spaniards that prospered under the protection of the community:

> A great number of other Spanish persons had come to start their own business: Alfredo López was El Zapatero, the shoe man; Victoria Inclan had her Carrito, her wagon services; and Rodolfo García had his barbería (barbershop) and his *mesa de billar* (billiard table). Agustín Pelaez, known as El Pintor, was a muralist whose son became one of the busiest men in town by virtue of his ability to paint portraits, landscapes and other scenery. (49)

With the ample success of their businesses, in 1906 a moderate number of new members joined the community. Cecil Applewhyte, M.D., and his wife were two of the few additions of people of non-Spanish nationalities. The fact that a non-Spanish doctor decided to become part of a community made up mostly of Spanish immigrants shows that the process of acculturation of the community to American culture was underway and was to continue over the next few years. José María Castillo came along, along with Juan's brother-in-law, with his wife Angela, and their daughter Angelita. José became the first dairyman in the area.

First-generation immigrants acclimatized with varying degrees of success to life in the United States. The fact that most of them lived in a community in Pinnick Kinnick Hill meant that the acculturation process was not as aggressive as elsewhere. The acquisition of the English language was limited by the Asturians' need to use it outside the community. Most of them lived on the hill around the zinc factory, socialized with other Spanish or Italian neighbors who spoke Spanish, shopped in their businesses, and even went to mass in the Spanish parish with a Spanish priest who had settled on the hill. Moreover, the few non-Spanish members of the community, such as Dr. Applewhyte or Mr. Ahrens, also ended up learning Spanish, so that the language issue as the main means of acculturation was not possible in most cases.

The case of Juan Villanueva's family, as with the other elements of the novel, was the exception that proves the rule. Juan spoke English, which he had learned during his work between Gijón and Liverpool on board *La Mariposa*. The job of brewer that he took upon his arrival in the Pinnick Kinnick Hill community allowed him to situate himself outside the ghetto created by the "Tizadores" in the furnace of the zinc company, which isolated the Asturians from any contact with the rest of the workers. Juan was able to interact not only with his community but also with suppliers and other non-Spanish consumers by selling beer. Before his death in 1935, Juan had become a mainstay of his community, drawn to both Spaniards and citizens of other nationalities because of his know-how and the ease with which he had acquired traits of the American culture such as entrepreneurship and work-oriented lives. These two characteristic American values became an integral part of Juan's and his family's successful acculturation process in the United States.

The Villanueva family's deculturation process was progressive and was facilitated by the fact that Juan, the head of the family, already spoke English before arriving in the United States. However, in the case of most families, and especially first-generation immigrants, this process was slower for several reasons. On the one hand, most of the men in the Spanish community of Pinnick Kinnick Hill worked in the furnaces, which functioned as working ghettos; on the other hand, Spanish workers tended to interact only with other Spaniards in the factory. As a result, both their acculturation and deculturation were complicated:

> Most of the old-line Spaniards that came from Asturias to work in the smelters in America had a way of life that followed a pattern from cradle to grave. They were hard-working, honest men, mostly unschooled, who raised large families. One of the first things most of them did was to buy a house. They went to work in the morning and came home after work. Depending on the season of the year, they planted a garden, took their siestas, had their dinner, took a snort of whiskey, went to bed, got up in the next morning and went to work, a routine that varied none from the first day. They paid off the mortgage, save every check the boys brought home, deposited them in the bank and accumulated $50,000 to $55,000. They never took their wives to a movie or a restaurant. They didn't live to be much older than fifty. Soon after their deaths, their widows died, leaving the house or money to the children, who fought over who should get what and, after squabbling over the remains, never spoke to each other again. (115)

The immigrants working in the zinc industry, who were the most integrated group in American culture, were also the most despised by their own compatriots: the "Tizadores." By overseeing the Spanish workers who could only occupy the furnace, the "Tizadores" spoke some English and did not interact with the majority of the Spanish community. The Spanish saw the "Tizadores" as traitors. This favored their assimilation into the dominant American culture while losing their Spanish one. This can be perceived when Juan Villanueva must go to the factory to represent the interests of the Spanish workers against the will of the Spanish Tizadores: "When they arrived for the meeting with Mr. Ahrens, three of the most powerful Tizadores were there: Agustin Gutierrez, Manuel Moran and Miguel Costa" (55). The Tizadores were not pleased with Juan representing the other Spanish workers as he spoke both English and Spanish and could indicate why they wanted more rights and freedom against the Tizadores' rule.

It is interesting to note that the process of transculturation also affected those immigrants who were not Spaniards but were in constant contact with the Spanish community. This was the case of people such as Dr. Applewhyte, who learned some Spanish, but especially of Mr. Ahrens, who enjoyed the presence of Juan Villanueva and many other Spaniards and would eventually learn how to speak Spanish properly: "Although Mr Ahrens was beginning to understand the Spanish spoken by Agustin Gutierrez and the other Spaniards in town, he could not yet carry on a conversation. He was, however, to become quite fluent as the years went by" (González 2003, 55).

The narrator indicates how his father, Juan Villanueva, stood out above the standard of "the old-line Spaniards." He also became interested in the American way of life, its culture, and even its medical benefits:

> My mother was the first Spanish lady in the town of Glenncoe to have her teeth extracted and fitted with dentures... Father also would take her and the children to eat at Anderson's Restaurant in Clarkston or to the Manhattan Greek Restaurant... He also took her to Parsons-Souders, the largest department store in Clarkston, and bought tailor-made suits for her. (115)

For the Villanueva family, the process of cultural change was a continuous one. As they became more successful in their businesses and in their integration into the new American way of life, they moved away from the Spanish customs that ruled the lives of many workers, especially furnace workers. The narrator points out that one of the reasons for their deculturation that was especially evident in the following generations of Spanish origin was disaffection, a disaffection that the author seems to share:

> Today there are grandchildren and great-grandchildren of original Spanish smelter workers scattered throughout the United States engaged in every aspect of American life.
>
> There is no viable reason why the descendants of the Asturian smelter workers should keep saying they are proud of being Spanish. Spain never did a thing for them. In fact, if their ancestors had stayed in Spain, they never would have existed. Their ancestors would have starved to death before they could have been conceived. (243)

This feeling of resentment toward the Spanish homeland, a homeland that most Americans of Spanish origin never knew, is transmitted from González to the narrator and Juan's son as an inhabitant of the "Third Space" of Pinnick Kinnick Hill. This was a space imagined by a community based mainly on Asturian immigrants who arrived in the United States and adapted to the American way of life in a process of transculturation that lasted decades. The stages of acculturation and deculturation went hand in hand, exchanging some typical traits of the Spanish community, such as spending more time at home with the family and saving money, for others more typical of the American way, such as staying less time at home and spending part of their salaries on leisure outside the Spanish area. However, it was the generations that followed the first Spanish immigrants who suffered the most from deculturation to the point of often losing the Spanish culture that their parents and grandparents had brought with them when they first crossed the Atlantic Ocean.

The first two stages of transculturation, acculturation and deculturation, gave way to the construction of a new hybrid subject not devoid of its contradictions and mixed feelings between the Spanish and the American cultures. As the narrator explains, neoculturation had two of its key manifestations in the outbreak of the Spanish Civil War and in the subsequent Second World War in the late 1930s and early 40s. According to the narrator, most of the Asturians who lived in America were ideologically loyal to the Spanish Republic, organizing rallies, meetings, fundraising activities, and other initiatives to support its government. However, very few decided to return to Spain to defend the Republic's cause. Most of them decided to stay in the United States as American citizens and did not want to get further involved in the conflict. However, after 1939 and the subsequent entry of the United States into the world conflict in 1941, many citizens of Spanish origin enlisted to lend their helping hands to the American army:

> Thousands of American-born sons and hundreds of daughters of Spanish immigrants from the province of Asturias entered the service to do what was asked of them. The greatest number of the men were drafted, although many of them volunteered. A few of those eligible to be drafted where deferred because of being employed in vital industries, but none of the men called to active duty refused to go. None of them deserted or left the country to keep from going to serve when they were called. (241)

Unlike the first generation of Spaniards who had fled the Iberian Peninsula to escape the "quintos" system in the early twentieth century, naturalized Spaniards in the United States and their children chose to participate in the global conflict on behalf of their host country. Their new cultural identity allowed them to support the Republican cause in the Spanish Civil War without engaging directly in the conflict, but at the same time also to volunteer to take arms for America in World War II. However, the narrator points out that only those who had arrived in the American country when they were children or were born there achieved a full neoculturation stage, and not all of them either. Most adults experienced both acculturation and deculturation with irregular success: "Some of the Spanish men waited years before applying for citizenship because of their inability to learn English. In fact, many of the men and women who came to America never learned English well enough to be understood" (213). It is also pointed out how some of the American-born characters, like González, had lost their identity: "Thousands of girls married 'American' boys and had children who lost their identity as 'Spics' " (213), while others were able to keep it despite the difficulties:

> Meanwhile, the children of "Spanish" boys and "American" girls continued to be discriminated against in many areas because of their surnames. Unlike a lot of other immigrants who Anglicized their last names to disguise their country of origin, few Spanish people changed their name regardless of how difficult it would be for them to get ahead. (213)

In other words, despite the difficulties and problems that could have caused having a surname of Spanish origin, most Spaniards decided to keep their real and original one, thus maintaining their hybrid identity not only through their Spanish traditions and customs but also through their family's name. There is a clear example of the hybrid subject's struggle between their American culture and their culture of origin. In Pinnick Kinnick Hill, there was a family, the Alonzo García family, who had two sons: Benjamin and Salvador. Benjamin had died during World War II in the invasion of Italy, but Salvador had been rejected in the army due to an asthmatic condition. However, when Salvador decided to apply for work in a new defense plant in Phoenix, he was rejected by the personnel man due to his Spanish origin. Although he was born in the United States and considered himself American, he was also proud of his Spanish culture:

> "Mr. Garcia, I'm sorry, we cannot hire you."
> "Why not? You told me to come ready for work."
> "Well, I have nothing to do with this, you understand, but we can't hire Mexicans."
> "But I'm not Mexican. I'm an American."
> "The name Garcia is not an American name."
> "The name Garcia happens to be my father's name and I'm proud of it."
> "Then you must be Spanish. You don't look like a Spaniard."

> "I was born in this country, and I'm just as American, or more so, than you are! One of my brothers gave his life in the war, and if I hadn't been classified 4-F, I would be defending our country right now. And now you tell me you won't hire me because my name is Garcia!"
> After this exchange, the personnel man turned to walk away. (215–219)

Salvador's discrimination shows that even those American-born descendants of Spanish immigrants could be marginalized despite being born in the United States, bilingual, and fully assimilated into American society, having even defended their country during the latest war. The new cultural subject that resulted from the combination of the Spanish and the American cultures suffered the shortcomings of being in-between cultures and the "otherness" of those who considered themselves part of the dominant American culture and decided what names were and were not "American," who was eligible for work, and which individuals were on the borderlines of acceptance or rejection by the American society.

5.3. Morell's Lower East Side Kid: From Spain to New York and Back Again

> My name is Claude Morell, in Spanish, the name is Claudio. To many of my American boyhood friends this name was difficult to pronounce, so it was decided to make a convenient and simple change. The name chosen was Larry, and it stuck, but only in the neighbourhood. Everywhere else the name remained Claude.
>
> — *Claude Morell, The Lower East Side Kid That Made It Good*

Claudio, hereafter Claude, Morell was born in Spain in 1928. When he was 11 months old, he and his parents immigrated to the United States, specifically to New York City, and settled on the Lower East Side of Manhattan between the Brooklyn and Manhattan bridges. He lived the first thirty-five years of his life in Little Italy, where, besides Italians, there were immigrants of other nationalities such as Chinese, Poles, Irish, Greeks, Jews, and Spaniards. He attended New York University, where he received a Bachelor of Arts degree, majoring in Business Administration and Liberal Arts as a minor. Then, he went to the School of Pharmacy of Long Island University, obtaining a Bachelor of Science degree. He was a pharmacist, and later, when he was 37 years old, he became a science and Spanish teacher at a high school in New York City. He got married in 1957 and had three children with his wife Mercedes: Angela, Claude, Jr., and Teresa (Morell 2008, i–iii).

The Lower East Side Kid That Made It Good (2007) is Morell's memoir of his life when Spanish immigration in New York City was still a relevant social phenomenon. In 1983, Morell moved with his wife to Spain to live on the Mediterranean coast. This book is written from the first-person perspective of the narrator, Morell himself, first as a kid, later as a young man, and finally as an adult. Most of the events described happened between the 1930s and the 1960s, when Spanish immigration in the metropolis had reached its peak and then began to decrease. As a result, Morell's testimony is a unique document, not only for the narration of his life in New York City as a descendant of Spanish immigrants but also for his description of events taking place in the Spanish community as seen from the perspective of a hybrid figure who moves seamlessly in-between worlds, between the American and the Spanish cultures. Morell presents a description of himself who, unlike his parents, inhabits New York City as a "Third Space," as something natural to his identity that can only be appreciated in other authors like de Pereda.

Morell begins his story with his parents' arrival in New York City. It is the first moment in the book where the author introduces the sense of "otherness" felt by Morell's parents upon their arrival in the United States, especially his mother's. During the author's life, there were other situations of marginalization, but this is one that his mother must have told him about, as Claude was only eleven months old when he was taken to New York City:

> According to my mother, at Ellis Island we were given a quick medical examination, our emigration cards were checked for our names, the name of the ship and from what port of Europe we began our trip. My mother was annoyed that an inspector had placed his fingers through my hair. The man was doing his job looking for fleas, lice or ticks. (2008, 2)

Morell and his parents were treated as was customary by the American authorities when immigrants arrived in New York City. All immigrants, regardless of their origin or nationality, were examined to check their state of health and whether they were fit to enter the United States. It was at this moment that they were treated as "Others" for the first time. The unequal relationship of power between the agent of the host country and the Spanish immigrant is evident. The equilibrium of forces is skewed because the Spanish immigrant has not yet been accepted as an individual worthy of being part of the dominant American culture. The immigrant depends on the agent's decision and is made to await his arbitrary decision that will allow them to enter or not in the United States.

The physical boundaries are delimited by Ellis Island. It works as a symbol of the dominance of American culture that all immigrants begin to recognize after seeing the Statue of Liberty. Ellis Island shepherded immigrants into the United States as its agents decided who could enter and who could not, who was worthy of enjoying the American way of life, and who was left out because of their physical, mental, or economic flaws, even because of their way of thinking. Poor and illiterate people, for example, were some of the main victims of these deportation practices:

> My father had made four round-trip journeys (Orba-NY, NY-Orba), his first in 1916 at the age of twenty. The first two voyages were made as a single man and his last two as a married man. Dad had very little schooling in his youth but he was smart enough to do the following --for all his trips he purchased second class tickets. He went through customs with no difficulties wearing a jacket with a pen in the front pocket and a newspaper under his arm. (2)

Aware of the possibility of being marginalized, Claude's father uses the picaresque, also seen in the case of Agapito López in *Windmills in Brooklyn*, to evade the American culture's control over the Spanish immigrant, who had already been to his native Spain four times. First, his father always buys second-class tickets to make it easier for him and his family to enter the United States through customs. Secondly, he puts a pen in his front pocket jacket and a newspaper under his arm to appear to be more educated, evading possible marginalization because of his little schooling.

However, this is not the only time that Claude's father is treated as an "Other." During his first trip to the United States in 1916, he and his young uncle Fabián had migrated looking for "riches" (22). Both made some money working "in the construction of new roads" and "working on new railroad tracks" (22), which means that they were able to find work easily. However, at this point, Claude explains that his father had to return to Spain unexpectedly:

> But after a year of success, my father quickly returned to Spain in 1917. That year the United States entered into World War I, which had begun in 1914. He was aware that immigrants were asked to volunteer their services in the military,

> and if they refused, they were deported to their homeland and never permitted to return. So he speedily came back to Spain, with the hope of another visit to the United States in the future. It was a wise decision. (22)

Claude's father knows American culture as a marginalizing agent due to his experience as a nomadic Spanish immigrant before moving there for the fourth time with his family. This creates a new ambivalence between the American culture and other foreign cultures, such as the Spanish one. Claude's father refused to participate in these recruitment techniques that produced "otherness" among those immigrants who refused to join the army. He returned to Spain as soon as this military service was imposed and came back to the United States after the end of the war in 1920.

During their first stay in the country, Claude's father and his uncle also described a group of men as "Others." They were near a pier on South Street next to the East River. A ship was on the dock, and a group of men were walking up and down a gangplank between the ship and the dock transporting bananas. They thought they were "strange men" because they "were shirtless and appeared very dark and shiny. Were they perspiring or did they have grease on their bodies?" (23). Neither man "had never seen an African-American" before (23). They considered the workers "strange" simply because Claude's father and his uncle had never seen Black people before. However, another Spaniard who was nearby understood what was happening and explained to them who they were: "He informed them that that these men were born in the United States, but their ancestors were brought here, from Africa, as slaves many years ago" (23). These Black men were not treated as socially different by the two Spaniards but were described according to their ethnic identity as a "strange" group of men, an identity that could be labeled as different and separated from the rest of the people and cultures that Claude's father and his uncle had seen in the United States.

The main method of acculturation for the youngest Spanish immigrants was school. As Morell points out, from the age of four or five, it was normal for children to start going to school. In kindergarten, little Claude's classes were all in English, which was the first tool employed to assimilate non-American cultures. In chapter three, "My Youthful Summer Years," Morell describes his process of acculturation during the summer months in the 1930s of a group of seven or eight youngsters that did one of the most culturally accepted things in American society during the hot months in New York City, i.e., to use the fire hydrants. Something unthinkable in Spain at the time. Fire hydrants had become a symbol of hot summer days to the American kids, boys and girls playing in the street who, instead of going "home and use the bathtub, go to the pool, or jump into the East River" (27), would use a wrench and a wooden plank to open the fire hydrant of their street and refresh themselves either "fully or partially dressed" (27). As Morell points out, this activity became a "ritual" that all the immigrant kids of the neighborhood enjoyed "if you lived in the city during the months of July and August" (28), until the police cars would arrive to close the fire hydrants to prevent the waste of water and to maintain the pressure.

After describing the fire hydrant practice by young American kids in the metropolis, Morell also mentions two other options for staying cool in the summer: swimming in the East River and using the Pitt Street pool. In the 1930s, the city of New York had begun the construction of public parks and pools. Morell indicates that two miles away from the neighborhood there was a new swimming pool built during the offices of Mayor LaGuardia and Robert Moses, the Parks Commissioner. It was common for families and groups of friends to go to the pool for the day: "The pool was filled with people, and several lifeguards were carefully observing the immense activity" (29)

As part of the routine of going to the pool, there was also time for food, another way of acculturation, which some scholars have described as "dietary acculturation," as the process of embracing the eating patterns of the dominant culture (Satia et al. 2001, 548). On the way back home from the pool, the youngsters would stop on Clinton Street for a typical American meal:

> Our first visit to the Pitt Street pool was not pleasurable, plus we had to walk a long distance. But on the way back to our neighbourhood we stopped on Clinton Street and sat down at a soda fountain to savor some freshly made French fries with a glass of Coca Cola on ice. Somehow, we always were hungry after spending some time in water! (29).

Morell adds that this "dietary acculturation" was already part of the young people's routine. This does not mean that young people of Spanish origin automatically stopped consuming the Spanish products that arrived in New York or the typical Spanish dishes that were homemade:

> My parents and I had just finished a hearty meal that Mom customarily prepared on Sundays. In Spanish it is called *cocido*; a three-course dinner in which all the ingredients are cooked in a large pot the pot contains some water, carrots, potatoes, celery, chickpeas, chicken, beef, pork and a meatloaf. (140)

However, it is true that regularly consuming food popularly established as characteristic of the United States, such as sodas and French fries, meant that these became part of their diet and, therefore, of their newly acquired culture. On several occasions, Morell describes other typical dishes of Spanish culture, such as *paella* or *flan*, indicating the *importance* that Spanish food has in his hybrid identity, to the extent of never making him forget his Spanish culture:

> When we arrive home it is evident that my parents are happy because I have been prompt to enjoy a tasty dish of *PAELLA* that Mom has prepared. Boy, am I lucky! This is delightful and savory dish made with rice, pork, shrimps, chicken, garlic and peppers. It is not cooked in a pot, but in a special pan, which is called the paella. (52)

Morell always pays attention to how meals are made and the typical ingredients of Spanish culture they include in each of his food descriptions. This demonstrates the narrator's interest in his culture of origin, as well as suggests an ongoing bond that keeps him close to his parents, with whom he often shares these dishes: "I see that my mother has brought us a delicious dessert that I still have room for after that splendid paella. It is *flan*, a Spanish cream custard made with eggs, milk and sugar" (53), he recalls.

These Spanish meals do not mean, however, that there is no more acculturation in relation to gastronomy. Another example of "dietary acculturation" is described in the section about Coney Island, a popular place for children like young Claude, where they would go, taking the BMT train from Little Italy through Kings County to the beach. Little Claude visited the place for the first time in 1933 when he was around five years old: "I was amazed to see such a large and long beach, but most of all, of the very large amusement centers with rides, exhibitions, concerts, souvenir shops, inexpensive restaurants and snack bars" (30), he writes. Morell emphasizes the magnificence of the place, especially the wide variety of places to eat in Coney Island. One of them, Nathan's restaurant, became one of the landmarks of American fast food in the area thanks to its hot dogs, which Claude and his friends enjoyed so much every time they went to the boardwalk of the beach: "The sea air brought on hungry sensations so you stopped at the famous Nathan's stand to munch on their well known frankfurter" (30).

This second example of how Morrell and his friends adopted cultural food elements from the American culture from a young age points out that the process of acculturation that the school had initiated continued developing outside the official institutions of the state and, on many occasions, as was the case with food, without any significant imposition by the culture of dominance. The different levels of "dietary acculturation" could vary depending on the frequency that immigrants consumed fast food and how used they were to eating their home country's traditional meals. In any case, the fact that food became an element in the process of cultural transformation of immigrant communities, as was the case of the Spanish, informs about the extent to which the environment facilitated or impeded further cultural assimilation in New York City.

The change of residence of Claude Morrell and his parents accelerated the process of loss of many original cultural traits maintained in Little Italy and its surroundings thanks to the presence of other Spanish families. One of them was the friendship of Spanish kids like little Claude, who had arrived in the city when they were very young or had even been born there: "My enjoyable world with all my friends at 54 Market Street would be a thing of the past" (37). Little Claude lost one of the main cultural connections to his primary Spanish culture, his community, by leaving behind a multicultural neighborhood where the presence of Spaniards was *important* for the maintenance of his Spanish identity. This change, according to Morell, was negative for the whole family, not just for him. His parents did not get used to the new neighborhood; they lost contact with most of their previous neighbors, and, even Morell openly points out, his mother "was unhappy" (37).

The isolation of the Morell family, separated from their Spanish culture, increased during the second half of the 1930s when Spanish immigration was at its peak. According to Rueda Hernanz (1993), the U.S. Census indicated a constant growth of the number of Spaniards from the late nineteenth century to 1930, after which the figures began to diminish (1993, 93). Political instability in Spain affected Claude's constant contact with his parents' family, especially with his grandmother, which led to a further deculturation that became rather significant to little Claude himself: "I will now describe the events that occurred in the latter years of the 1930s, which had an effect on my life. That's a long time ago, but I still remember them because they were significant to me" (57). After Morell's father's fourth trip to the United States with his family, he maintained a constant correspondence with his mother, who lived in Spain. It is the same kind of correspondence that Ros Varona indicates in *Fiesta* that ceased to occur when he stopped writing to his family, leading to a significant deculturation in him. On this occasion, the interruption is due to the death of Claude's grandmother, who dies before his father's planned trip to Spain in the summer of 1936, eliminating the reason to remain directly connected to the country: "Unfortunately, my grandmother died before the war had begun, so that my dad's aspirations of a future visit where abandoned" (57).

Both the change of neighborhood and the death of Claude's grandmother marked the deculturation phase of the protagonist, who lost contact with the closest Spanish community in Little Italy and a direct family anchorage with the Iberian Peninsula. This situation gave rise to Claude's distancing from his culture of origin and accelerated the process of cultural change in favor of the dominant American culture. This does not mean, however, that the author definitively lost contact with the Spanish immigrants, but only that his cultural ties became weaker. Besides, Morell mentions the *importance* for him and for many immigrants of Manhattan of the first Spanish community that established itself in New York City, which reached its peak between the 1920s and 1950s in the area of Cherry Street between the Brooklyn Bridge and the Manhattan Bridge. He mentions some of the most relevant businesses in the area, such as *La Ideal*, "a butcher shop," "*LA FARMACIA ESPAÑOLA*," and a Spanish establishment called "*LA VALENCIANA*" (105) in the southwest corner of Cherry and Roosevelt Street, which indicates that he and his family were still in touch with several Spanish communities in the metropolis that might have contributed to preventing Claude's deculturation from being as aggressive and radical as in other similar cases.

Claude Morrell's experience in the army in the 1950s and his subsequent nineteen-month stay in Europe further contributed to establishing his hybrid identity. Like Ros Varona, the return to Spain and the encounter with his roots helped Morrell to reconnect with his origins. Undoubtedly, the most transcendental moment for him and his neocultural identity was his marriage to Mercedes, a Spanish girl from Ondara, a village next to Orba, his parents' village in Alicante. On his journey from New York City as a "Third Space" to Ondara in mid-April of 1957, Claude tells his barber during his stopover in Madrid that he is not Spanish:

> He knew that I was not from Spain, but I quickly satisfied his wishes and told him where I was from. I was also proud to say to him that I soon would marry a young lady from Spain. He wished me luck when I departed and was pleased with my gratuity. (284)

The fact that both the barber and the protagonist himself agree that he is not Spanish suggests that, initially, the deculturation to which he has been subjected has been such that Claude has lost touch with his roots. However, the arrival of Mercedes in his life and the protagonist's contact with a new family that, unlike his own, has always lived in Spain, make the couple's wedding in Valencia even more culturally essential to consolidate his hybridism.

Claude's marriage reinforces his ties with Spain. From then on, they will be linked to the figure of Mercedes. When his father-in-law's friend asked him at the wedding banquet: "*Claudio*, I want to thank you for a wonderful wedding. I would like to ask you for your opinion on the following question. How do you compare the American woman with the Spanish girl?" (286). Claude has understood that he is now part of two worlds and answers accordingly:

> Don Vicente, I returned to Spain after an 8 month absence. I did not come back because she was Spanish; I return because she was the girl that I loved and I wanted to marry. I hope that answers your question (287).

After their honeymoon, the couple stayed during the summer months and up to the month of October in Orba. Then, they departed to the United States, and Claude began working at the pharmacy while Mercedes was pregnant. First, they lived with his parents for several months before moving to an apartment in Knickerbocker Village, between the Manhattan and Brooklyn Bridge. Five years later, when the three children of the family had been born, they decided to move to a house in Queens.

The construction of the new hybrid self during the neoculturation phase also affected the rest of the family. The three children were named Angela,

Claude Jr., and Teresa and were educated both in Spanish and English. They did "annual voyages to Spain" (301) to remain in touch with the family. After the pharmacy and his work for two city agencies, Morrell became a Spanish teacher at Bryant High School in Queens and later a science teacher at the Aviation High School. He was a teacher for eighteen years, although he always kept his part-time job as a pharmacist. When asked, Claude always considered himself an American:

> "The young girl laughed heartily and surprised me when she asked, "Mister Morell, are you from New York City?" I answered, "Yes." How did she know that I was a New Yorker? Is it because we are direct and blunt in our opinions or is it our indistinct and peculiar way of speaking the English language?" (339)

However, when the couple had vacations or a sabbatical year, they always returned to Spain, where they felt at home: "My wife and I traveled to all parts of Spain visiting numerous historic places... Fortunately, during our many trips throughout Spain we always had the opportunity to return to Orba, our home base" (340). Claude and Mercedes considered Orba their "home base," so when he retired in 1983, they decided to reside permanently in Spain. Claude was still attached to his family and his friends in New York City, a space that he considered as his own. However, when he decided where to settle permanently after so many years of experiences and travels, the author and his wife chose Spain, as it was their homeland for both, completing the last stage of transculturation where he accepted his ambivalence as a hybrid individual that was constructed over the years in New York City as a "Third Space."

5.4. Felipe Alfau's creation of the Americaniard

> This is something that we frequently do when abroad, so that one has the strange situation of two Spaniards posing before each other as Latin Americans and both being surprised at their accent and suspecting that after all the parents of both were gallegos.
>
> — *Felipe Alfau, Chromos*

Felipe Alfau and his family migrated to the United States in 1916. They settled in New York City, where Alfau worked for a brief period writing for *La Prensa*, the first Spanish-speaking newspaper in the metropolis (Alfau 1999, vi). However, Alfau spent most of his life working as a translator for Chase Bank and writing. In the 1920s, when he was only fourteen, he wrote *Locos: A Comedy of Gestures*. The novel, one of the two he wrote in English, would take eight years to be published, as it was not until 1936 that it reached the American bookstores. Twelve years later, in 1948, Alfau wrote his *magnum opus*, *Chromos* (Alfau 1999, vi). However, the novel was not rediscovered until 1990, when Dalkey's Editor Steven Moore rescued it from oblivion and decided to publish it for the first time (Alfau 1999, vi). As a result, Alfau's figure as a novelist and as a poet was revived, and his literary contribution became part of postcolonial and migration literature in the United States.

In his *magnum opus*, Alfau is presented both as a narrator and protagonist of the story, breaking partially the fourth wall between him as an author and his audience. At the beginning of the story, the process of cultural transformation of Doctor Don José de los Ríos, Don Pedro Guzman O'Moore Algoracid, and the author himself is so advanced that the three men can already be considered hybrid individuals. Alfau is aware of this cultural hybridization and coins the term "Americaniard" to name the transformation of the cultural identity of his characters. Under these premises, the three friends are portrayed as unique individuals that inhabit the space of Spanish immigrants in the city that became their "Third Space." Anderson (2006) explains that the conception of space has always been subject to the dominant culture. The metropolis is thus a location of unstable boundaries where the "Americaniards" are hybrid individuals moving in-between boundaries of two cultures that they seem to have intermingled as one.

In postcolonial representation, the figure of the "Other" in the metropolis as "Third Space" becomes even more relevant in shaping the situation of these characters. On this occasion, the figure of the "Other" in the United States is epitomized by three Spanish immigrants: the narrator, Don José, and Don Pedro. In the United States, one of the most common representations of the "Other" is the migrant, as this nation of émigrés has become a theater of constant clash of cultures that seem to be overcome by the process of assimilation and the speed at which the new settlers adapt to the dominant culture of the host country. As a result, from the beginning of the story, Alfau vocalizes through his characters how the national construction of the American identity around the wider English-speaking community forces immigrants to assimilate the language of the culture of dominance and to keep any other language separated from the Anglo-American culture controlling the First Space.

At the beginning of the novel, Alfau uses the term "Americaniard" to define Spanish immigrants who live in the United States, especially in New York City. His definition refers to the hybrid result of the combination of the culture of the Spanish immigrants, the "Other," and the dominant Anglo-American culture of the United States. Spaniards are occupying the Third Space, while the First Space is inhabited by the American nation imagined by the previous immigrants that managed to establish an English-speaking community. The Americaniard's feeling of "Other" is made evident several times in the novel. Because of the time spent in the metropolis, the three friends have already negotiated the boundaries between their native and host cultures. All three have accepted the conventions established in New York as a "Third Space," and their identity has been shaped by the interactions between them as Spanish immigrants and the reception of them as individuals, initially "othered" and now established as an integral part of the metropolis. Don Pedro Guzman O'Moore Algoracid comes from an earlier hybridization due to his British and Moorish origins, embodied in his surnames and further evidenced by the nickname "The Moor." It is Don Pedro who, at the beginning of the story, expresses his refusal to accept English as part of the process of animalization in the American culture: "According to Don Pedro, a Spaniard speaking English is indeed a most incongruous phenomenon, and the acquisition of this other language, far from increasing his understanding of life, if this were possible, only renders it hopelessly muddled and obscure" (Alfau 1999, 26). Throughout the novel, the rejection of the English language as the spearhead of the culture of reception is repeated constantly by Alfau, although it has already become part of the identity of his "Americaniard" protagonists.

In *Chromos*, the cultural conflict between the Spanish and the American cultures continues due to the hybrid identity of the protagonists. Alfau uses the streets of New York to represent the narrator's conflict to write a novel inside a novel, explaining, in part, the relevance of the work as a thread of the dominant culture over the Spanish one: "He held and shook before us like a marionette his straw man: the 'Americaniard'" (1999, 31). Eventually, the metropolis becomes an instrument for the author to capture the cultural implications that the boundaries between the Spanish culture of origin and the American culture of reception permeate the construction of the new hybrid identity of his characters through their location in the temporal space of the city:

> Doña Rosario had once said almost prophetically: "The place where people are brought up has a decided influence upon their lives, it charts their existence which acquires in time almost the same shape that their place of origin and early development presents" (1999, 54).

To conclude, it can be argued that Alfau uses his own characters to justify his creation of a work that was already written:

> He concentrated on me: "You should write a book about the Americaniards, somebody should, but you have not written for a long time—anyway you could not write anymore about your people in Spain—have been too long away, forgotten too much—don't know what it's all about and you could not write about Americans—don't know enough— impossible ever to understand another people." (Alfau 1999, 32–33)

The author desires to engage the reader in the phenomenon of postmodernist absurdity in which the characters of *Chromos* move within the metropolis. From the beginning of his story, Alfau is aware of the complexity of his novel, which encompasses the cultural assimilation of Spanish immigrants as they become hybrid American and Spanish subjects. However, this change in his own identity keeps the Americaniard in-between cultures, as he will never again be considered a Spaniard if he returns to Spain or as another American if he ultimately decides to remain in the United States as a citizen.

5.5. Victoria, Mona, and Luz Arenas: Americaniard Women

> Probablemente la culpa la tuviera el hecho de haberse instalado en un cuarto de alquiler en la zona de Cherry Street, el asentamiento de españoles más antiguo de la ciudad. Allí, en el extremo sureste de la isla de Manhattan, frente al waterfront, junto a los muelles, bajo el ruido estrepitoso del arranque del puente de Brooklyn, se concentraban desde finales del siglo pasado varios miles de almas procedentes del mismo rincón del globo.[80]
>
> — *María Dueñas, Las hijas del Capitán*

80 This was probably because they had moved into a rented room in the Cherry Street area, the oldest Spanish settlement in the city. There, on the south-eastern side of Manhattan Island, facing the waterfront, next to the docks, under the thundering noise of the Brooklyn Bridge, several thousand souls from the same corner of the globe had been gathering since the end of the last century.

In 1936, New York was the city with the largest number of Spanish immigrants in the United States (Rueda Hernanz 1993). Most of them had settled there due to its proximity to the Iberian Peninsula, being the main port of entry for immigration from Europe, and the initial ease at finding a job after their arrival. The 1930s was one of the last relevant decades for Spanish immigration to the United States. The economic problems and the political instability brought about by the Spanish Civil War provoked an abundant migration of Spaniards to America, but they found greater restrictions in Latin America between 1936 and 1945 with harsh controls and measures aimed at selecting immigrants according to the needs of each country and always in favor of the interests of their own national population (Sallé et al. 2009, 28).

Dueñas's *Las hijas del Capitán* is the only work analyzed that is not based on a true story but inspired both by the lives of many Spaniards who arrived in New York and by the historical background of authors such as Fernández and Argeo (2014), who had rediscovered essential archival material to reconstruct the lives of these immigrants in the metropolis in the 1930s. The story of the Arenas sisters begins like most of the lives of Spanish immigrants: in their home country. The maternal grandmother Mamá Pepa, with whom her daughter Doña Remedios and granddaughters live, dies, and they are forced to leave the *corralón* that has sheltered them. Torn away from their native Málaga and their provincial life in the neighborhood of La Trinidad, Doña Remedios and her three daughters Victoria, Mona, and Luz take on a new life in New York City. The unexpected decision of the father to finally settle down and run a restaurant, El Capitán, on 14th Street in Manhattan leads them to make the decision to travel to the other side of the Atlantic, cutting ties with what had been their world till then.

Shortly after settling down as a real family and starting the business, their father suffers a fortuitous and unexpected fatal accident. His widow and daughters are left without the mooring of the person who connected them with New York, her husband and their father, Emilio Arenas, whom the girls were beginning to get to know after a series of comings and goings that had turned him into an intermittent figure in their childhood. They then make the decision to face their new destiny and stay in the city at least until the conflict with the Compañía Trasatlántica Española is settled, with the confident hope of returning to Spain at some point in the future.

The arrival of Emilio Arenas in New York meant a change in the Arenas family. Emilio found a place where he could settle permanently and, in time, also bring his family. However, outside the Spanish quarter, his work, like that of many Spaniards of his time, was almost on the margins of society. They were the hardest, lowest-paid, and least regarded jobs in American society. To protect each other, the Spaniards concentrated in the neighborhood around Cherry Street, where the sense of belonging and community was greater while remaining on the fringes of others. New York City as a Third Space created ghettos for immigrants; they were the "Other" and therefore not a desired part of the American culture:

> La colonia fue después creciendo y diversificando ocupaciones, llegaron parientes, paisanos, cada vez más mujeres, hasta familias enteras que se amontonaron en pisos baratos por las calles cercanas: Water, Catherine, Monroe, Roosevelt, Oliver, James…[81] (Dueñas 2018, 19).

This concentration of Spaniards in the neighborhood was followed by the establishment of businesses dedicated to covering all the needs of immigrants who, on settling in the metropolis, longed for the company, the language, and the food of a far-off Spain to which many would never return:

> En La Ideal compraban chuletas, mollejas y morcillas; con el pulpo se hacían donde Chacón; para el jabón, el tabaco y los trajes hechos iban a Casa Yvars y Casasín; para los remedios, a la farmacia española. Los tragos y el café los tomaban en el bar Castilla, en el café Galicia o en El Chorrito, donde su dueño, el catalán Sebastián Estrada, los atendía con sus más de cien kilos de energía contagiosa y les recordaba un día sí y otro también que la gran Raquel Meller era clienta asidua cada vez que pisaba la ciudad. El Círculo Valenciano, el Centro Vasco-Americano y algunas sociedades locales gallegas tenían por allí sus cuarteles; había sastres, barberías, fondas y tiendas de comestibles como Llana o La Competidora Española en donde hacerse con garbanzos, habichuelas y pimentón. Había en definitiva, entrelazando las idiosincrasias regionales, un mullido sentimiento de comunidad. (Dueñas 2018, 19–20)[82]

81 "The colony then grew and diversified its occupations, relatives arrived, fellow countrymen, more and more women, even entire families that crowded into cheap apartments in the nearby streets: Water, Catherine, Monroe, Roosevelt, Oliver, James…"

82 At La Ideal they bought chops, sweetbreads, and black pudding; they got hold of octopus at Chacón's; for soap, tobacco, and ready-tailored suits they went to Casa Yvars and Casasín; for medicines, to the Spanish pharmacy. For drinks

The marginalization of Spanish immigrants as the "Other" provoked a strong sense of community among them that favored the preservation of their culture for decades, even though their proportion among other dominated cultures was rather small. It was the younger ones, like the Arenas sisters, or those already born on American soil, who, in their capacity as Americaniards, exploited their bilingualism to assimilate into the American host culture. If Emilio Arenas always seemed like a passing visitor in all the ports he called at, including New York, his daughters managed to step into a world that allowed them to enter American culture more easily.

Indeed, one of the most representative cases of this migration can be found in the daughters of Emilio Arenas, Victoria, Mona, and Luz, who arrived in New York with their mother in the 1930s when the bulk of Spanish emigration was at its peak. Like most women who appear in the files of La Nacional, at the beginning of the story Emilio's daughters have a close relationship with the Spanish Benevolent Society, so much so that their father's death is notified in that institution at the beginning of the novel: "Ellas lanzándose escaleras abajo detrás del muchacho y corriendo luego arrebatadas hacia La Nacional, donde se recibió el aviso" (Dueñas 2018, 14).[83]

If we observe, for example, the cases of the protagonists of Dueñas's *Las hijas del Capitán*, the changes that the Arenas sisters undergo take place in a very short period, while Prudencio's evolution from a child to a young man and then to an adult is described over different decades and the length of two novels. This contrast between the process of transculturation of the Arenas sisters and Prudencio can also be perceived even among the sisters

---

and coffee, they went to bar Castilla, or café Galicia or El Chorrito, where its owner, the Catalan-born Sebastián Estrada, served them with his more than one hundred kilos of contagious energy and reminded them day in and day out that the great Raquel Meller was a regular customer every time she visited the city. The Círculo Valenciano, the Centro Vasco-Americano and some local Galician societies had their headquarters around there; there were tailors, barbers, inns, and grocery shops such as Llana or La Competidora Española where you could get hold of chickpeas, beans and paprika. There was, in short, intertwined with regional idiosyncrasies, a gently sense of community.

83 They rushed down the stairs after the boy and then ran wildly after him to La Nacional, where the notice was received.

themselves, as Victoria, Mona, and Luz will evolve differently, and, as a result, the final hybrid subject is unique in each case. In all the stories, the cultural identity of the characters changes. As there is a transition between cultures, the identity is not static and is naturally affected by the personality of each of the protagonists, by the interactions they engage in, and by the evolution of the story, which influences their cultural behavior. They undergo acculturation because they are constantly in contact with the American dominant society. The identities of each character experience a transformation. This transformation is different in the case of Prudencio, born in the United States and a son of Spanish emigrants living in one of New York's Spanish colonies, and in the case of the Arenas sisters, who belong to a very young but already adult first generation, what we could consider a 1.75 generation type of immigrant. The lack of scholarship on *Windmills in Brooklyn* and *Las hijas del Capitán* in relation to the process of transculturation of their main characters through the interactions between their traditional culture of origin and their culture of reception requires a thorough study of the influence of this phenomenon on the formation of their identities.

Victoria, Mona, and Luz belong to the 1.75 generation (Rumbaut 2004, 1167). Having arrived in New York City at a young adult age, they begin their evolution and assimilation into the American culture while trying to maintain their Spanish identity, represented by their family—especially their mother—their language, and their contact with the Spanish immigrant community spread throughout the different neighborhoods of the metropolis. The Arenas sisters are older than little Prudencio, and their age is closer to that of young Prudencio. This makes their social interactions with their environment different, as is their process of transculturation. In this case, the process of assimilation of the Arenas sisters takes place at a later age, which means that their evolution as subjects is more complex and framed in a shorter space of time in the novel. Each of the three sisters experiences the process of transculturation differently, transforming their culture of origin and their individual identity while maintaining different features within their new hybrid self. They go through hard and painful moments of uncertainty, anguish, insecurity, and hesitation, like all the immigrants who left their homeland in search of a better life, and feel the uncertainty of not knowing if they were doing the right thing. Pérez Firmat points out that "only the 1.5 generation is marginal to neither culture... unlike younger and older compatriots" (1996, 8). This may be the case for the Arenas sisters, who

> may actually find it possible to circulate within and through both the old and the new cultures. While one-and-a-halfers may never feel entirely at ease in either one, they are capable of availing themselves of the resources—linguistic, artistic, commercial—that both cultures have to offer. In some ways they are both first and second generation. (1996, 8)

They go through certain moments of inner heartbreak that push them to lean on compatriots who, like them, go through similar experiences of uprooting and initial helplessness. As a result, "at some point... the immigrant begins to find it impossible to sustain, even precariously, the fiction of rootedness" (1996, 8), which can also be perceived in the figure of the Arenas sisters as multicultural circumstances surrounding the evolution of the characters.

If Spanish migration to the United States has been marginalized for decades, the obliviousness of the role Spanish women played is not an exception. According to Cagiao Vila,

> cuando en las últimas décadas del siglo XIX las mujeres comienzan a participar directamente en los flujos de salida hacia América se enfrentaron a los problemas que ya eran habituales para los hombres añadiéndose a ellos los inherentes a la condición de su género. (Liñares Giraut et al. 2007b, 161)[84]

Six women allow us to see through their eyes and deeds the transculturation of Spanish immigrants in American society. In her novel, María Dueñas uses an encounter between Victoria and some of her husband's fellow countrywomen to describe the first generation of women who arrived from the other side of the Atlantic:

> Ellas, por su parte, se quedaban en casa al tanto de todo, a veces incluso compartían las viviendas llenas de muebles de segunda mano. Con un ojo puesto en aquellos que dejaron y otra atento en los hijos que crecían, desayunaban tazones de leche caliente con pan migado, guisaban con aceite Ybarra, compraban en las tiendas de los italianos, lavaban la ropa a mano en las pilas de las cocinas,

84 When in the last decades of the nineteenth century women began to participate directly in the outflows to America, they faced the problems that were already common for men, but also those inherent to their gender.

> se resistían a aprender inglés y cosían en casa para talleres ajenos a centavo la pieza. No se concedían ni lamentos ni caprichos, se apoyaban unas a otras en los quebrantos, pagaban religiosamente sus alquileres, usaban a sus niños como intérpretes cuando necesitaban abrirse al mundo y tiraban hacia adelante con coraje y dignidad, enviando cada tanto al otro lado del océano cartas que narraban pequeños y grandes aconteceres mientras se escondían zozobras con las preocupaciones y melancolías. (Dueñas 2018, 400)[85]

They were daughters of the Spanish culture, and the change of country had not meant a change in their customs, for they behaved as if they were still living in their homeland: they bought products from their land, they cooked traditional dishes, they did not learn the new language, they only interacted with the colony, and they celebrated their patron saint festivals surrounded by popular folklore; they had simply changed their location. A good example of this type of non-integrated woman is Remedios, Emilio Arenas's wife, a quiet, hard-working, practical woman who sees in her daughter Victoria's wedding economic stability and well-being that she lacked, and which she also wishes for her other two daughters: "Y la única solución que usted ve para que las niñas sienten la cabeza son unos maridos que las aten cortas, ¿no?" (317).[86] Some, like Milagros, the Arenas family's downstairs neighbor, had to face life with two young children to care for after her husband had abandoned her:

> Así que decidió vestirse de luto ignorando si realmente era una viuda, y se lanzó a trabajar: acabó como costurera en un taller del Garment District, como tantas inmigrantes españolas e italianas, y así logró sacar adelante a sus hijos y después

85 "They, for their behalf, stayed at home and kept an eye on things, sometimes even sharing their homes full of second-hand furniture. With one eye on those they left behind and the other on their growing children, they breakfasted bowls of hot milk with crusty bread, cooked with Ybarra oil, shopped in the Italian shops, washed clothes by hand in the kitchen sinks, resisted learning English and sewed at home for other people's workshops for one cent a piece. They did not indulge in whining or whims, they supported each other in times of hardship, paid their rents religiously, used their children as interpreters when they needed to open to the world and pushed forward with courage and dignity, sending letters from time to time to the other side of the ocean that recounted small and big events while hiding their worries and melancholy."

86 "And the only solution you see for girls to settle down is husbands who tie them up short, right?"

> cuando ellos formaron sus propias familias y ella podría haber vuelto a disfrutar de sus ahorriños porque todos los que la precavieron estaban ya muertos y nadie le daría la monserga ni la haría avergonzarse por su torpeza, fue cuando quebró el Banco de Lago en el que tantos compatriotas tenían sus ahorros, y ya no hubo opción. Se quedó en Nueva York, haciendo en el salón de su casa flores de papel que después vendía a una tienda a tres centavos la pieza. (106)[87]

Milagros Couceiro takes a step forward in her cultural transition as she faces the new society in which she lives on her own. She works, interacts, and lives with immigrants who are no longer only her compatriots, and she intermingles with the environment. Others, though born in the land of opportunity, survive in the squalid world of Mulberry Bend, in the Five Points neighborhood:

> Nacida en un burdel del infame vecindario de Five Points, hija de una prostituta canaria y el órgano reproductor de un cliente cualquiera que una noche imprecisa pagó unos centavos por aliviarse dentro de ella sobre un mugriento jergón: ese era el origen de sor Lito (116).[88]

And, indeed, it is the land of opportunity, or at least that is how it is presented: "Sor Lito había acabado siendo la primera religiosa católica que se sentó en las aulas de la cercana Universidad de Nueva York" (141).[89] Unaware that she has Spanish blood in her, until one day, by chance, he understands a few words in Spanish: "Dos religiosas católicas de hábito impoluto que hablaban entre sí en una lengua que a la joven le evocó

87 "So she decided to dress in mourning, not knowing if she was really a widow, and started to work: she ended up as a seamstress in a Garment District workshop, like so many Spanish and Italian immigrants, and so she managed to raise her children, and then, when they had raised their own families and she could have gone back to enjoying her savings because all those who had forewarned her were already dead and no one would give her a hard time or make her feel ashamed of her clumsiness, that was when the Banco de Lago, where so many of her compatriots had their savings, went bankrupt, and there was no other choice. She stayed in New York, making paper flowers in her living room, which she then sold to a shop for three cents apiece." [My translation]

88 "Born in a brothel in the infamous Five Points neighbourhood, the daughter of a Canadian prostitute and the reproductive organ of a random customer who one vague night paid a few cents to relieve himself inside her on a filthy mattress: that was the origin of Sister Lito."

89

tiempos perdidos" (117).[90] Consuelito, or Sister Lito, unwittingly returns to her mother's culture, but this does not prevent her from going a step further in her integration into American culture, and, in addition to taking the religious habit, she graduates from New York University with a law degree.

The three Arenas sisters begin their social and working lives in the city at the same time. Three different characters who evolve at different paces, whose integration into New York society is unequal. One of "the beneficial consequences of this intermediate location" as part of the 1.5 generation is the fact that "they may actually be able to choose cultural habitats" (Pérez Firmat 1996, 5). Victoria, the eldest, prudent, responsible, and rational, develops her daily life within the Spanish community: she is the one who helps the most in the family business when they lost their father. She marries a Spanish widower and goes to live with him in the vicinity of the Spanish community in Park Slope. It seems that her world evolves in a calm, natural, and more anodyne way until she meets her husband's son, Chano.

When Victoria meets him, the reader understands the words of Pérez Firmat when he points out that "one-and-a-halfers are translation artists. Tradition bound but translation bent, they are sufficiently immersed in each culture to give both ends of the hyphen their due" (1996, 5). Chano belongs to a second generation who considers themselves American. Besides his name, there is little trace of his Cuban origin. His father had no choice but to be Cuban; however, it seems that Chano has chosen his Americanness over his "cubanía" as "only those immigrants who arrived here between infancy and adulthood share both the atavism of their parents and the Americanness of their children" (1996, 5).

Mona, the middle sister, is the most pragmatic one. She is the first sister to take a casual job because she knows how necessary money is at that moment. And she is the one to come into close contact with another community of Spaniards: those who live on the Upper West Side. When Mona agrees to look after Doña Maxi, a supposedly wealthy old Spanish woman who only retains her social position, she meets important people and moves around a much more cosmopolitan area of New York than the simple

90 "Two Catholic nuns in immaculate habits who spoke to each other in a language that reminded the young woman of lost times."

working-class neighborhood of 14th Street. But at the same time, she also meets unsavory people linked to the Italian mafia and encounters the world of illegal gambling organized by Puerto Ricans.

Mona experiences biculturalism not onlybecause of her contact with two different cultures but also because she experiences "a situation where the two cultures achieve a balance that makes it difficult to determine which is the dominant and which is the subordinate" (Pérez Firmat 1996, 6). All this provides her with a global, current, and fresher vision of American society, which encourages her to modernize her business, behaving like a real enterprising woman who tackles problems head-on, looking for resources wherever she can find them. Mona is also the one to provide her sister Luz with the balance and good sense she lacks, always supporting and advising her.

Luz, the youngest, is the most cheerful and lively, but also the most unconscious and impulsive. She starts working in a neighborhood laundry owned by a Basque couple and soon develops her vocation as an artist, even if she must use deception and lies to do so. She undergoes not only the most radical physical change in accordance with Broadway fashion at the time but also in her cultural transition as a nomadic subject. Her search for an equilibrium between her culture of origin and her culture of reception is the most complicated one. The balance of power between both cultures affects her actions, while her naivety and lack of common sense sometimes turn her into a victim of the circumstances, from which she emerges a stronger woman thanks to her sister Mona's resolute help.

The three young women begin a progressive cultural transformation as soon as they arrive in the metropolis:

> La evidencia creciente de que sus hijas iban cambiando con los días: Victoria ya con casa propia y su nuevo papel de mujer casada, Mona escapándose constantemente como una lagartija, Luz con esos pelos teñidos y esos descoques que cada vez les recordaban más a las mujeres sin asomo de vergüenza que se veían en los anuncios colgantes, hasta un sombrero se había comprado últimamente. (Dueñas 2018, 415)[91]

91 The growing evidence that their daughters were changing as the days went by: Victoria with her own house and her new role as a married woman, Mona constantly running away like a lizard, Luz with that dyed hair and those unbowed looks that reminded them more and more of the shameless women seen in the hanging advertisements, she had even bought a hat lately.

Some changes have to do with their relationships and behavior with their surroundings, and others with their physical appearance. After their father's death, they no longer are the unfriendly, ill-mannered, and proud young women who did not relate to the community in which they lived, hurt as they were at having been dragged to that continent. "Y sus tres hijas, con esa actitud tan insolente y farruca que ninguna se molestaba en disimular, se habían ganado a pulso una fama que bien poco contribuía en su beneficio" (35).[92] From that moment on, they begin to open to the world: first to the neighborhood, starting to get in touch with their neighbor Doña Milagros, who in turn puts them in contact with Sister Lito, then with the landlady Moneo and the Iragaray couple, owners of the laundry, and even patronizes, as also does Luz, the Nacional.

The next step takes them out of their comfort zone of 14th Street: Mona to the Upper West Side and Luz to Broadway and West Ninth Street in Hispanic Harlem, while Victoria sees to the clientele of El Capitan and later moves to her husband's neighborhood. With the second blow to their morale, the attack on the shop on the day of its reopening, it is confirmed that the change in the girls' behavior has been perceived by the people of the neighborhood; they are now part of it, and as such, they help them:

> Pronto hubo dentro ocho o nueve mujeres, luego una docena, luego casi veinte, y Las Hijas del Capitán se convirtió de repente en uno de esos pequeños milagros de solidaridad colectiva tan comunes entre los inmigrantes. Así funcionaban siempre, en los buenos ratos y en las adversidades, frente a las alegrías y ante los derrumbamientos: al fin y al cabo, eran como una balsa de compatriotas que flotaban contra viento y marea en la inmensidad de Nueva York. Si no se amparaban entre ellos, invisibles como eran tan a menudo, nadie más los iba a ayudar. (519)[93]

---

92 And his three daughters, with that insolent and farcical attitude that none of them bothered to conceal, had earned themselves a reputation that did little to help them.

93 "Soon there were eight or nine women inside, then a dozen, then almost twenty, and Las Hijas del Capitán suddenly became one of those small miracles of collective solidarity so common among immigrants. This is how they always functioned, in good times and in adversity, in the face of joys and in the face of breakdowns: after all, they were like a raft of compatriots floating against the odds in the immensity of New York. If they did not shelter each other, invisible as they often were, no one else would help them."

The first physical change of the young women took place at Victoria's wedding, leaving behind their worn-out Spanish clothes and changing them for light dresses, gloves, and silk stockings: "…y las hermanas de la novia, por supuesto, deslumbrantes las dos con sus vestidos de seda floreada, los guantes claros de primavera y las vistosas pamelas de Nortons que les había regalado el novio" (289).[94] The next transformation is much more cosmopolitan and luxurious but less lasting in time, barely one night, and will bring them into contact with people and places unimaginable for girls from La Calle Catorce: the glamor of the dresses and their accessories, even if they come from the pawnshop of an old Jew: "sandalias de piel teñida, escarpines forrados, calzado cerrado y abierto, tacón alto, tacón medio, tacón bajo" (392),[95] the sophistication of the hairstyles and make-up that Adela, the Puerto Rican, manages to do for them: "¿un recogido o cabello suelto, qué prefieren? Suelto, dijeron las dos a la vez" (394).[96] And, above all, that dinner in the Sert Room of the Waldorf Astoria with the heir to the Spanish crown, Don Alfonso de Borbón, accompanied by Xavier Cugat's orchestra: "levita negra con faldones y solapas de seda, chaleco de piqué marfil, white tie y zapatos de charol: el clásico attire masculino para acudir en la ciudad a cualquier entorno de empaque después de las seis" (404),[97] and the look of the director: "cara ancha, nariz prominente, calvo y con bigote fino; sobre la camisa blanca plagada de chorreras, llevaba puesta una extravagante chaqueta de lentejuelas" (412).[98] Dueñas is clear about this cultural transformation in Chapter 69 when Luz and Tony are dancing:

94 "and the bride's sisters, of course, both dazzling in their flowered silk dresses, light spring gloves and the colorful Nortons pamelas given to them by the groom."

95 "dyed leather sandals, lined booties, closed and open shoes, high heels, medium heels, low heels."

96 "An updo or loose hair, which do you prefer? Loose, they both said at the same time."

97 "black frock coat with silk lapels, ivory pique waistcoat, white tie and patent leather shoes: the classic men's attire for going out in the city in any sophisticated ambiance after six o'clock."

98 "broad face, prominent nose, bald and thin moustache; over his white shirt riddled with splotches, he wore an extravagant sequinned jacket."

> Luz y Tony bailaban con una gracia y un desparpajo que llamaba la atención. El bolitero lo hacía con cuerpo ágil, frescura y buen ritmo; al fin y al cabo, él mismo era hijo de cubana, como lo eran también miles de vecinos de su Tampa natal. Pero la que verdaderamente deslumbró fue Luz: como si a través del baile sacara de su cuerpo los demonios que llevaba dentro, pareció transmutarse en otra mujer (420).[99]

But Luz had already shown a new version of herself a few days before: "Su melena castaña había pasado a ser pelirroja, se había depilado las cejas hasta dejarlas convertidas en dos finos trazos arqueados que parecían pintados con un pincel" (332).[100] She had become fashionable, as young American show business hopefuls were wont to do, and had undergone a change that made her resemble Rita Hayworth, also the daughter of a Spaniard (333). On the other hand, in the universe of the Arenas sisters, men started to revolve around them, attracted by the beauty and hybrid personality of these three women. One of the first to appear was the shy César Osorio, a boy with a pleasant and well-groomed appearance:

> Por eso también había invitado esa noche al corresponsal de su diario de cabecera, Fernández Arias, y ahí estaba el hombre tan satisfecho, charlando con unos y otros frente a un bargueño de taracea después de haberse quitado de encima a Máxima Osorio, la señora de la silla de ruedas, esa plasta de mujer que cada vez que lo pillaba por banda le insistía machacona para que comentara en sus crónicas sociales los avances de su ahijado como asistente del doctor Castroviejo, ambos presentes, y del que se decía que llevaba un carrerón espectacular. (84)[101]

---

99 "Luz and Tony danced with a grace and enthusiasm that attracted everyone's attention. The *bolitero* did it with an agile body, freshness, and good rhythm; after all, he was himself the son of a Cuban lady, as were thousands of his neighbours in his native Tampa. But it was Luz who really dazzled: as if in her dance she was getting rid of the demons inside her, she seemed to transmute into another woman."

100 "Her brown hair had changed to red; her eyebrows had been plucked to become two thin arched strokes that looked as if they had been drawn with a brush."

101 "That is why he had also invited that night the correspondent of his favorite daily newspaper, Fernández Arias, and there he was, so satisfied, chatting with everyone in front of an inlaid *bargueño* after having got rid of Máxima Osorio, the lady in the wheelchair, that annoying woman who every time she corned him persistently insisted that he comment in his social chronicles on the progress of his godson as assistant to Dr Castroviejo, both present, and of whom it was said to enjoy a spectacular career."

César Osorio represents part of the Spanish upper class of the time, assimilated into American society: "En general el profesor español se mantuvo alejado de la colectividad,"[102] as mentioned by Rueda Hernanz (1993, 91). Well positioned socially, living in the Upper West Side, with excellent academic preparation that allowed him to work as an ophthalmologist assistant to Dr. Castroviejo, he was unable to win Mona's love; neither the supposedly casual encounters that he provoked, nor the details he gave her, nor the job he offered her of looking after the doctor's elderly aunt made her feel true love for him, despite being aware of his intentions. César Osorio represents the type of person whose integration is due not only to his social status but also to his academic training, something like what happens nowadays when the younger generations find greater support in looking for job opportunities outside their borders.

Another interesting man is Luciano Barona. He is a widower of Almerian origin with a son of a similar age to the Arenas sisters. He works as a representative of a tobacco factory selling tobacco in bars and restaurants, like a *teveriano*, which is why one day he entered El Capitán: "El tabaquero había vuelto a aparecer ese mediodía por El Capitán; tras otro rato de conversación supieron que se llamaba Luciano Barona, que sufría de acidez de estómago y que nació en Alhama de Almería" (148).[103] Although at first it is believed that he intends to marry the mother, it was Victoria, the eldest of the sisters, who finally became his wife. Luciano is a good person who assumes the responsibility of being the only man and head of the family. Brave, he is not afraid to defend the honor of women when necessary, which will bring him fatal consequences. Luciano is described as a calm, thoughtful, splendid, and affable man who is happy to have a young and beautiful woman by his side. He embodies the example of many Spaniards who decided to move to the United States looking for a better life and became part of those immigrants who were assimilated by the culture of origin, holding the low paying jobs: "lavó platos, fregó suelos, picó verduras, selló paquetes de azúcar en la Domino Sugar Refinery, entró

102 "In general, the Spanish professor stayed away from the community."

103 "The tobacco seller had reappeared at El Capitan that afternoon; after another chat they learned that his name was Luciano Barona, that he suffered from heartburn and that he was born in Alhama de Almería."

después como dependiente en una pequeña tienda de tabacos en Atlantic Avenue en la que vendían cigarros de manufactura casera,"[104] as he moved between borders trying to establish himself as part of American society and to create a Spanish family inside the community.

Tony, the *tampeño* or *bolitero*, is the son of Antonio Carreño, from Asturias, a friend of Luciano's who, like him, worked as a representative for a tobacco company until one day he decided to leave New York and settle in Tampa, Florida. He set up a place that served food during the day and at night, in the middle of Prohibition. He fell into gambling and alcohol until one day the mafia shot him twice. Little Tony's mother's Cuban family then decides to send him away to study in another state, with mixed results. When he turned up in New York, he was already in his thirties and was overseeing a group of *boliteros*:

> los vendedores de lotería clandestina que poblaban las calles de Nueva York, al olor de la fiesta ya estaban allí también. Desde Cuba había venido el juego de la bolita años atrás y, tras arraigarse, no paraba de crecer. Prohibida y perseguida por la ley, condenados sus responsables hasta con penas de cárcel, su popularidad resistía contra viento y marea. La lotería de los pobres, la llamaban algunos, a base de pequeñas apuestas, uno podía acostarse pobre como una rata y levantarse a la mañana siguiente dueño de una suma medianamente sustanciosa. (297–98)[105]

Tony's friendship with Barona brought him closer to Mona. On the other hand, Chano, Luciano's boxer son, appears just as a guest as the bride and groom are having their wedding photo taken, and the newlyweds' thoughts at that moment are premonitory:

> El fotógrafo ya había apretado el obturador y en esa placa quedarían grabadas para la eternidad la imagen borrosa de un novio maduro al que su propio

104 "He washed dishes, scrubbed floors, chopped vegetables, sealed sugar packets at the Domino Sugar Refinery, then became an assistant at a small tobacco shop in Atlantic Avenue that sold home-made cigars."

105 "the clandestine lottery sellers who populated the streets of New York were already there too, on the scent of the party. The game had come from Cuba years before and, after taking root, it continued to grow. Banned and persecuted by the law, its perpetrators even sentenced to prison, its popularity resisted against all odds. The poorman's lottery, as some called it, by means of small bets, one could go to bed poor as a rat and wake up the next morning with a relatively substantial sum of money."

> movimiento difuminó como la tinta en el agua, y la de una joven novia que plasmó en su rostro un abismal desconcierto cuando súbitamente se dio cuenta de que el matrimonio en el que acababa de comprometerse ante Dios y ante los hombres podía haber sido un descomunal error. (291)[106]

Both Chano and Tony are part of the second generation of Spaniards or descendants of Spaniards integrated into American society, as it is never made clear whether they were born in the country or whether either of them could have been born in Spain and traveled to America as children. The difference between them lies in the unclear origin of Tony's mother; the only information provided is that his mother's family is Cuban, while Chano's parents are Spanish. Both boys have received an American upbringing, and they are able to get by in this society quite naturally. Being bilingual gives them the opportunity to participate in a specific culture without forgetting that of their parents because language was the main barrier that immigrants encountered when they arrived in the United States.

The endogamy of the neighborhoods was due not only to the immigrants' longing for their distant homeland but also to the difficulty of making themselves understood by the host society because they lacked the instrument that would allow them to open to the new English world. This language barrier was not only suffered by the Spanish but also by other ethnic groups: Italians, Jews, Africans, Chinese, Indians, etc., the entire range of cultures that populated the American territory. Hence, the *importance* of mastering the language, as it was the main knot of intercultural union and integration.

The American Frank Kruzan was the destabilizing element in Luz's life. He first appeared as a talent scout, who saw in the girl a promising aptitude for the world of show business. With the skills of an experienced manipulator and his false promises, he gradually subjected her, first to physical and then to moral changes. However, Luz was not entirely innocent, and although she was aware of what was happening, she eventually succumbed. When the situation became violent, it was Mona who insisted, encouraged, and supported her

106 "The photographer had already pressed the shutter, and on that plate the image of a mature groom blurred by his own movement as ink on water, and that of a young bride whose face showed abysmal bewilderment as she suddenly realised that the marriage would be etched for eternity she had just entered before God and man might have been a huge mistake."

sister to abandon that professional and sentimental relationship; however, in Luz's head there was always this characteristic dependence on violence and the feeling of being the one to blame for Frank's aggressive responses:

> Los españoles con posibles que viven en el Upper West Side y en el Midtown; los empresarios, los que tienen intereses comerciales, los cultos y bien alimentados, bien preparados y bien relacionados, van a las galas y a las óperas del Met, a los conciertos del Carnegie Hall y a las grandes producciones de Broadway. Si de tanto en tanto hay algo interesante de lo nuestro, si tocan por ejemplo Pau Casals o Andrés Segovia en el Town Hall o si la Argentinita monta un espectáculo, allí acuden también ellos, claro. Pero en caso de que no haya nada con sabor a patria, sobreviven sin el menor problema entre los espectáculos para americanos y lo mismo de contentos acuden a disfrutar de un ballet ruso que de la orquesta de Duke Ellington. (185–86)[107]

Many Spaniards begin to neglect their compatriots and only take an interest in them when there is someone of interest to them, such as Pau Casals or Andrés Segovia's acts. The rest of the time, they enjoy American culture at the Metropolitan Museum of Art, on Broadway, or even at Carnegie Hall in Midtown Manhattan. By attending these performances, immigrants are showing their adaptation to the receiving culture while demonstrating the *importance* of cultural events as a sign of clear and voluntary assimilation in the context of New York City as a "Third Space."

Throughout the novel *Las hijas del Capitán*, the Arenas sisters evolve and go through the different stages of transculturation. First, they experience acculturation at the hands of other immigrants or descendants of immigrants like themselves, who teach them the first ins and outs of American culture and how the Spaniards as nomadic subjects are adapting

107 "The well-off Spaniards who lived in the Upper West Side and in Midtown; the businessmen, those with commercial interests, the learned and well fed, the well-educated and well connected, go to the galas and the operas at the Met, the concerts at Carnaghi Hall and the big Broadway productions. If from time to time there is something interesting of our own if, for example, Pau Casals or Andrés Segovia play at Town Hall or if La Argentinita puts on a show, there they go too, of course. But in case there is nothing with a homeland flavour, they survive without the slightest problem among the shows for Americans and are just as happy to come and enjoy a Russian ballet as they are to enjoy Duke Ellington's orchestra."

throughout the American geography, settling in places where there is work, where they are needed, and accepted by the American society:

> —Por todo ello, chiquillas, ando con la idea de montar una compañía; una pequeña compañía con la que hacer una larga gira por lugares donde hay colonias de trabajadores españoles: empezaríamos aquí, en New York, para viajar después a la parte de las canteras de granito de New England, subir hasta Maine y Vermont, hacer luego el cinturón industrial entero: ir a Canton, a Dayton y a Cleveland en Ohio, a actuar para los de la metalurgia, que ésos ganan buenos jornales, y después seguir por Donora, en Pennsylvania, y por la zona de las minas de West Virginia, que me imagino yo cómo van a agradecerlo las pobres criaturas, con lo solos que por allí están metidos días y noches en esos socavones... A las praderas y a California no llegaríamos aunque por allí haya también buenos montones de compatriotas, pero aquello está a tomar viento; a donde sí a lo mejor podríamos ir es a Saint Louis, Missouri, que por allí andan todos los del zinc, o tal vez bajar a Tampa, en la Florida, donde se ganan buenos dólares en las fábricas de tabaco. (187)[108]

Secondly, the sisters begin to experience a process of deculturation as they integrate into New York society, leaving the safe shelter of their Spanish community on 14th Street and beginning to participate in the nightlife of the city with its shows, parties, and endless evenings: "Esa noche no tenían ningún sitio mejor al que acudir más que a aquella inclasificable mezcla de cabaret, mesón sofisticado, pequeña sala de fiestas y célebre night-club" (197).[109] This process of deculturation continues throughout the novel, albeit with resistance from the protagonists' lack of interest in

108 "—That's why, girls, I'm thinking of starting a company; a small company with which to make a long tour to places where there are colonies of Spanish workers: we would start here, in New York, and then travel to the granite quarries of New England, go up to Maine and Vermont, and then do the whole industrial belt: we'd go to Canton, Dayton and Cleveland in Ohio, to work for the metallurgists, who earn good wages, and then on to Donora, Pennsylvania, and the mines of West Virginia, as I can imagine how grateful these poor creatures will be, when they're so lonely down there, stuck for days and nights in the pits... We wouldn't get to the prairies and California, although there are plenty of compatriots too, but that's a hell of a long way off; where we could perhaps go is Saint Louis, Missouri, where all the zinc people are, or maybe down to Tampa, Florida, where they earn good dollars in the tobacco factories."

109 "that night they had nowhere better to go than this unclassifiable mixture of cabaret, sophisticated inn, small boîte, and famous night-club."

learning English: "Se arreglaban el pelo entre ellas, no tenían ni una sola amiga, se negaban a aprender inglés. Y como consecuencia de tan patente terquedad, a sus espaldas dejaban casi siempre un murmullo indisimulado de cuchicheos" (400).[110] It is not until the epilogue of the novel that the reader can appreciate the transition to the neoculturation stage of the sisters after they embraced their hybrid selves in New York as the "Third Space."

Mona and Tony decide to stay in 14th Street for decades. The neighborhood evolved until the Spanish presence practically disappeared, and it stopped being an enclave for Spanish immigrants. Coinciding with their retirement, Mona and Toni leave their apartment in New York as their "Third Space" and move to St. Petersburg in Tampa, Florida. Victoria stays with Chano in New York City and only misses him when he was fighting in the Spanish Civil War with the Lincoln Brigade and then, in World War II, when he was sent to the Philippines. After that, the narrator highlights that they stayed together.

Finally, it is Luz who becomes the embodiment of the complete transculturation process of the three sisters. After their initial and slow acculturation process, Luz decides to frequent New York's nightlife, taking an interest in show business, and even seeks a life as an artist:

> A Luz aún le escocía la actitud del buscador de talentos; el desconocido Frank Kruzan que, tan sólo un rato antes y con tan sólo unas cuantas frases contundentes, había logrado hacer temblar los cimientos de su candorosa seguridad y la había lanzado de cabeza hacia la duda. (253)[111]

In her process of deculturation, she gradually leaves behind part of her "Spanishness" to dive into the dominant American culture. The epilogue of the book gives the reader clues about her last stage, the creation of a hybrid self in the neoculturation phase.

It is only at the end when Luz seems to accept the usefulness of the English language to evolve as a nomadic subject and as an individual as a means of integrating into mainstream American society: "Y cuando los Irigaray decidieron retirarse a Long Island y cerraron la lavandería apenas un año

---

110 "They did each other's hair, didn't have a single friend, refused to learn English. And because of such blatant stubbornness, behind their backs they almost always left an undisguised murmur of whispering."

111

después, ella empezó a aprender inglés y encontró trabajo en un salón de belleza junto a Union Square" (614).[112] This shows the future of hybrid identity, which depends on the familiarity of the dominant language. As a result, Luz manages to integrate fully into the Anglo-Saxon dominant culture, not only by learning the English language but also by being the only sister who does not marry a Spanish-speaking man:

> Los gritos de Remedios se oyeron hasta en el Hudson cuando supo que la menor de sus hijas pretendía casarse con un tal Henry, banquero judío de ascendencia polaca que no hablaba ni papa de español, mantenía a un par de exmujeres en sendos apartamentos e iba a llevarse a su criatura a vivir al Upper East Side. (615)[113]

The fact that she did not marry a Spanish-speaking person demonstrates Luz's flexibility in integrating into the American culture. She leaves the neighborhood and in doing so leaves behind part of her culture to the point of adapting her name to a more English one, "reconvertida para entonces en Lucy Janowski" (615),[114] but without forgetting her Spanish origins:

> Se encerraría en su dormitorio enmoquetado con vistas a Central Park, pondría un disco de Xavier Cugat y su orquesta, y bailaría rumbas en combinación delante del espejo, moviendo una melena ahora teñida de rubio ceniza y unas caderas que serían ya un tanto voluminosas, mientras las lágrimas le rodaban por las mejillas, recordando aquel tiempo que se le escapó de entre los dedos sin darse cuenta apenas, los días crudos, turbulentos e inolvidables de su juventud. (615)[115]

---

112 "And when the Irigarays decided to retire to Long Island and closed down the laundry just a year later, she began learning English and found work in a beauty salon next to Union Square."

113 "Remedios' cries were heard even in the Hudson when she learned that the youngest of her daughters intended to marry a certain Henry, a Jewish banker of Polish descent who did not speak a word of Spanish, kept a couple of ex-wives in two apartments and was going to take his child to live on the Upper East Side."

114 "transformed by then into Lucy Janowski."

115 "She would lock herself in her carpeted bedroom overlooking Central Park, play a record by Xavier Cugat and his orchestra, and dance rumbas in front of the mirror, moving her now dyed ash blonde hair and hips already be a bit voluminous, while the tears rolled down her cheeks, remembering that time that slipped through her fingers without hardly even realizing it, the hard, turbulent, and unforgettable days of her youth."

In the end, Luz achieves complete linguistic and cultural hybridization while maintaining her Spanish identity, integrating into American society, and experiencing a mixture of sadness, longing, and happiness for having managed to combine both cultures to create a new individual to be proud of.

Conclusions

In the introduction, I referred to the *importance* of the concept of culture as a crucible of behaviors, beliefs, and ideas of a community of human beings. In the case of Spanish immigrant communities, created from a diaspora in the United States, their culture was affected by a series of changes between the dominant Anglo-American culture of reception and the Spanish culture of origin. To analyze the literary representation of these changes through the characters and the language used by the authors in the selected literature, I have applied the term "transculturation," created by Cuban anthropologist Fernando Ortiz, the concept of hybridization, understood as the combination of Spanish and American culture in the creation of a new hybrid individual, and the theory of the Third Space, developed by the critical theorist Homi K. Bhabha.

When we think about twentieth-century migration in the United States in the first half of the century, we usually think of waves of people who arrived in the country from other parts of America, Asia, Africa, and Europe. In the latter case, countries such as Italy, Ireland, or Germany inevitably come to mind as responsible for some of the biggest flows of human beings to the States (Dolan 2010). Although this is true, the fact that there have been minor migrations from other nations, such as Spain, has produced a small literary production. This Spanish migrant literature has been produced by immigrants such as Morell, de Pereda, Alfau, and González, or other fictional narrators such as Dueñas. In a setting like the United States, the theme of identity is essential for the understanding of how these Spanish communities evolved from the displacement of their country of origin to their integration in the American host country.

This book began by noting that besides the nearly 320,000 Spanish immigrants that officially arrived in the United States of America between 1820 and 1977, roughly 250,000 did it before 1950 (Rueda Hernanz 1993, 74). The memory of this event and its subsequent representation in literature have been rather scarce. Only six texts centered on the period from 1900 to 1950 have been chosen specifically for this analysis because of their historical basis and their testimonies, worthy of representing in literary form the lives of the immigrants of Spanish origin in the communities they created in the aforementioned time span in the American country. The theoretical framework and the historical background on the origin of how these Spanish communities were built in the United States have created a basis for my exploration of the degree of *importance* of memory and its embodiment in the literature of the time. In the introduction of this thesis, the relevance of literary representation of the past was highlighted. As this book has endeavored to show, it is now plausible to sustain that the construction of the collective identity of the Spanish immigration in the United States represented by González, de Pereda, Morell, Alfau, and Dueñas is essential to understand these communities, as testimonies of a past partially invisibilized by other waves of immigration that should never be forgotten.

These works constitute an example of the under-representation of this community in the United States, hence their value to provide a close examination of the in-between/hybrid space created by the Spanish culture and the American culture, indeed a place where the first and the second spaces clash to generate a new mixture of cultures, a hybrid immigrant self. The information that we may extract from these texts creates a background that facilitates the analysis of the five selected works. This book has shown that the process of transculturation undergone by the main characters can be considered a constructive and positive representation of the phenomenon of cultural hybridity experienced by Spanish immigration in the United States during the first half of the twentieth century.

The use of both New York City and Mozares as "Third Spaces" shows the ambivalence of a writer like de Pereda, who can create a different framework depending on the level of transculturation of his characters, especially the protagonists, Prudencio and Ros. These two characters represent the most elaborate evolution of the writer's alter ego in his novels *Windmills in Brooklyn* and *Fiesta*. The use of these two "Third Spaces" to portray the cultural transition of those Spaniards who migrated to the United States allows the reader to discover the different stages of acculturation, deculturation, and neoculturation as they progress through the reading of de Pereda's novelized biography in two parts. In his works, de Pereda uses Spanish migration literature to show his own round trip as an Americaniard while being surrounded by the rest of the Spanish community, both in New York and Mozares. Both urban spaces participate directly in the construction of his hybrid identity, as he inhabits the "Third Space" in the capacity of both an author and a character in his narrations.

De Pereda's novels describe New York City and Mozares as "Third Spaces" by using different elements such as the dual use of the Spanish and English languages and his construction of the hybrid individual as the final and successful triumph of transculturation, where two cultures are combined while elements of both are maintained. De Pereda's version of the "Third Space" creates a complex structure of cultural inequalities where the Americaniards interact with the environment, and they constantly evolve as the result of the contact between two cultures that certainly modify their always-changing cultural identity. The postcolonial value of these two works becomes even more evident when the author bases his whole narration on his personal experience as an immigrant. He recreates his life as a second-generation Spaniard in New York City who finally returned to his parents' village in Mozares in search of his long-forgotten roots due to his deculturation in the United States. He recovered them during his return to the motherland, where he culminated the development of his hybrid self, the same way that Ros Varona reencountered his hybrid identity at the end of a path of self-discovery.

Claude Morell's depiction of his cultural transformation in New York as a "Third Space" shows the evolution of a character located in the boundaries between his Spanish culture of origin, mainly represented by his Valencian parents, and the American culture of dominance, embodied by the metropolis and transmitted through such vital elements as education, food, neighborhoods, and the English language. English represents the ultimate weapon of colonization of the American dominant culture. Morell's work shares many characteristics with Gonzalez's autobiography. Both are narrated in the first person, from the point of view of an omniscient intradiegetic narrator who knows everything about the story and characters, who is also at the same time its protagonist. Morell is undoubtedly more of a protagonist than González, the latter being a complement to the Villanueva family rather than a separate entity from his parents, as is the case with Morell.

On the other hand, despite being two decades apart from each other, de Pereda and Morell use New York City for their respective childhood and youth, that is, their first and second stages of transculturation, acculturation, and deculturation, accompanied by their return to their motherland as part of their third phase of transculturation, neoculturation. They both return to their parents' village looking for answers. There they reconnect with their roots and establish a dialogue between their American and Spanish cultures that makes them reconsider their hybrid identity. Morell sees himself as an American with Spanish roots who finally ends up accepting Spain as his home. De Pereda's alter ego, Ros, goes back to Spain with no set return date. Ros is treated by older Spanish people in the village as a lost immigrant who has come back home and by those who belong to his same generation as an American, a simple "*Inglés*" who has come to occupy the space as an unwelcomed "Other."

Morell's *The Lower East Side Kid That Made It Good* depicts the triumph of a cultural process of transformation toward transculturation that started with his arrival at Ellis Island as a baby and spanned toward the final return to Spain of a retired Claude who has decided to settle in the country for good after decades in the United States. He has become the epitome of the polyglot nomadic subject. Claude's evolution takes place within the gears of the dominant American culture versus a Spanish culture that struggles to survive in a foreign environment where immigrants experience the challenges of identity construction. Morell's narrative uses New York City as a "Third Space" where a narrator like Claude, also the protagonist, undergoes a transformation that shows his comfort not as an immigrant, but as an Americaniard—partly a New Yorker and partly a Spaniard—who is happy with the memories of his cultural transformation, finally creating an identity that makes him feel proud of his hybrid self.

Gavin W. González died in 1988. The discovery of his manuscript after his death was the basis for the creation of this bilingual novel based on the lives of the members of the Spanish colony of Pinnick Kinnick Hill. They had created their own imagined community to replicate their original Asturian communities. Pinnick Kinnick Hill's literary representation as a "Third Space" changes the way of analyzing the process of transculturation of its inhabitants. The creation of ghettos in the working space, the use of othering to reject someone simply because of their alien origin, and the emergence of a new hybrid identity after the cultural transformation of the individual are just some of the elements that can be learned from the Spanish immigrants' experience in the United States of America.

Pinnick Kinnick Hill, An American Story is also a Spanish story that reflects the narrative construction of González, who used the "Third Space" to inhabit the reality that he experienced as a first-generation American-born son. He described it through the experiences of the fictional Villanueva family. This story represents the hybridity of the protagonists, Americaniards who do not live in New York City. They have become a perfect example of characters in migrant literature that tell their story of immigration and displacement, where the Spanish immigrants are depicted as struggling to succeed, while assimilation to the American culture is transforming and weakening their Asturian culture. The uniqueness of González's work is his ability to provide a faithful portrait of those Spanish immigrants who, at the beginning of the twentieth century, decided to pursue the American dream by escaping from a Spain impoverished by its wars and its erratic administration in the wake of an old empire that no longer existed. González's representation of the "Third Space" in Harrison County, where these nomadic subjects adapt to the representation that the writer chooses to convey, becomes his own reality of the life of a Spanish-imagined community in West Virginia that no longer exists.

Las hijas del Capitán by María Dueñas is the most different of the works analyzed. It is the only work originally written in Spanish and the only one whose author is also a narrator who does not inhabit the "Third Space." Dueñas's novel is based on the archived work of Professor James Fernández and on the testimonies of those Spanish immigrants and their descendants who arrived in the United States in the early twentieth century. In addition, Dueñas explains that in order to write her novel, she read Morell's *The Lower East Side Kid That Made It Good* and de Pereda's *Windmills in Brooklyn*. With such precedents, her readers are not at all surprised by the presence of *teverianos* in her work, by the similarities in the descriptions of the Cherry Street neighborhood in Manhattan, or by the way her characters evolve in New York City as a "Third Space," where they go through a process of transculturation with all their due stages of acquisition of the dominant American culture specified. The novel dwells on the characters' gradual loss of the Spanish culture of origin and the progressive neoculturation of the Arenas sisters as they move between borders, just like many other nomadic subjects belonging to the first and 1.75 generations who arrived in the United States and assimilated to American society in the first half of the past century.

At the beginning of the story, Luz, Mona, and Victoria seem to resist American culture: they show no interest in learning the English language, they relate only with Spanish-speaking people, mostly of Spanish origin, and they hardly ever leave their communities. However, little by little, the three women let American culture become a part of them, leaving their comfort zone in the Spanish colony, learning some English words and sentences, and even interacting with the American culture in New York. They work, interact with New Yorkers, and enjoy the freedom of the 1930s in the United States. Thus, the Spanish culture of origin and their memory of the Iberian Peninsula gradually fade until they become part of the past. The death of their father, though sad, forces the Arenas sisters to become independent, forge their own character, and develop their hybrid selves. Luz, Mona, and Victoria become independent nomadic subjects by moving between two worlds that will shape their behavior until they end up experiencing the metropolis as a "Third Space," where their inherited Spanish culture and the newly acquired one create a new, more flexible subjectivity. This is a place where the clash of cultures and the possibilities that it entails, i.e., cultural death or cultural evolution, are in favor of the latter. The protagonists leave behind the condition of those Spaniards who cannot be assimilated, like their mother. They are now able to negotiate for themselves by creating a new hybrid product.

In Alfau's *Chromos*, Mary Louise Pratt's theory of the bilingual nomadic subject can be applied, provided that we consider Spanish immigrants in the United States as nomadic individuals that did not hesitate to move to New York, New Jersey, and then Idaho to find a better life. The language transculturation of the Spanish immigrants in New York City is not only represented by their use of the language of the dominant culture, English, but also by the use of their native languages of origin, Spanish and Basque. These native languages are now fighting to survive as their speakers keep evolving through the different stages of their cultural transformation. However, it will not be until the last phase of this transculturation, neoculturation, that the new hybrid individual will be able to combine both languages indistinctively. Alfau is the result of that transition. As a Spanish immigrant himself who arrived in the metropolis in his teenage years, he developed a marked bilingualism represented by the way he expressed himself, with a clear influence of his native Spanish, but also correctly in English. The "Iberian" English that Alfau uses for *Chromos* and the references to the use of other languages, such as Spanish and Basque, show that transculturation also implies being bilingual, even trilingual, in the final stage of the linguistic hybridization. The use of language, both Spanish and English, by the authors of the texts selected and by the characters of Spanish origin that appear in them is the successful representation of a last phase of transculturation where Spanish immigrants and their descendants become, finally, complete hybrid individuals.

This research paves the way for scholars interested in the literary representation of Spanish communities in the United States of America in different periods and places. The texts selected reinforce the *importance* of literature as a way of remembering people's past. The best evidence of this is that no matter how much documentation, such as photographs, membership cards, or even letters, appeared in the primary sources, I would have never been able to do research on the literary representation of Spanish immigration in the United States in the first half of the twentieth century if the English/Spanish literature I have read and consulted did not exist. The representation of the linguistic and cultural hybridization experienced by the Spanish immigrants as portrayed in the given texts, even the very coining of the term "Americaniard" to define this type of immigration, would have never happened. The fictional-autobiographical works of González, de Pereda, Morell, Alfau, and Dueñas are impressive in their scope and unmistakable in their originality, rendering them the authoritative and indelible reference points of the Spanish-American immigrant experience of the first half of the nineteenth century. These authors have immortalized these stories in their own idiosyncratic way, rich with linguistic interplays of words, best fully appreciated by a bilingual reader, cementing a literary gold standard of what it means to do justice to the written preservation of the stories produced by a minority migrant group in the United States.

Works Cited

Acheaïou, Amar. 2011. *Questioning Hybridity, Postcolonialism and Globalization*. London: Palgrave Macmillan.

Acheaïou, Amar. 2008. *Rethinking Postcolonialism: Colonialist Discourse in Modern Literatures and the Legacy of Classical Writers*. London: Palgrave Macmillan.

Aguirre, Anna M., and Koldo San Sebastián. 2018. *NEW YORK TARRAK: Origen de la Comunidad Vasca de Nueva York, 1880–1955*. Colección Urazandi Bilduma. Servicio Central de Publicaciones del Gobierno Vasco. Accessed March 21, 2021. https://www.euskadi.eus/contenidos/informacion/06_urazandi_coleccion/es_712/adjuntos/urazandi30.pdf

Alfau, Felipe. 1988. *Locos: A Comedy of Gestures*. Champaign-London: Dalkey Archive Press.

Alfau, Felipe. 1990. Chromos. Dalkey Archive Press.

Alfau, Felipe. 1999. *Chromos*. Normal: Dalkey Archive Press. Illinois State University.

Allolio-Näcke, Lars. 2014. "*Transculturalism*." In *Encyclopedia of Critical Psychology*, ed. Teo, T. New York: Springer. Accessed March 21, 2021. https://doi.org/10.1007/978-1-4614-5583-7_316

Amate Martínez, María del Carmen. 2011. *El Grupo Salmerón en Nueva York*. Almería: Instituto de Estudios Almerienses.

Armstrong, John A. 1976. "Mobilized and Proletarian Diasporas." *The American Political Science Review* 70 (2): 393–408. Accessed March 21, 2022. https://doi.org/10.2307/1959646.

Álvarez Gila, Ó., Angulo Morales, A., & Ramos Martínez, J. A. (Coords.). (2007). Emigración vasca y asociacionismo en América: El caso de Uruguay. Universidad del País Vasco.

Anbinder, Tyler. 2001. *Five Points: The Nineteenth-Century New York City Neighborhood that Invented Tap Dance, Stole Elections, and Became the World's Most Notorious Slum*. New York: The Free Press.

Anderson, Benedict. 2006. *Imagined Communities: Reflections on the Origin and Spread of Nationalism*. London: Verso.

Anzaldúa, G. 2016. Borderlands / La Frontera: La nueva mestiza (C. Valle, Trans.; Saldívar Hull, Intro.). Madrid: Capitán Swing.

Arguedas, José María. 1976. *Formación de una cultura nacional indoamericana*. Madrid: Siglo Veintiuno de España Editores, S.A.

Arnedo-Gómez, Miguel. “The Afrocubanista Poetry of Nicolás Guillén and Ángel Rama’s Concept of Transculturation.” *Afro-Hispanic Review*, vol. 26, no. 2, 2007, pp. 9–25. JSTOR, http://www.jstor.org/stable/23054617. Accessed 26 Mar. 2025.

Ashcroft, Bill, Gareth Griffiths, and Helen Tiffin. 2013. *Post-Colonial Studies: The Key Concepts*. Third ed. Abingdon: Routledge.

Ashcroft Bill. 2001. *Post-Colonial Transformation*. London: Routledge.

Azancot, Pedro A., Pepa Vega Vives, and Jesús Oyamburu, eds. 1992. *Historia general de la emigración española a Iberoamérica*. 2 vols. Madrid: Ministerio de Trabajo y Asuntos Sociales.

Bagelman, Jennifer J. 2015. *Sanctuary City: A Suspended State (Mobility & Politics)*. London: Palgrave Macmillan.

Benessaieh, Afef. “II. Multiculturalism, Interculturality, Transculturality”. *Amériques Transculturelles Transcultural Americas, edited by Afef Benessaieh*, Les Presses de l’Université d’Ottawa | University of Ottawa Press, 2010, https://books.openedition.org/uop/356.

Barbulescu, Roxana. 2019. *Migrant Integration in a Changing Europe: Immigrants, European Citizens, and Co-Ethnics in Italy and Spain*. Paris: University of Notre Dame Press.

Bargatzky, Thomas, Myrdene Anderson, Timothy Earle, Azzo Ghidinelli, Walter Goldschmidt, James G. Peoples, Glenn Petersen, Antonio Santangelo, and M. Estellie Smith. 1984. “Culture, Environment, and the Ills of Adaptationism [and Comments and Reply].” *Current Anthropology* 25 (4): 399–415. Accessed March 20, 2021. http://www.jstor.org/stable/2742901.

Bartlett, Frederic Charles. 1995. *Remembering: A Study in Experimental and Social Psychology*. Cambridge: Cambridge University Press.

Bau, Ignatius. 1985. *This Ground is Holy: Church Sanctuary and Central American Refugees*. New York/Mahwah: Paulist Press.

Benessaieh, Afef, editor. Amériques transculturelles / Transcultural Americas. University of Ottawa Press, 2010.

Bercovici, Konrad. 1924. *Around the World in New York*. New York: Century.

Berger, Arthur Asa. 2000. "The Meanings of Culture: Culture: Its Many Meanings". *M/C Journal* 3 (2). Accessed May 21, 2021. https://doi.org/10.5204/mcj.1833.

Berger, A. A. 2000. *The Meanings of Culture: Culture: Its Many Meanings*. M/C Journal, 3(2). https://doi.org/10.5204/mcj.1833

Bhabha, Homi K. 1990. "The Third Space. Interview with Homi Bhabha." In *Identity, Community, Culture, Difference*, ed. Jonathan Rutherford, 207–21. London: Lawrence and Winhart.

Bhabha, Homi K. 1994. *The Location of Culture*. London: Routledge.

Bhabha, Homi K. 2004. *The Location of Culture*. London: Routledge.

Bhabha, Homi K. 2006. "Cultural Diversity and Cultural Differences." In *The Post-Colonial Studies Reader*, ed. Bill. Ashcroft, Gareth. Griffiths, and Helen. Tiffin, 155–57. New York: Routledge.

Blanda Sallé, María Ángeles, and Ángeles Van den Eynde. 2009. *La emigración española en América: historias y lecciones para el futuro*. Madrid: Ministerio de Trabajo e Inmigración, Fundación Directa.

Blázquez Domínguez, Carmen, Yovana Celaya, and José Velasco. 2011. *Veracruz: Historia Breve*. Ciudad de México: Fondo de Cultura Económica.

Boas, Franz. 1898. *Jesup North Pacific Expedition (1897–1903)*. Facial Paintings of the Indians of Northern British Columbia. Memoirs of the AMNH; v. 2, pt. 1. Publications of the Jesup North Pacific Expedition; v. 1, pt. 1. Accessed June 29, 2022. https://digitallibrary.amnh.org/handle/2246/10

Bolles, Edmund Blair. 1988. *Remembering and Forgetting: An Inquiry into the Nature of Memory*. New York: Walker and Company.

Braidotti, Rosi. 2011. *Nomadic Subjects: Embodiment and Difference in Contemporary Feminist Theory*. New York: Columbia University Press.

Cagiao Vila, P. 2001. Género y emigración: las mujeres inmigrantes gallegas en la Argentina. En X. M. Núñez Seixas & P. Cagiao Vila (Eds.), *La Galicia austral: la inmigración gallega en la Argentina* (pp. 107–136). Buenos Aires: Editorial Biblos.

Cagiao Vila, P. 2008. *Una perspectiva histórica de la emigración de las mujeres españolas*. En Acogida. Cuaderno de la emigración española y el retorno, 2-5. http://www.espanaexterior.com/upload/pdf/50-acogida4.pdf

Cahoone, Lawrence E. *Cultural Revolutions: Reason Versus Culture in Philosophy, Politics, and Jihad*. Penn State University Press, 2005. JSTOR, http://www.jstor.org/stable/10.5325/j.ctt1wf4csh. Accessed 26 Mar. 2025.

Cahoone, L. E. 2005. *Cultural Revolutions: Reason Versus Culture in Philosophy, Politics, and Jihad*. University Park, PA: Pennsylvania State University Press.

Camba, Julio. 2008 (1932). *La ciudad automática*. Madrid: Alhena Media.

Camba, Julio. 2013 (1917). *Un año en el otro mundo*. SergioS: epublibre.

Carmen González López-Briones Fin de siglo, crisis y nuevos principios: Actas del III Congreso de la Sociedad Española para el estudio de los Estados Unidos (SAAS), celebrado en León, 19-21 marzo 1997 / coord. por María José Álvarez Maurín, Manuel Broncano Rodríguez, Camino Fernández Rabadán, Cristina Garrigós González, 1999, ISBN 84-7719-751-2, págs. 171-182

Casa Galicia de Nueva York. 1941. *Libro de Memoria 1941*. New York: Unity Gallega. Accessed March 20, 2021. https://www.casagaliciany.com/up/memorias/Memoria-1941.pdf

Casa Galicia de Nueva York. 1944. *Libro de Memoria 1944*. New York: Unity Gallega. Accessed March 20, 2021. https://www.casagaliciany.com/up/memorias/Memoria-1944.pdf

Casa Galicia de Nueva York. 1945. *Libro de Memoria 1945*. New York: Unity Gallega. Accessed March 20, 2021. https://www.casagaliciany.com/up/memorias/Memoria-1945.pdf

Casa Galicia de Nueva York. 1946. *Libro de Memoria 1946*. New York: Unity Gallega. Accessed March 20, 2021. https://www.casagaliciany.com/up/memorias/Memoria-1946.pdf

Casa Galicia de Nueva York. 1948. *Libro de Memoria 1948*. New York: Unity Gallega. Accessed March 20, 2021. https://www.casagaliciany.com/up/memorias/Memoria-1948.pdf

Casa Galicia de Nueva York. 1949. *Libro de Memoria 1949*. New York: Unity Gallega. Accessed March 20, 2021. https://www.casagaliciany.com/up/memorias/Memoria-1949.pdf

Casa Galicia de Nueva York. 1951. *Libro de Memoria 1951*. New York: Unity Gallega. Accessed March 20, 2021. https://www.casagaliciany.com/up/memorias/Memoria-1951.pdf

Casa Galicia de Nueva York. 1952. *Libro de Memoria 1952*. New York: Unity Gallega. Accessed March 20, 2021. https://www.casagaliciany.com/up/memorias/Memoria-1952.pdf

Casa Galicia de Nueva York. 1953. *Libro de Memoria 1953*. New York: Unity Gallega. Accessed March 20, 2021. https://www.casagaliciany.com/up/memorias/Memoria-1953.pdf

Casa Galicia de Nueva York. 1955. *Libro de Memoria 1955*. New York: Unity Gallega. Accessed March 20, 2021. https://www.casagaliciany.com/up/memorias/Memoria-1955.pdf

Casa Galicia de Nueva York. 1956. *Libro de Memoria 1956*. New York: Unity Gallega. Accessed March 20, 2021. https://www.casagaliciany.com/up/memorias/Memoria-1956.pdf

Casa Galicia de Nueva York. 1958. *Libro de Memoria 1958*. New York: Unity Gallega. Accessed March 20, 2021. https://www.casagaliciany.com/up/memorias/Memoria-1958.pdf

Casa Galicia de Nueva York. 1959. *Libro de Memoria 1959*. New York: Unity Gallega. Accessed March 20, 2021. https://www.casagaliciany.com/up/memorias/Memoria-1959.pdf

Casa Galicia de Nueva York. 1960. *Libro de Memoria 1960*. New York: Unity Gallega. Accessed March 20, 2021. https://www.casagaliciany.com/up/memorias/Memoria-1960.pdf

Casa Galicia de Nueva York. 1961. *Libro de Memoria 1961*. New York: Unity Gallega. Accessed March 20, 2021. https://www.casagaliciany.com/up/memorias/Memoria-1961.pdf

Casa Galicia de Nueva York. 1962. *Libro de Memoria 1962*. New York: Unity Gallega. Accessed March 20, 2021. https://www.casagaliciany.com/up/memorias/Memoria-1962.pdf

Casa Galicia de Nueva York. 1962. *Libro de memoria 1962*. New York: Unity Gallega. Recuperado el 20 de marzo de 2021, de https://www.casagaliciany.com/up/memorias/Memoria-1962.pdf

Casa Galicia de Nueva York. 1964. *Libro de Memoria 1964*. New York: Unity Gallega. Accessed March 20, 2021. https://www.casagaliciany.com/up/memorias/Memoria-1964.pdf

Casa Galicia de Nueva York. 1967. *Libro de Memoria1966–67*. New York: Unity Gallega. Accessed March 20, 2021. https://www.casagaliciany.com/up/memorias/Memoria-1966-67.pdf

Casa Galicia de Nueva York. 1970. *Libro de Memoria. 1969–70.* New York: Unity Gallega. Accessed March 20, 2021. https://www.casagaliciany.com/up/memorias/Memoria-1969-70.pdf

Casa Galicia de Nueva York. 1972. *Libro de Memoria. 1971–72.* New York: Unity Gallega. Accessed March 20, 2021. https://www.casagaliciany.com/up/memorias/Memoria-1971-72.pdf

Casa Galicia de Nueva York. 1973. *Libro de Memoria. 1972–73.* New York: Unity Gallega. Accessed March 20, 2021. https://www.casagaliciany.com/up/memorias/Memoria-1972-73.pdf

Casa Galicia de Nueva York. 1974. *Libro de Memoria. 1973–74.* New York: Unity Gallega. Accessed March 20, 2021. https://www.casagaliciany.com/up/memorias/Memoria-1973-74.pdf

Casa Galicia de Nueva York. 1976. *Libro de Memoria. 1975–76.* New York: Unity Gallega. Accessed March 20, 2021. https://www.casagaliciany.com/up/memorias/Memoria-1975-76.pdf

Casa Galicia de Nueva York. 1977. *Libro de Memoria. 1976–77.* New York: Unity Gallega. Accessed March 20, 2021. https://www.casagaliciany.com/up/memorias/Memoria-1976-77.pdf

Casa Galicia de Nueva York. 1978. *Libro de Memoria. 1977–78.* New York: Unity Gallega. Accessed March 20, 2021. https://www.casagaliciany.com/up/memorias/Memoria-1977-78.pdf

Casa Galicia de Nueva York. 1980. *Libro de Memoria. 1978–80.* New York: Unity Gallega. Accessed March 20, 2021. https://www.casagaliciany.com/up/memorias/Memoria-1978-80.pdf

Casa Galicia de Nueva York. 1983. *Libro de Memoria. 1981–83.* New York: Unity Gallega. Accessed March 20, 2021. https://www.casagaliciany.com/up/memorias/Memoria-1981-83.pdf

Casa Galicia de Nueva York. 1996. *Libro de Memoria. 1993–96.* New York: Unity Gallega. Accessed March 20, 2021. https://www.casagaliciany.com/up/memorias/Memoria-1993-96.pdf

Casa Galicia de Nueva York. 2000. *Libro de Memoria 2000.* New York: Unity Gallega. Accessed March 20, 2021. https://www.casagaliciany.com/up/memorias/Memoria-2000.pdf

Casa Galicia de Nueva York. 2002. *Libro de Memoria 2002.* New York: Unity Gallega. Accessed March 20, 2021. https://www.casagaliciany.com/up/memorias/Memoria-2002.pdf

Casa Galicia de Nueva York. Unity Gallega. 2016. *Libro de Memoria. 75 años. 1940–2015*. New York: Unity Gallega.

Casa Galicia de Nueva York. 2018. *Libro de Memoria 2017–2018*. New York: Unity Gallega. Accessed March 20, 2021. https://www.casagaliciany.com/up/memorias/Memoria-Casa-Galicia-2017-2018.pdf

"Castelao, Propagandista Da República En Norteamérica". *Emilio González López*. Ediciós do Castro, 2000. Serie Documentos.1ª edición.

Castillo, Debra A. 2005. "Latina or Americaniard?" *Revista Canadiense de Estudios Hispánicos* 30 (1): 47–59.

Charity Organization Society of the City of New York. Directory of Social and Health Agencies of New York City. Charity Organization Society, 1914.

Clifford, James. 1988. *The Predicament of Culture: Twentieth-Century Ethnography, Literature, and Art*. Cambridge, Massachusetts: Harvard University Press. Accessed July 10, 2021. www.jstor.org/stable/27764035

Coatsworth, John H., and Alan M. Taylor. 1999. *Latin America and the World Economy Since 1800*. Cambridge, Massachusetts: Harvard University Press.

Columbia University Graduate School of Architecture, Planning, and Preservation. 2006. 14th Street and Union Square: Preservation plan. New York City: Historic Preservation Program, Graduate School of Architecture, Planning, and Preservation, Columbia University.

Columbia University Graduate School of Architecture, Planning, and Preservation. 2010. '14th Street and Union Square, Preservation Plan' New York City: Historic Preservation Program, Graduate School of Architecture, Planning and Preservation, Columbia University. 2006.

Community Council of Greater New York, Association of Catholic Day Nurseries, Charity Organization Society of the City of New York, and Welfare Council of New York City. *Directory of Social And Health Agencies of New York City*. New York: Columbia University Press.

Community Council of Greater York. *Directory Social and Health Agencies of New York City Volume 23: 1914*. New York: Rare Books Club.

Côté, James E. 2006. "Acculturation and Identity: The Role of Individualization Theory." *Human Development* 49 (1): 31–35. Accessed May 17, 2021. www.jstor.org/stable/26763866.

Côté, Jean-François. 2010. "From Transculturation to Hybridization: Redefining Culture in the Americas In: Amériques transculturelles/ Transcultural Americas." Ottawa: Les Presses de l'Université d'Ottawa / University of Ottawa Press. Accessed March 20, 2021. http://books.openedition.org/uop/363

Crittenden, Ann. 1988. *Sanctuary: A Story of American Conscience and the Law in Collision*. New York: Grove Press.

Cuccioletta, Donald. 2001/2002. "Multiculturalism or Transculturalism: Towards a Cosmopolitan Citizenship". *London Journal of Canadian Studies* 17: 1–11.

Culture Is Destiny (1994): *A Conversation with Lee Kuan Yew. Foreign Affairs*, 73, 109-126.

Cunningham, Hilary. 1995. *God and Caesar at the Rio Grande: Sanctuary and the Politicization of Religion in the United States*. Minneapolis: University of Minnesota Press.

Davidson, Miriam. 1988. *Convictions of the Heart: Jim Corbett and the Sanctuary Movement*. Tucson: University of Arizona Press.

De Pereda, Prudencio. 1953. *Fiesta*. London and Southampton: The Camelot Press.

De Pereda, P. 1953. Fiesta: A novel of modern Spain. A. A. Wyn.

De Pereda, Prudencio. 1960. *Windmills in Brooklyn*. New York: New York Atheneum Publishers.

Diamond, Jared. 1999. *Guns, Germs and Steel: The Fates of Human Societies*. New York: W. W. Norton.

DiMaggio, Paul. 1997. "Culture and Cognition." *Annual Review of Sociology* 23: 263–87. Accessed September 29, 2021. www.jstor.org/stable/2952552

Dolan, Jay P. 2010. *The Irish Americans: A History*. New York: Bloomsbury Press.

Duany, Jorge. 1999. "Cuban Communities in the United States: Migration Waves, Settlement Patterns and Socioeconomic Diversity". *Pouvoirs dans la Caraïbe* [Online] 11. Accessed April 20, 2021. https://core.ac.uk/reader/224122080

Duany, Jorge. 2007. "Nation and Migration: Rethinking Puerto Rican Identity in a Transnational Context." *None of the Above: Puerto Ricans in the Global Era. New Directions in Latino American Cultures*. 51–63. Accessed April 20, 2022. https://www.researchgate.net/publication/305246252_Nation_and_Migration_Rethinking_Puerto_Rican_Identity_in_a_Transnational_Context

Duany, Jorge. 2010. "Anthropology in a Postcolonial Colony: Helen I. Safa's Contribution to Puerto Rican Ethnography." *Caribbean Studies* 38 (2): 33–57. Accessed April 20, 2022. www.jstor.org/stable/41220535.

Dueñas, María. 2018. *Las hijas del Capitán*. Madrid: Planeta.

Dueñas, M. 2018. *Las hijas del Capitán*. Editorial Planeta.

Ebbinghaus, Hermann. 2011. *Memory: A Contribution to Experimental Psychology*. Reprint of 1913 Edition. New York: Columbia University.

Ellis, Mark, and Jamie Goodwin-White. 2006. "1.5 Generation Internal Migration in the U.S.: Dispersion from States of Immigration?" *The International Migration Review* 40 (4): 899–926.

Faber, Sebastiaan, and Cristina Martínez Corazo. 2010. *Contra el olvido. El exilio español en Estados Unidos*. Biblioteca Benjamin Franklin. Madrid: Universidad de Alcalá.

Federal Writers Project. 1995. *The WPA Guide to New York City: The Federal Writers' Project Guide to 1930s New York*. New York: New Press.

Felman, Shoshana, and Dori Laub. 1992. *Testimony: Crises of Witnessing in Literature, Psychoanalysis, and History*. New York: Routledge.

Fernández, James D. 2007. *Facing Facism: New York and the Spanish Civil War*. New York: New York University, Museum of the City of New York.

Fernández, James D. 2011. *La colonia: un álbum fotográfico de inmigrantes españoles en Nueva York 1898–1945*. Valey Centro Cultural de Castrillón. Gijón: Imprenta Mercantil Asturias. Accessed March 20, 2021. https://jamesdanielFernández.files.wordpress.com/2011/09/la-colonia-espac3b1oles-en-ny.pdf

Fernández, James D., and Luis Argeo. 2014. *Invisible Immigrants: Spaniards in the US (1868–1945)*. New York: White Stone Ridge.

Ferrer Álvarez, Mireia. 2016. *Segrelles. Un pintor valenciano en Nueva York. 1929–1932*. Valencia: Institució Alfons el Magnànim.

Federal Writer's Project. 1939. *New York City Guide*. New York: Random House. Accessed March 20, 2021. https://archive.org/details/newyorkcityguide00federich/mode/2up

Gaite, Carmen Martín, and Ilan Stavans. 1993. "The Triumph of the Exception." *The Review of Contemporary Fiction* 13 (1): 174. *Gale Academic OneFile*. Accessed March 19, 2021. https://gale.com/apps/doc/A13663055/AONE?u=anon~f14f17d8&sid=googleScholar&xid=eb58726f.

García Canclini, Néstor. 2005 (1995). *Hybrid Cultures: Strategies for Entering and Leaving Modernity*. Translated by Christopher. L. Chiappari, Silvia. L. Lopez. Minneapolis: University of Minnesota Press.

García Cárcel, Ricardo. 2013. *La herencia del pasado: Las memorias históricas de España*. Barcelona: Galixia Gutenberg.

García Lorca, Federico. 2017. *Poeta en Nueva York: Cartas de Lorca desde Nueva York* (1929–1930). Edición Bilingüe. New York: Grove Atlantic.

Geertz, Clifford James. 1973. *Interpretation of Cultures*. New York: Basic Books.

Gloria Anzaldúa, Borderlands/ *La Frontera: The New Mestiza* (2016), Capitan Swing S.L

Golden, Penny Golden, and Michael N. McConnell. 1986. *Sanctuary: The New Underground Railroad*. New York: Orbis Books.

Gómez, Rosendo A. 1962. "Spanish Immigration to the United States." *The Americas* 19 (1): 59–78.

González, Cristina Garrigós. 2018. "Felipe Alfau's Parodisatirical Fiction and the Reconstructive Memory of Spain from the United States." In *A Critical Gaze from the Old World: Transatlantic Perspectives on American Studies*, eds. Isabel Durán G.-Rico, Rebeca Gualberto, Eusebio De Lorenzo, Carmen Méndez, and Eduardo Valls, eds. 309–24. Frankfurt: Peter Lang.

González, Gavin W. 2003. *Pinnick Kinnick Hill: An American Story/Las colinas sueñan en español*. Morgantown: West Virginia University Press.

González López, Emilio. "Galician Exile to New York." Galician New York: A Cultural History / Database, 2000, https://newyork.gal/en/galician-exile-to-new-york/.

González López, Emilio. 2000. *Castelao, propagandista da República en Norteamérica*. Sada: Ediciós do Castro.

González López-Briones, Carmen. 2019. "Windmills in Brooklyn: A Story of the Spanish Immigrants in New York". *Revista de Estudios Norteamericanos* 5. Accessed June 24, 2021. https://revistascientifi

cas.us.es/index.php/ESTUDIOS_NORTEAMERICANOS/article/view/10634.

Goodenough, W. H. 1957. *Cultural Anthropology and Linguistics*. In *Report of the Seventh Annual Round Table Meeting on Linguistics and Language Study*, ed. P. Garvin. Washington: Georgetown University Press. The Institute of Languages and Linguistics. Accessed March 3, 2021. https://repository.library.georgetown.edu/bitstream/handle/10822/555451/GURT_1956.pdf;sequence=1

Gunaratnam, Yasmin. 2014. "Rethinking Hybridity: Interrogating Mixedness." *Subjectivity* 7: 1–17. Accessed January 11, 2021. https://doi.org/10.1057/sub.2013.16

Gutiérrez, David G. 1996. *Between Two Worlds: Mexican Immigrants in the United States*. Lanham: Rowman & Littlefield.

Hatton, Timothy J., and Jeffrey G. Williamson. 1998. *The Age of Mass Migration: Causes and Economic Impact*. New York: Oxford University Press.

Horn, James, and Philip D. Morgan. 2005. "Settlers and Slaves: European and African Migrations to Early Modern British America." In *The Creation of the British Atlantic World*, eds. Elizabeth Manke and Carole Shammas: 19–45. Baltimore: Johns Hopkins University Press.

Hobsbawn, Eric. 1996. "Language, Culture, and National Identity." *Social Research* 63 (4): 1065–80. Accessed May 18, 2021. www.jstor.org/stable/40971324.

INE (Instituto Nacional de Estadística). 2001. "Censos de Población y Viviendas de 2001." Accessed March 6, 2021. https://www.ine.es/censo2001/historia.htm#:~:text=La%20poblaci%C3%B3n%20censada%20en%20Espa%C3%B1a,(18.830.649%20habitantes).

Innes, J. H. 1902. *New Amsterdam and its People; Studies, Social and Topographical, of the Town under Dutch and Early English*. New York: Charles Scribner's Collection. Library of Congress. Accessed March 6, 2021. https://archive.org/details/newamsterdamitsp01inne

Jäger, Friedrich, and Ora Wiskind. 1991. "Culture or Society? The Significance of Max Weber's Thought for Modern Cultural History." *History and Memory* 3 (2): 115–40. Accessed March 10, 2021. www.jstor.org/stable/25618620.

James, Rian. 2017. *Dining in New York* (1930). Review of El Chico. New York: John Day.

Joyner, Brian Peyton, and Donna Carol Voss. 2017. *Deep Dive: Sanctuary Cities*. New York: Golden Rule Omnimedia.

Keesing, Roger M. 1974. "Theories of Culture." *Annual Review of Anthropology* 3: 73–97. Accessed September 11, 2021. www.jstor.org/stable/2949283.

Koestler, A. 1964. *The Act of Creation*. New York: Penguin.

Kooyers, Jessie. 2015. "The United States and Spain: A Comparison of Cultural Values and Behaviors and their Implications for the Multi-Cultural Workplace". *Honors Projects*. 399. Grand Valley State University. Accessed March 6, 2021. https://scholarworks.gvsu.edu/honorsprojects/399

Kraut, Alan. 1982. *The Huddled Masses: The Immigrant in American Society, 1880–1921*. Arlington Heights: Harlan Davidson.

Krishnamurti, Yamini. 1993. "What Is Culture?" In *World Affairs: The Journal of International Issues* 2 (2): 73–74. Accessed March 10, 2021. www.jstor.org/stable/45083502.

Kroeber, Alfred. L, and Clyde Kluckhohn. 1952. *Culture: A Critical Review of Concepts and Definitions*. Peabody Museum of American Archeology and Ethnology Papers 47, 1. Cambridge: Harvard University.

Kundera, Milan. 2000. *Ignorance*. Translated by Linda Asher. New York: HarperCollins.

Kuper, Adam. 1999. *Culture: The Anthropologist's Account*. Cambridge: Harvard University Press.

La Nacional. 2015. "Spanish Benevolent Society of New York." Accessed March 6, 2021. http://lanacional.org/es/sobre-la-nacional-spanish-benevolent-society-nyc/

La Nacional. 2018. "Spanish Benevolent Society of New York Archive." New York.

Lentz, Carola. 2017. "Culture: The Making, Unmaking and Remaking of an Anthropological Concept." *Zeitschrift Für Ethnologie* 142 (2): 181–204. Accessed March 10, 2021. www.jstor.org/stable/26607020.

Lévi-Strauss, Claude. 1963. *Structural Anthropology*. New York: Basic Books. Accessed April 5, 2021. https://monoskop.org/images/e/e8/LeviStrauss_Claude_Structural_Anthropology_1963.pdf

Liñares Giraut, X. Amancio and Óscar Álvarez Gila. 2007a. *Ciudadanos españoles en el mundo: Situación actual y recorrido histórico*. Vigo: Grupo España Exterior.

Liñares Giraut, X. Amancio and Óscar Álvarez Gila. 2007b. *El protagonismo de la mujer en las corrientes migratorias españolas*. Vigo: Grupo España Exterior.

Liñares Giraut, X. Amancio and Óscar Álvarez Gila. 2007c. *La memoria de la emigración. Fuentes históricas, centros y archivos para el estudio de los flujos migratorios españoles*. Vigo: Grupo España Exterior.

Liper, Randy, and Sean Rehaag. 2013. *Sanctuary Practices in International Perspectives: Migration, Citizenship and Social Movements*. London: Routledge.

Literary Digest. 1919. "Education in Americanism, Lessons in Patriotism Prepared for The Literary Digest and Especially Designed for High School Use: Spaniards in the United States." March 22, 1919, 40. Accessed April 10, 2021. https://archive.org/details/literarydigest60newy/page/n1321/mode/2up

Little Spain. 2011. Directed by Artur Balder. New York: Bluechromatic Productions, Chinstrap Films, Meatpacking Productions.

López, Iraida H. 2012. "The Notion of 'Volver' in Cuban-American Memoirs: Gustavo Pérez Firmat's 'Next Year in Cuba' as a Case of Mistaken Coordinates." *South Atlantic Review* 77 (3/4): 59–76. Accessed March 10, 2021. www.jstor.org/stable/43739010.

Lull, James. 1990. *Media, Communication, Culture: A Global Approach*. New York: Columbia University Press.

Lynch, John. 1973. *The Spanish-American Revolutions, 1808–1826*. New York: Norton.

MacDonald, George F. 1991. "What Is Culture?" *The Journal of Museum Education* 16 (1): 9–12. Accessed March 9, 2021. www.jstor.org/stable/40478873.

Mack, Edward. 2022. "Culture: Samurai, Spies, and Serialized Fiction." In *Acquired Alterity: Migration, Identity, and Literary Nationalism*, ed. iEdward Mack, 41–66. Berkeley: University of California Press. Accessed June 10, 2021. www.jstor.org/stable/j.ctv2rb75tc.8.

Marotta, Vince. 2014. "The Multicultural, Intercultural and the Transcultural Subject." In *Global Perspectives on the Politics of Multiculturalism in the 21st Century: a Case Study Analysis*, eds. Boulou Fethi and Ebanda de B'beri, 90–102. New York: Routledge.

Marquart, Sharon. 2011. "Authoritative Witnessing and the Control of Memory: On Jorge Semprun's 'L'écriture Ou La Vie.'" *French Forum* 36 (2/3): 147–61. Accessed October 13, 2021. www.jstor.org/stable/41708756.

Martí, Alberto. 2018. *Os adeuses: Fotografías de Alberto Martí*. Consello de Cultura Galega.

Mercado, Julio. 1923. *En torno a la vida y a lo bello*. In *Serie de Conferencias de 1922–1923*. New York: Unión Benéfica Española. Accessed January 12, 1923.

Millington, Mark. 2007. "Transculturation: Contrapuntal Notes to Critical Orthodoxy" *Bulletin of Latin American Research* 26 (2): 256–68. Accessed May 15, 2021. www.jstor.org/stable/27733922.

Morell, Claude, and Teresa Morell Moll. 2008. *The Lower East Side Kid That Made It Good: The Autobiography of Claude Morell*. Denver, Colorado: Outskirts Press.

Morell Moll, T. (1991). La interacción en la clase magistral. Universidad de Alicante.

Morell Moll, Teresa. 2007. La difusión oral del conocimiento: las clases magistrales y las ponencias en congresos. In E. Alcaraz, J. Mateo, & F. Yus (Eds.), Las lenguas profesionales y académicas (pp. 247–258). Barcelona: Ariel Lenguas Modernas.

Morell Moll, Teresa. 2017. *Valencians to New York: The Case of La Marina Alta*. Valencia: Edicions 96.

Municipal Archives. 24 October 1831. *Petition to Have the Five Points Opened*. Board of Assistant Aldermen documents New York City. Accessed March 10, 2021. https://web.archive.org/web/20110928231235/http://cahotest.cc.columbia.edu/dbq/11003.html#B

Muñoz Sánchez, Antonio. 2012. "Una introducción a la historia de la emigración española en la República Federal de Alemania (1960–1980)." *Iberoamericana* XII (46): 23–42. Accessed May 9, 2021. https://www.iai.spk-berlin.de/fileadmin/dokumentenbibliothek/Iberoamericana/46-2012/46_Munoz_Sanchez.pdf

Nader, Laura. 2002. "Missing Links: A Commentary on Ward H. Goodenough's Moving Article 'Anthropology in the 20th Century and

Beyond.'" *American Anthropologist* 104 (2): 441–49. Accessed February 19, 2021. www.jstor.org/stable/683996.

Nagel, Joane. 1994. "Constructing Ethnicity: Creating and Recreating Ethnic Identity and Culture." *Social Problems* 41 (1): 152–76. Accessed July 21, 2021. https://doi.org/10.2307/3096847.

Nevius, Michelle and James Nevius. 2009. *Inside the Apple: A Streetwise History of New York City*. New York: Free Press.

Ng, Wen Lee. 2015. "Transculturation in *The Gift of Rain* and *The Calligrapher's Daughter*." Master's Thesis. Universiti Putra Malaysia.

Ng, Wen Lee, Manimangai Mani, and Roselezam Yahya. 2016. "Transculturalism in Tan Twan Eng's the Gift of Rain." *International Letters of Social and Humanistic Sciences* 74: 1–15. Accessed April 5, 2021. https://ssrn.com/abstract=3013511

Núñez Seixas, Xosé M., ¡Fuera el invasor! *Nacionalismos y movilización bélica durante la guerra civil española* (1936-1939), Madrid, Marcial Pons, 2006, 477 págs.

Núñez Seixas, X. M. 2007. El asociacionismo de la emigración vasca en América: El caso de Uruguay. Universidad del País Vasco.

Núñez Seixas, X. M. 2007. Imperios de muerte: La guerra germano-soviética, 1941–1945. Madrid: Alianza Editorial.

Onghena, Yolanda. 2008. "Transculturalism and Relation Identity" *Intercultural Dialogue Between Europe and the Mediterranean* 10: 181–84.

Ortiz, Fernando. 2012. *Cuban Counterpoint, Tobacco and Sugar*. New York: Knopf Doubleday.

Ortiz, F. (2012). Contrapunteo cubano del tabaco y el azúcar. Madrid: Cátedra.

Ortiz, Fernando. Cuban Counterpoint: Tobacco and Sugar. Translated by Harriet de Onís, preface by Fernando Fernández Retamar, Duke University Press, 1995. Originally published in 1940.

Ortner, Sherry B. 1984. "Theory in Anthropology since the Sixties" *Comparative Studies in Society and History* 26 (1): 126–66. Accessed April 5, 2021. http://www.jstor.org/stable/178524.

Palacios Bañuelos, Luis. 2013. "Las relaciones entre España y China, una larga historia" *Historia Actual Online* 30: 151–163. Accessed June 15, 2021. dialnet.unirioja.es/servlet/articulo?codigo=4198150

Pardo Bazán, Emilia. 2007 (1889). *Morriña*. Madrid: Cátedra.

Pares. "Portal de Archivos Españoles." Ministerio de Cultura y Deportes. Accessed March 5, 2021. http://pares.mcu.es/ParesBusquedas20/catalogo/autoridad/143196?nm

Parekh, Bhikhu. 1991."British Citizenship and Cultural Difference." *In Citizenship*, ed. Geoff Andrews. London: Lawrence & Wishart.

Pavel, Thomas. "Søren Frank, Migration and Literature: Günter Grass, Milan Kundera, Salman Rushdie, and Jan Kjærstad." *Modern Philology*, vol. 110, no. 2, 2012, pp. E139–42. JSTOR, https://doi.org/10.1086/667943. Accessed 26 Mar. 2025.

Payne, Stanley G., Richard L. Kagan, James D. Fernández, Lola Jiménez-Blanco, Ignacio Suárez-Zuloaga, Eugenia Querci, Suzanne L. Stratton-Pruit and Elizabeth Boone. 2010. *When Spain Fascinated America*. Madrid: Fundación Zuloaga.

Pérez Firmat, Gustavo. 1996. *Life on the Hyphen: The Cuban-American Way*. Austin: University of Texas Press.

Pérez, Lisandro. 1965. "Cuban Catholics in the United States." *Puerto Rican and Cuban Catholics in the US, 1900–1965* (1): 147–208.

Perlmann, Joel, and Roger Waldinger. 1997. "Second Generation Decline? Children of Immigrants, Past and Present – A Reconsideration." *International Migration Review* 31 (4): 893–922. Accessed March 7, 2021. https://doi.org/10.1177/019791839703100405

Peyton Joyner, Brian, and Donna Caro. 2017. *Deep Dive: Sanctuary Cities*. New York: Golden Rule Omnimedia.

Plato. 2008. *The Complete Works of Plato*, Compiled by Dr Mohamed Elwany. Translated by Benjamin Jowett. Oxford: Oxford University Press. Accessed March 5, 2021. https://www.holybooks.com/wp-content/uploads/plato-complete-works.pdf

Portes, Alejandro, and Rubén Rumbaut. 2001. *Legacies: The Story of the Immigrant Second Generation*. Berkeley: University of California Press.

Portes, Alejandro, and Rubén Rumbaut. 2014. *Immigrant America: A Portrait*. Berkeley: University of California Press.

Powell, John. 2005. *Encyclopedia of North American Immigration*. New York: Facts on File.

Pratt, Mary Louise. 2007. *Imperial Eyes: Travel Writing and Transculturation.* London: Routledge.

Prudencio de Pereda Papers: 1935–1973. *Manuscript Collection. MS-01107.* Harry Ransom Center: University of Texas at Austin. Accessed March 20, 2021. https://norman.hrc.utexas.edu/fasearch/pdf/00033.pdf

Rabben, Linda. 2016. *Sanctuary and Asylum: A Social and Political History.* Washington: University of Washington Press.

Rama, Angel. 2012. *Writing across Cultures: Narrative Transculturation in Latin America.* Durham and London: Duke University Press.

Radstone, Susannah, and Bill Schwarz. 2010. *Memory: Histories, Theories, Debates.* New York: Fordham University Press.

Rao, Sai. 2019. *USA's Red Card Immigration: Examining Cryogenic Immigration Options for the Racially Discriminated. (Immig-Rant Book 1).* Kindle.

Redondo Carrero, Emilio. 2017. *Migrantes y refugiados en la posguerra mundial: la corriente organizada de españoles hacia Argentina, 1946–1962.* Madrid: Sílex.

Regazzoni, Susanna. 2006. *Transculturation, Mestizaje and Hybridism. (Teoría y crítica de la cultura y literatura).* Madrid: Iberoamericana Editorial Vervuert.

Ricoeur, Paul. 2006. *Memory, History, Forgetting.* Chicago: University of Chicago Press.

Riis, Jacob A. 1890. *How the Other Half Lives: Studies among the Tenements of New York.* New York: Charles Scribner's. Bookbiding Company. Accessed March 7, 2021. www.gutenberg.org/files/45502/45502-h/45502-h.htm

Riis, J. A. 1902. *The Battle with the Slum.* Macmillan Company.

Rogers, Richard. 2006. "From Cultural Exchange to Transculturation: A Review and Reconceptualization of Cultural Appropriation." *Communication Theory* (16): 474–503. Accessed March 7, 2021. https://doi.org/10.1111/j.1468-2885.2006.00277.x

Rossington, Michael, and Anne Whitehead. 2007. *Theories of Memory: A Reader.* Baltimore: The John Hopkins University Press.

Rueda Hernanz, Germán. 1993. *La emigración contemporánea de españoles a Estados Unidos. 1820–1950. De «Dons» a «Misters»*. Madrid: Colecciones Mapfre 1492.

Rueda Hernanz, Germán. 2000. *Españoles emigrantes en América (Siglos XVI–XX)*. Madrid: Arco.

Rumbaut, Rubén G. 2004. "Ages, Life Stages, and Generational Cohorts: Decomposing the Immigrant First and Second Generations in the United States." *The International Migration Review* 38 (3): 1160–1205. http://www.jstor.org/stable/27645429

Said, Edward W, *Orientalism*. Pantheon Books, 1978.

Said, Edward W. 1979. *Orientalism*. New York: Vintage.

Said, Edward W. 1990. "Figures, Configurations, Transfigurations." *Race & Class* 32 (1): 1–16, Accessed May 21, 2021. https://doi.org/10.1177/030639689003200101

Said, E. W. 1993. Culture and Imperialism. New York: Knopf.

Said, E. W. 1994. Representations of the Intellectual: The 1993 Reith Lectures. New York: Pantheon Books.

Said, Edward W. 1993. *Culture and imperialism*. 1 New York: Vintage Books.

Said, Edward W. 1994. *Culture and Imperialism*. New York :Vintage Books.

Said, E. W. 1978. Orientalism. New York: Pantheon Books.

Santí, Enrico Mario. 2002. *Fernando Ortiz: Contrapunteo y transculturación*. Madrid: Editorial Colibrí.

Sapir, Edward. 2013 1924. "Culture, Genuine and Spurious." *American Journal of Sociology* 29: 401–29. Accessed May 21, 2021. https://evols.library.manoa.hawaii.edu/bitstream/10524/35859/1/SM%205%20Culture%20Genuine%20and%20Spurious.pdf

Satia Jessie A., Ruth E. Patterson, Alan R. Kristal, T. Greg Hislop, Yutaka Yasui, Victoria M. Taylor. 2001. "Development of Scales to Measure Dietary Acculturation among Chinese-Americans and Chinese-Canadians." *Journal of the American Dietetic Association* 101 (5): 548–53. Accessed May 21, 2021. https://www.jandonline.org/article/S0002-8223(01)00137-7/fulltext

Schneider, David M. 1980. *American Kinship: A Cultural Account*. Chicago: The University of Chicago Press.

Shukla, Nikesh, and Chimene Suleyman. 2019. *The Good Immigrant USA: 26 Writers on America, Immigration and Home.* London: Dialogue Books.

Siegel, Dina, and Veronika Nagy. 2018. *The Migration Crisis?: Criminalization, Security and Survival.* The Hague: Eleven International.

Silva, Víctor, and Rodrigo Browne. 2011. "'Transculturación literaria' y 'elogio del mestizaje' en La ciudad letrada los intersticios en las escrituras de José María Arguedas y de Ángel Rama." *Estudios Ibero-Americanos* 37 (1): 86–104.

Smith, Daniel Scott. 1972. "The Demographic History of Colonial New England." *The Journal of Economic History* 32 (1): 165–83. Accessed March 15, 2022. http://www.jstor.org/stable/2117183.

Smokowski, Paul R., Roderick Rose, and Martica L. Bacallao. 2008. "Acculturation and Latino Family Processes: How Cultural Involvement, Biculturalism, and Acculturation Gaps Influence Family Dynamics." *Family Relations* 57 (3): 295–308. Accessed March 15, 2022. http://www.jstor.org/stable/20456794.

Sollors, Werner. 1986. *Beyond Ethnicity: Consent and Descent in American Culture.* New York: Oxford University Press.

Spivak, G. C. 1999. A Critique of Postcolonial Reason: Toward a History of the Vanishing Present. Cambridge, MA: Harvard University Press.

Spivak, Gayatri Chakravorty. 1988. "Can the Subaltern Speak?" *Die Philosophin* 14 (27): 42–58.

Spivak, Gayatri Chakravorty. *A Critique of Postcolonial Reason: Toward a History of the Vanishing Present* (Cambridge, Massachusetts: Harvard University Press, 1999.

Stavans, Ilan. 1993. "Anonymity: An Interview with Felipe Alfau." *The Review of Contemporary Fiction* 13 (1): 146. Gale Academic OneFile. Accessed June 12, 2022. https://link.gale.com/apps/doc/A13663053/AONE?u=anon~aa3c8534&sid=googleScholar&xid=03faac3e.

Stavans, Ilan, and Gail Sheehy. "Memory and Literature." *Agni*, 48 (1998): 79–90. www.jstor.org/stable/23007941.

Suarez-Orozco, Marcelo M. 1998. *Crossings: Mexican Immigration in Interdisciplinary Perspectives.* Cambridge, Massachusetts: Harvard University Press.

Suárez-Orozco, C., Suárez-Orozco, M. M., & Todorova, I. (2008). *Learning a new land: Immigrant students in American society*. Belknap Press/ Harvard University Press.

Subcommittee on Immigration and Border Security of the Committee on the Judiciary House of Representatives. 2015. *Sanctuary Cities: A Threat to Public Safety*. Washington: Independent Publishing Platform.

Sullivan, Edward J. 2010. *Nueva York: 1613–1945*. London: New York Historical Society, Scala.

Taylor, Diana. 1991. "Transculturating Transculturation." *Performing Arts Journal* 13 (2): 90–104. Accessed May 21, 2021: https://doi.org/10.2307/ 3245476.

The Making of an American by Jacob A. RIIS First edition, fifth printing. Macmillan, 1902.

Tienda, Marta, and Susana M Sánchez. 2013. "Latin American Immigration to the United States." *Daedalus* 142 (3): 48–64. Accessed March 10, 2021. https://doi.org/10.1162/DAED_a_00218.

Tomsho, Robert. 1987. *The American Sanctuary Movement*. Texas: Texas Monthly Press.

Toro, Alfonso de. 2006. "Figuras de la hibridez: Ortiz: transculturación – Paz: hibridismo–Fernández Retamar: Calibán." In *Alma cubana: transculturación, hibridez y mestizaje. The Cuban Siprit: Transculturation, Mestizaje, and Hybridism*, ed. Regazzoni, Susanna, (1), 15–36. Madrid/ Frankfurt am Main: Iberoamerican/Vervuert.

Totoricagüena, Gloria. 2003. *The Basques of New York: A Cosmopolitan Experience*. Colección Urazandi Bilduma. Vitoria: Servicio Central de Publicaciones del Gobierno Vasco. Accessed March 21, 2021. https:// www.euskadi.eus/web01-a2aznscp/es/k75aWebPublicacionesWar/ k75aObtenerPublicacionDigitalServlet?R01HNoPortal=true&N_LIBR= 024599&N_EDIC=0001&C_IDIOM=en&FORMATO=.pdf

Tylor, Edward B. 1920. *Primitive Culture: Researches into the Development of Mythology, Philosophy, Religion, Language, Art, and Custom*. London: John Murray. Accessed March 10, 2021. https://archive.org/ details/primitiveculture01tylouoft/page/n9/mode/2up?ref=ol&view= theater

United States. National Labor Relations Board. 1961. *Decisions and Orders of the National Labor Relations Board*. National Labor Relations Board.

U.S. Department of Homeland Security. 2012. "Total Immigrants from each Region and Country, by Decade, 1820–2010." Accessed May 21, 2021. http://teacher.scholastic.com/activities/immigration/pdfs/by_region/region_table.pdf

U.S. Department of Justice. 1996. "Statistical Yearbook of the Immigration and Naturalization Service." Accessed May 21, 2021. https://digitallibrary.utah.gov/awweb/pdfopener?sid=4701EA760AA30AB8844311143F50734C&did=82160&fl=%2Fpublications%2Fpdf%2Frm005887.pdf#toolbar=0

Varela-Lago, Ana María. 2008. "Conquerors, Immigrants, Exiles: The Spanish Diaspora in the United States (1848–1948)." PhD diss. University of Chicago.

Villanueva López, Claudio Vicente. 2001. "Los modelos de aculturación e intervención psicosocial en la inmigración." *Gazeta de Antropología* 17 (6): Accessed April 2, 2022. http://hdl.handle.net/10481/7470

Wayne Powell, Philip. 1971. *Tree of Hate: Propaganda and Prejudices Affecting United States Relations with the Hispanic World.* New York: Basic Books.

Weber, James. 2016. *History: American History in 50 Events: From First Immigration to World Power*. Scotts Valley, California: CreateSpace.

Weber, James (2016). *American history in 50 events: From first immigration to world power.* Scotts Valley, CA: CreateSpace.

Wepman, Dennis. 2008. *Unanue, Prudencio (1886–1976), Founder of Goya Foods, Inc.* American National Biography. Accessed March 22, 2021. https://www.anb.org/view/10.1093/anb/9780198606697.001.0001/anb-9780198606697-e-1002298

Wiesel, Elie. 2002. *¿Por qué recordar?* Academia Universal de las Culturas. Barcelona: Ediciones Granica.

Zaballa Beascoechea, Ana de. 1990. *Transculturación y misión en Nueva España. Estudio histórico-doctrinal del Libro de los "Coloquios" de Bernardina de Sahagún.* Pamplona: Ediciones Universidad de Navarra.

Zakaria, F. (1994). Culture is destiny: A conversation with Lee Kuan Yew. Foreign Affairs, 73(6), 122–135.

CONTRIBUTIONS TO ENGLISH AND AMERICAN LITERARY STUDIES (CEALS)

Edited by Ingo Berensmeyer, Christoph Ehland,
Julika Griem, Andrew S. Gross and Antje Kley

Vol. 1 Ottilie P. Klein: Lethal Performances. Women Who Kill in Modern American Drama. 2017.

Vol. 2 Antje Kley / Kai Merten (eds.): What Literature Knows. Forays into Literary Knowledge Production. 2018.

Vol. 3 Florian Zappe / Andrew S. Gross (eds.): Surveillance – Society – Culture. 2019.

Vol. 4 Sascha Klein: Skyscraping Frontiers. The Skyscraper as Heterotopia in the 20th-Century American Novel and Film. 2020.

Vol. 5 Teona Micevska: Modernist Women Dandies. Poetry, Photography, Authorship. 2021.

Vol. 6 Nasrin Babakhani: Cultural Realism: Reconsidering Magical Realism in the Works of Contemporary American Women Writers. 2022.

Vol. 7 Francisco Javier Plañxart Pérez-Santalla: Literary Representation of Spanish Immigration in the United States of America (1900–1950) Transculturation, Hybridization, and the Third Space 2025.

www.peterlang.com

Printed by
CPI books GmbH, Leck